*W*ildlife
Travelling Companion

SPAIN

*W*ildlife
Travelling Companion

SPAIN

John Measures

The Crowood Press

First published in 1992 by
The Crowood Press Ltd
Ramsbury, Marlborough
Wiltshire SN8 2HR

Field Guide plates 1–12 by **Michael Benington** and
plates 13-20 by **Amanda Yektaparast**.
Maps by **Kathy Merrick**.

Title page photograph: tranquil Embalse de Riaño in
the early morning.
Photograph this page: Greater Flamingos.

Dedication
To my mother and my uncle, Victor Allan, for stimu-
lating my interest in natural history from an early age.

Acknowledgements
During the research for this book, I have travelled over
15,000km, revisiting places I have known over the
past thirty-five years and exploring many more remote
and exceptionally beautiful areas. Throughout Spain, I
received help, kindness and hospitality. In particular I
would like to thank the directors and guides in the
many nature reserves I visited, all of whom were
extremely helpful.

   David and Namrita Goodfellow of D & N
Publishing have given advice and encouragement
during the preparation of the book and I am greatly
indebted to them. I thank Michael Benington and
Amanda Yektaparast for their brilliant work.

   Above all my grateful thanks to my wife, Madge,
who accompanied me on all my trips. Without her
encouragement and help, plus the unenviable task of
typing the manuscript, this book would never have
been completed.

British Library Cataloguing in Publication Data

A catalogue record for this book is available from the
British Library.

ISBN 1 85223 610 8

Edited and designed by:
D & N Publishing
DTP & Editorial Services
5 The Green
Baydon
Wiltshire SN8 2JW

Phototypeset by FIDO Imagesetting, Witney

Printed and bound by Times Publishing Group,
Singapore

CONTENTS

INTRODUCTION: HOW TO USE THIS BOOK

Within this book I have tried to bring together 150 of the best places to find the extremely varied wildlife of Spain. Many of the sites are well known for one or more aspects of natural history, either for vast quantities of rare birds which winter in some remote marsh or for a rare species of butterfly, only found in one valley in a particular mountain region. Within your holiday zone or journey if travelling by car, you should be able to find a number of sites which suit your personal interest.

In addition, a number of subsidiary sites have been mentioned. These are not too far from the main site and do not necessarily have a similar habitat. The subsidiary site may be an interesting valley within an Alpine zone or some unusual caves of geological significance, for example. Throughout, the Michelin maps 1/400,000, numbers 441 to 446 inclusive, have been used. I have found these superb and therefore have used them for map co-ordinates within the text for each site. For accommodation and restaurants in the larger towns I recommend the *Michelin Red Guide* which has also proved invaluable on many occasions.

Many of the sites are in fact quite large, not one specific point, more a general area, like Covadonga which is a large mountainous zone and is good for all aspects of mountain wildlife. All the sites are easy to find by using the map references and there should hopefully be no difficulty. The majority of sites do require a car for visiting them, but others are accessible from tourist centres or are easily reached by local transport. Tourist information centres can usually help with bus and train timetables. Town and area names throughout have been used in accordance with the Michelin maps, with the exception of Cataluña where occasionally I have used the local names to try to avoid confusion when travelling in that region.

The photographs show the various types of habitat, exciting views of many of the main sites and some of the animals and plants that you might hope to see. I hope these will encourage you to visit and see for yourselves the wonders of each area and the wealth of wildlife that Spain has to offer the naturalist.

It is difficult to give precise details for finding the rarer species of wildlife. Most are highly protected and for birds in particular some areas are restricted during the breeding season. Most of the mammals are nocturnal and often difficult to locate, with the best time of day being early morning or late evening when a large number will be feeding and drinking. Rare plants can be found by searching in suitable habitats, but it must be remembered that these plants are protected and must not be picked or dug up.

For the identification of the commoner birds, mammals, reptiles, amphibians, butterflies and plants the identification plates at the back of the book showing many aspects of the species depicted have been designed to assist you. Nearly 200 species are shown in this field guide section. Some of the rare or more interesting species are illustrated photographically throughout the book in *Special Species Boxes*.

Before looking at the sites in detail, let us take a look at Spain as a whole: its countryside, agriculture, conservation record and of course its wildlife.

Opposite: the deep gorge at Ronda, taken from the bridge looking towards Serranía de Ronda.

SECTION I.
COUNTRY GUIDE

GEOGRAPHY

Spain is like a saucer, high mountains around the edges and a lofty plateau in the centre. It is a land of great contrasts with surprising vistas at every turn. There are the high snow-capped mountains of the Pyrenees; the very moist limestone and granite peaks of the Cantábrican mountains with lush verdant pastures and woodlands; dry, arid, desert-like wastes in the Ebro Valley and in Almería; the flat grain- and grape-growing areas of the central plateau where the landscape is relieved here and there by small hills crowned with one or two 'Don Quixote' windmills; the huge snow-covered bastion of the Sierra Nevada, only 40km from the subtropical zone lapped by the gentle warm Mediterranean; the natural wilderness of the Coto Doñana with its flocks of Greater Flamingo and herds of Wild Boar; and the cold Alpine heights in northern Spain where Wolves and Brown Bears roam the deciduous forests.

The coastline is rugged and severe in the north, washed by the Atlantic in the Bay of Biscay, but in the south and east it is lapped by the gentle waters of the Mediterranean Sea. Of the five great rivers, four disgorge into the Atlantic and one into the Mediterranean Sea. Spain is certainly a country of contrasts and it is more diverse geographically than any other country in Europe. This is emphasized when it is realized that rice and citrus can be grown in the south, while rye and oats are grown in the north.

Opposite: the beautiful area of the Río Tajo near Almaraz, bounded by Poplars (Populus alba).

MOUNTAIN RANGES AND THEIR ROCK TYPES

Spain is the second highest country in Europe, averaging 660m (2165 feet), and is second only to Switzerland. It also boasts the highest capital in Europe with Madrid at 660m as well. Much of the land is taken up with the high plateaux known as the Mesetas, these being traversed by a series of high mountain ranges. The most important are the high Pyrenees which rise to 3404m (11,168 feet) and extend for 435km from the Bay of Biscay to the Mediterranean coast forming a natural boundary between France and Spain. The basic core of these mountains is granite and schist, with lower ridges of limestone which give a very diverse flora. The Cantábrican mountains stretching right along the north of Spain are really a western extension of the Pyrenees. Both of these ranges act as a barrier to the cold north and north-west winds and depressions, and therefore receive substantial rainfall.

To the south are the dry plains of 'Old Castile' broken by the Montes de León to the west composed of crystalline rock. Across the centre of Spain are two high mountain ranges, the Sierra de Gredos and the Sierra de Guadarrama. They are old fold mountains having a hard core of crystalline rock and rising up to 2592m (8504 feet) in the Sierra de Gredos.

Further to the east, the Iberian Mountains, with the Montes Universales in the centre, are composed of the same hard core rock with areas of limestone. These rise to a height of 2313m (7589 feet) at Moncayo on the extreme northern end. This range is

Looking towards Maladeta from Vall d'Aran. Here Alpine pastures hold sheep which produce milk for magnificent cheeses. Vall d'Aran is a wonderful area for butterflies. Many species, such as Alpine Grizzled Skipper (Pyrgus andromedae), Clouded Apollo (Parnassius mnemosyne) and the rare Silvery Argus (Pseudaricia nicias) may be found here.

characterized by a high moorland landscape with very well-wooded sides, deep canyons and high rugged cliffs.

To the south and west there are the Toledo mountains and the Sierra Morena, which are old fold mountains rising to 1323m (4341 feet) in the Sierra Morena. The Andalucían Baetic mountain chain, including the Sierra Nevada, is relatively new geologically and runs from Gibraltar to the Cabo de la Nao and continues under the sea to appear again in the Balearic Islands. This chain has the highest mountain in mainland Spain at Mulhacén in the Sierra Nevada (3478m; 11,411 feet) and the highest European road.

In the south-east of Spain there are small mountain masses, the Sierras de Ronda and Cazorla y Segura, all of which are composed of limestone.

VOLCANIC ACTIVITY

There are no active volcanoes on mainland Spain, but the area known as Garrotxa near Olot was the centre of a very active volcanic zone 11,000 years ago, which geologically is very recent. The whole area is covered with cones of volcanic ash which supports lush vegetation. Most of these cones can easily be seen and almost all contain a distinct crater depression.

GORGES

Spain is a country of gorges, many deep and long. Over the centuries the sudden violent storms have swollen the small rivers into swirling torrents sweeping everything before them, eroding deep canyons where the softer strata occur. The most notable are in the Montes Universales and the Cantábrican mountains where limestone predominates.

CAVES

The largest cave in Spain is in western Andalucía at Aracena and is known as the Gruta de las Maravillas. Most caves are formed in limestone areas where water has eroded a passageway, giving rise to stalagmites, stalactites and underground lakes. Many of the larger ones are open to the public. Mallorca and the mainland have many caves.

In some areas these caves have been adapted by man for many thousands of years. There are a series of very famous ones in northern Spain which were inhabited by man 25,000 years ago. On the walls he has left primitive decorations and frescos depicting hunting scenes. The most famous of these is the Cueva de Altamira to the west of the coastal town of Santander.

MINES

Spain is rich in minerals, especially coal, iron and zinc. These have been exploited in the north near Oviedo which has resulted in the growth of heavy industry along the northern coast. Silver and lead is also mined in many areas. In the Sierra Morena the huge Río Tinto opencast mine has formed a great scar on the landscape. Here copper pyrites is mined in large quantities supplying a high percentage of Spain's demand for copper. Manganese is also mined nearby. Mercury is produced in the plains of La Mancha, and supplies all of Spain's needs.

PEOPLE

Spain has been inhabited for at least 25,000 years, which is the age attributed to the evocative drawings found in a series of caves, especially those at Altamira. The ancient dolmen caves at Antequera prove that southern Spain was inhabited by an ordered society in 2500BC. It was not until 1000BC that the Phoenecians and Greeks formed trading posts along the coast. The Romans finally founded an administration in 151BC and elected Cordoba as their capital. The next great historical step was in 711AD when the Muslims landed here and rapidly occupied the whole peninsula. The uprising at Covadonga in 722AD began the reconquest by the Christians, but not until 1479AD was Spain completely united under one crown.

Spain is basically an agricultural community. In the Middle Ages, wool from the indigenous Merino sheep was exported to northern Europe which brought great prosperity to the Spanish landowners. The wool was shipped from the northern Spanish ports of Santander and Bilbao which were also prosperous fishing ports. With the discovery of large coal, iron and zinc deposits in the Cantábrican mountains these towns developed at a fast rate and are now the centre of Spanish heavy industry with vast iron and steel foundries rapidly expanding.

In the southern part of Spain, especially along the coastline, tourism is a major source of income, but this has a harmful effect by

The Río Tinto opencast copper mine in western Andalucía, showing multi-coloured rocks. Copper pyrites is mined here and supplies much of Spain's demand for copper. However, this is not without causing considerable damage to the environment.

The Bee-eater (Merops apiaster) *is a spectacular bird nesting in sandy areas throughout Spain.*

disfiguring the coastline and changing the environment. It also doubles the human population during the summer months, putting a strain on food resources and distribution. The average population density in Spain is seventy-four head per square kilometre, but in the pastoral areas, such as Extremadura, Castilla and Aragon the average is only twenty-five. In the north of Spain there are small villages within a short distance of one another, whilst in the centre and south the population is concentrated in larger towns.

Following a trend now common in most European countries there is a drift from the land resulting in some of the small villages in the more remote regions being completely abandoned. This leaves large areas untilled and they quickly revert to scrubland.

FLORA AND FAUNA

The flora and fauna of Spain belong to the geographical region known as the Western Palaearctic, which includes all of Europe and North Africa. The last ice age sent tongues of permafrost and glaciation well down into the Iberian Peninsula. Only the south and west escaped the worst effects of the ice age and

the plants were not destroyed here. When the ice receded, the Pyrenees acted as a barrier to plants dispersing northwards. This is why a large number of the approximately 5500 seed-bearing species found in Iberia are endemic to the peninsula. Almost 250 of these are on the endangered species list.

Animals on the other hand colonize and disperse in different ways than plants, and therefore the Spanish fauna is very similar to that which existed in the rest of Europe many hundreds of years ago, before much of it was exterminated by man. Brown Bear, Wolf, Pardel Lynx, Wild Cat, Genet and Wild Boar are still present in small numbers, but where man has disturbed them and moved within their domain their existence is precarious and they could still vanish like their ancestors further north.

Many of Spain's birds, like the mammals, have very specific habitat requirements and it is vital that such habitats are conserved, as in some cases the populations are dangerously low in numbers. Black Vultures prefer evergreen oak trees in which to build their nests; Black Storks nest on remote cliff ledges in Monfragüe; White-headed Duck, Purple Gallinule, Marbled Teal and Crested Coot need plenty of vegetation at the water's edge in which to breed; and the Greater Flamingo

The Marsh Fritillary (Eurodryas aurinia) *is frequent in the mountains and on rough ground.*

must have high salinity, as the organisms on which it feeds only live in such conditions.

Butterflies in a number of cases have been isolated in a particular valley for many thousands of years and have as a consequence developed special characteristics which have distinguished them as subspecies.

All these endangered groups are living on a knife edge, but with the conservation methods now being implemented the decline to extinction can be halted. Let us hope that it is just in time.

HABITATS

ALPINE AND SUBALPINE ZONE

Alpine habitat is usually found well above the treeline and is composed of rock and cliff face with scree. It is normally covered with snow for up to eight months of the year. It looks inhospitable but this habitat contains a number of real botanical gems. In general, small cushion plants cling precariously to the rock face with tiny hair-like roots which find purchase and nourishment in minute cracks. The flowers are often spectacular, especially when *en masse*. *Silene acaulis* and *Arenaria tetraquetra* are good examples with many other plants growing on the scree which provides ideal conditions for plants requiring good drainage.

In these areas few animals exist, but during the summer, when the snow has gone, Spanish Ibex, Alpine Marmot and Chamois make this their home. The larger birds of prey, such as Golden Eagle, Egyptian and Griffon Vultures and in the Pyrenees the very rare Bearded Vulture (Lammergeier), with their long and broad wings enjoy the swirling air currents and updraughts and use them to glide from peak to peak. The Alpine Accentor, a most trusting bird, inhabits this

A typical scene in the mountainous area of Cantábrica, depicting Alpine and subalpine habitats. As the snow recedes the pastures come alive with flowers.

type of terrain and will almost sit on your hand on the summit of the Sierra Nevada and share your lunch! Butterflies are present and are represented mainly by the Apollo and some of the blues.

Subalpine meadows, lower down but still above the treeline, are covered with short-growing, often boggy, pasture, which is of poorish quality and grazed only during the summer months. This region is botanically very rich, and immediately the snow recedes the plants appear. crocuses, narcissi, sundews, campanulas, gentians, soldanellas and a host of other colourful non-cushion plants. Where the land is dryer, hedgehog-like plants are common, such as *Vella spinosa*,

Bupleurum spinosum, Astragalus sempervirens and many more.

In Spain, these habitats are found in extensive areas of the Pyrenees, the Cantábrican range, Sierras de Guadarrama and Gredos, Sierra de la Demada, the Iberian Mountains, Sierra Nevada and the summit of Puig Major in Mallorca.

CONIFEROUS FOREST
Coniferous forests are found in most mountainous and hilly areas below the subalpine and scrub zones. In many regions there are vast coniferous plantations managed commercially for the timber industry.

Spain is a huge country with large climatic variations and therefore the forests are composed of many different species: the Silver Fir is common in the Pyrenees and the Iberian Mountains; the Spanish Fir, a handsome tree, is now very rare and only found naturally near Ronda in Andalucía; the Maritime Pine is often planted commercially for timber and resin collection, and it is also used as a sand binder commonly seen in coastal areas and mountains; the Umbrella Pine, an impressive and unmistakable tree with a large spreading crown, is usually grown near the sea (its seeds produce pine kernels which are commercially important); the Aleppo Pine, an attractive slender tree, often grown for timber, prefers warm sandy soils; the Black Pine, a mountain species, is found in the Pyrenees, central and eastern Spain and is grown commercially; the Scots Pine is easily recognized by its large size and ochre-red flaking bark, and is grown in the cooler moist areas in the mountains of north and east Spain; and the Mountain Pine species found in Spain is a form of the central European *Pinus mugo*, a small stunted tree usually found high in the mountains.

Coniferous forests usually produce dense shade and the undergrowth is hence sparse, except in the forest edges where Heather, Bracken and *Genista* generally occur. Red, Fallow and Roe Deer frequent these forests, as do the Red Squirrel, Wild Boar, Pine Marten and in parts the Wolf.

Many birds can be seen, especially in the natural forest areas. Black, Green, Great Spotted and Lesser Spotted Woodpeckers, Capercaillie, Crested Tit and Crossbill are all typical birds of this habitat. Butterflies are not generally abundant, but the Pine Processionary Moth is common and its larvae can cause considerable damage. The rare Spanish Moon Moth and the Pine Hawk Moth can also be found in coniferous forests.

DECIDUOUS BROAD-LEAVED FOREST
These are found mainly in the north of Spain in the mountains where there is high rainfall. In the Cantábrican and Basque regions, vast areas of Beech are the dominating feature of the landscape. In places this is mixed with the deciduous Pyrenean Oak. There are smaller areas of Poplars, mainly commercial plantations in river basins, and in some very wet zones willows are grown for basket making.

This habitat is notable for having a large variety of birds. Smaller birds of prey, such as Kestrel, Sparrowhawk, Buzzard and Red and Black Kite can often be seen perched or hunting. Typical woodland birds include Tawny Owl, Woodpigeon, Turtle Dove, Great Spotted, Lesser Spotted, Green and Black Woodpeckers, Golden Oriole, Short-toed Treecreeper, and Spotted and Pied Flycatchers, with Nightingales very common in the more moist valleys.

The mammal species here are very similar to those found in coniferous forests except that the Brown Bear prefers Beech forests and the Red Squirrel is more frequently seen as it feeds on Beech mast and Pyrenean Oak acorns. The Beech Marten, a pretty little animal, is found within these woods.

Marsh Frogs, newts and salamanders can be found in damper areas. A few snakes, such as Grass and Ladder Snake and Lataste's Viper, can be found in the more exposed areas but are not likely to cause a problem.

Heather, *Genista* and Bracken form an undergrowth. There are many woodland orchids, such as Lady's Slipper (mostly in Beech woods), Early Purple, Green-winged and Bird's Nest. Martagon Lilies, Bluebells and Foxgloves are common.

Some interesting butterflies, such as the large Great Banded Grayling, and Southern and Spanish Gatekeepers, are found in deciduous woods. The Silver-washed Fritillary can be found here laying eggs on tree trunks where violets are present as the food plant for the caterpillars the following season. Moths in this habitat include the Lime Hawk Moth, Poplar Hawk Moth and Oak Eggar.

STEPPE

This is a degenerate habitat produced in one of two ways. The first is climatic and occurs where the rainfall is below 30cm (12 inches) per year and there are over 200 days of sun annually. When rain does occur, it is usually violent, resulting in excessive erosion. These factors, coupled with the fact that extremes of temperature occur, make the habitat inhospitable for all but the most hardy animals. Some plant life has through many thousands of years evolved and adapted to survive. The second way the habitat is produced is through overgrazing, mainly by goats. They will eat almost anything, leaving only the spiny plants and unpalatable asphodels and Dwarf Fan Palms.

There are many areas in Spain which are designated as steppe. The Río Ebro on most

Above: *deciduous broad-leaved forest in the Garrotxa volcanic zone.*
Below: *typical dry steppe with thorny scrub and False Esparto Grass near Mengen in Almería.*

of its course passes through dry arid land which was at one time an immense lake. The river eventually cut through the limestone rock, which blocked its way, to what has now become the Ebro Delta. The lake slowly drained away leaving a vast, dry salty countryside. The La Mancha area of central Spain is another place where there are many tracts of steppe. The most extreme example is in the Cabo de Gata region of Almería, where there is a dry, almost desert-like landscape with deep canyons. There is scarcely any plant life here and herds of goats eat most of the remaining vegetation.

When rain does occur, the plains soon burst into life and annuals flower and seed within a few weeks. The bird life is very specialized with Great and Little Bustards, Black-bellied and Pin-tailed Sandgrouse, Stone Curlew, and Dupont's, Short-toed and Lesser Short-toed Larks. Other vertebrates are uncommon, but the Spur-thighed Tortoise may be seen.

MAQUIS SCRUB

This is a common habitat found throughout Spain. Wherever the natural forest has been felled the scrubland takes over. There is also often a zone of scrub above the tree line in the mountains.

Soil type and climate determine the major plant species of the scrub. In the south and in the generally warmer zones *Cistus* species, such as Gum Cistus, Sage-leaved Cistus, Grey-leaved Cistus and *Cistus crispus* predominate, with Lavender, Rosemary and Thyme. Where the soil is acid, various species of heather and *Genista* are added giving a very aromatic and colourful picture. In northern areas, *Cistus* is generally replaced by Gorse, Juniper, Heather and the larger Strawberry Tree. Orchids, gladioli, irises and Tulips can be found within the undergrowth as well as a multitude of other plants.

Small birds enjoy this habitat and many warblers nest here, for example Sardinian, Dartford, Subalpine and Spectacled. Flycatchers, finches and the Stonechat can also

Halimium halimifolium, a typical constituent of the maquis scrub in southern Spain.

be seen here. Butterflies are common as their caterpillars have a variety of plants on which to feed and grow. Fritillaries, the Swallowtail and Scarce Swallowtail, blues, skippers, Clouded Yellow and Cleopatra may all be seen, and along the southern coast the Two-tailed Pasha can be spotted searching for the Strawberry Tree on which to lay its eggs.

Smaller vertebrates are numerous. Fox, Hare, Rabbit, Genet and Wild Cat, and in the south the Egyptian Mongoose all hide in the undergrowth. Snakes also like this habitat and there are a number of species here such as Montpellier, Ladder and Viperine Snakes and also the Lataste's Viper, which can be nasty if trodden on!

LOWLAND MIXED FOREST

Throughout much of the lowlands and plains of Spain there are areas of old mixed woodland. These are usually composed of Cork Oak, the bark being stripped about once every ten years, and the evergreen Ilex Oak which is periodically pruned, the prunings used to produce the best charcoal. Often conifers have been planted for timber, and

Freshwater marshes on the Coto Doñana, which are often teeming with ducks and waders, with kites flying overhead. The Coto Doñana is one of the best wetland sites for wildlife in Europe. During summer, many species of birds nest here and during winter hundreds of thousands of waterbirds migrate here after breeding in northern Europe.

more recently Eucalyptus has been introduced to become pollarded every ten years, the timber being used for the wood-pulp industry.

Formerly a large part of Spain was covered with native natural woodlands; now many of these have vanished with areas reverting to maquis scrub. In zones where the trees are widely spaced, pasture has been planted and sheep, goats, cattle and some pigs are herded. Where the trees are thicker an interesting undergrowth occurs comprising many species of *Cistus*, Mastic Tree, *Daphne gnidium*, Strawberry Tree, Lavender, *Halimium halimifolium* and many others. Deer, Wild Boar and Fox roam these lowland woods, and butterflies, such as Swallowtail, Clouded Yellow, Cardinal, and Lulworth and Essex Skippers are abundant.

Birds of prey are common and Red and Black Kites (near water) circling on thermals can usually be seen. White Storks make their nests in trees as do Black Vultures especially in the Monfragüe Reserve.

Interesting areas of lowland mixed forest can be found at Coto del Rey, Sierra de Espuña, Montseny, Garrotxa, Baseit, Monfragüe, Sierras de Gredos and Guadarrama, and Peña de Francia.

SALTWATER AND FRESHWATER MARSHLAND

The largest areas of marshland are found at the estuaries of two of the great rivers of Spain, the Río Ebro which gives rise to the huge Ebro Delta, and the Río Guadalquivir which forms the famous Coto Doñana. Both these deltas are freshwater marshes composed of sediment brought down from the mountains over thousands of years. Large areas have been drained and the flow of water controlled. The resulting rich deep soil produces high-grade rice in the Ebro Delta, and cotton, millet, sunflower and sugar-beet in the eastern side of the Guadalquivir. The western side of the Guadalquivir is the renowned Coto Doñana Reserve, one of the great marshes of Europe, where hundreds of thousands of birds overwinter. During summer this marsh dries out leaving huge areas baked and cracked with just a few small water-holes. These are used by the hundreds of Wild Boar, Red and Fallow Deer, Pardel Lynx and Egyptian Mongoose, which live in the reserve.

The Ebro Delta is highly cultivated, but even so the wildlife is plentiful. It is a wintering ground for ducks and a breeding ground for amphibians, such as the European Pond

Terrapin and Western Spadefoot Toad, and reptiles like the Viperine Snake. Other fresh-water marshes are to be found at the Albufera de Valencia, Las Marismas del Odiel, and the important Aiguamolls de l'Emporda.

Salt-marshes on the other hand have been exploited mainly by the salt-making indus-try, and vast stretches of salt-pans produce an interesting avifauna. The short vegetation is composed mostly of glassworts, saltworts and Sea Purslane, which give cover for nesting Black-winged Stilt, Mallard and many others.

SAND DUNES

These are almost exclusively coastal areas de-rived from sand blown and deposited on the land. There are two types of dune formation: shifting or moving dunes and stabilized dunes. Shifting dunes usually move at a slow rate of 3–6m per year, covering everything in their path. Vegetation is found only in the hollows where water can stand during the winter if the clay substratum is near the surface. Snakes may be seen and also tracks of animals that have passed during the night.

Stabilized sand dunes have vegetation growing on them which has arrested move-ment by binding the sand together. In some areas the vegetation may be trees, usually Maritime Pine, with an abundant under-growth of *Cistus*, *Halimium*, Thrift, Sea Stock, large areas of Hottentot Fig and legu-minous plants. Amongst the trees are Bee-eater and Great Spotted Cuckoo.

Many varieties of butterflies can usually be found, especially blues and skippers, Swallowtails if Fennel is present and the Two-tailed Pasha if the Strawberry Tree is in the area. Birds of prey are fairly numerous, rising on warm air thermals from the hot sand.

The Coto Doñana in the Guadalquivir Delta has the most extensive and highest dune areas, where Red Deer, Wild Boar, Egyptian Mongoose and Pardel Lynx live. Other dune areas can be found on the coast north of Tarifa and the Ebro Delta.

SEA CLIFFS AND BEACH

Where the mountains of hard rock reach the coast, high sea cliffs occur often giving spec-tacular scenery. If the rock is soft, or where there are river estuaries, large expanses of sandy beaches are often produced. In the north-west of Spain the hard core of the Cantábrican mountains meets the sea. The cliffs have been worn by the relentless pounding of the Atlantic Ocean and in many cases a fiord-like coastline has evolved, with some very deep inlets and high cliffs.

All along the northern Spanish coast sea-cliff habitats occur with very few sandy beaches. These cliffs provide nesting ledges for many thousands of seabirds, such as Guillemot, Razorbill, Puffin and Shag. The south and eastern coasts also have spectacular sea cliffs at Gibraltar, the Costa del Sol, Cabo de Gata, Javea, and the Costa Brava where the Pyrenees meet the Mediterranean Sea. Often from these cliff tops, pelagic birds can be seen migrating along the coastline.

Sandy beaches have been formed by the incessant pounding of the sea over many thousands of years. There are some wonder-ful beaches on the Mediterranean coast, much loved by holiday-makers. From the naturalist's point of view, the most satisfying are the long sandy stretches of Tarifa and the 30km-long protected beach at Matalascañas on the Coto Doñana. These beaches provide nesting places for Little Tern, Caspian Tern and Kentish Plover, plus roosting places and feeding areas for Sandwich Tern, Oyster-catcher, many gulls, such as the Lesser Black-backed and Audouin's, and many others.

FRESHWATER LAKES AND RIVERS

There are few natural lakes, but a very large number of huge man-made reservoirs, or embalses, in Spain. Many more embalses are planned which will flood thousands of hectares and submerge many villages. The largest natural lake in Spain is at Gallocanta where thousands of ducks and Cranes over-winter. Most large embalses have little or no vegetation around the edges and are very deep. Therefore the bird population is low.

The rivers Tajo, Duero, Guadalquivir Ebro and Guadiana are the five great Spanish rivers. Four flow into the Atlantic and one, the Ebro, into the Mediterranean. They are all of great importance and the Río Guadalquivir is navigable as far as Sevilla. The river basins possess excellent fertile soil (except for the Río Ebro) and produce a variety of specialized crops. In various places, dams have been built to produce hydro-electric power as well as water for irrigation.

The wild northern coast of Galicia, a haven for nesting birds.

Along the edges of most rivers there is sufficient vegetation to provide nesting and feeding areas for a large number of birds, and of course, certain amphibians and reptiles live in the surrounding undergrowth. Butter-flies, dragonflies and moths inhabit the river basins and two notable moths may be seen: the Death's Head Hawk Moth caterpillar feeds on Potato and Jasmine, and the large Emperor Moth with its 12cm wingspan may be seen near willow, Poplar and fruit trees, all of which grow in the fertile river basins.

CLIMATE

The climate in Spain is as variable as the scenery, with extremes in the centre of the country, heavy rainfall in the northern

The Embalse del Tranco where the Río Guadalquivir cuts through a red sandstone seam, forming a large lake.

mountains and arid deserts in the south. Such a diversity of climate along with the varied geography has lead to a great variety of habitats each of which has its own ecosystem.

With the approach of winter, the shorter day length coupled with the onset of colder weather informs the Brown Bear in the north to begin to look for a dry nest in which to hibernate. This is either between or under rocks. During winter they give birth to their young, who make their first faltering steps into the outside world the following spring. The autumnal weather also tells the birds that it is time to make their long journeys southwards to warmer climates. Therefore migration can be spectacular, especially in the Gibraltar area where many thousands of birds can be seen passing over to Africa on this, the shortest route across the Mediterranean.

With the approach of spring, the reverse occurs and a few sunny days in January will bring everything to life again. This re-awakening moves progressively northwards until in June the Alpine meadows in the mountains are a riot of colour once again.

The table below gives you some idea of the climate of each area at various seasons. With its help you should be able to time your holiday to suit your own preferences.

REGIONAL CLIMATIC INFORMATION

	total annual rainfall (mm)	ave. annual temp. (°C)	ave. Jan. temp. (°C)	ave. July temp. (°C)	lowest temp. (°C)
Barcelona	526	15.2	9.0	23.0	−9.6
Cabo de Gata	122	18.6	13.0	26.5	
Cartagena	205	17.0	12.2	27.2	−1.2
Madrid	419	14.0	4.3	24.3	−12.5
Malaga	600	18.6	11.8	25.0	−0.9
San Sebastian	1396	14.1	9.9	22.3	−8.2
Santiago de Compostella	1655	12.9	9.7	19.9	−5.1
Sevilla	500	19.8	10.3	29.0	−2.7
Sierra de Guadarrama	780	8.7	2.0	18.0	−16.2
Valencia	472	16.9	10.0	25.0	−8.2
Valladolid	308	11.8	4.9	26.0	−21.0
Zaragoza	295	14.7	6.9	23.6	−16.6

CONSERVATION

Since 1985 there has been a great upsurge of national interest in wildlife and conservation to try to retain for the future the areas of natural beauty. It is very gratifying to note that every school-day throughout the year up to 200 school children are taken around the Coto Doñana reserve in safari trucks accompanied by qualified guides. They are introduced to the wonders of nature and shown the heritage which is theirs to preserve for future generations.

There are five national parks in mainland Spain: Covadonga, Ordesa, Aigües Tortes, Tablas de Daimial and Coto Doñana which in total extend to about 95,500ha. These important reserves are managed by the central organization ICONA (Instituto para Conservación de la Naturaleza).

In 1978 conservation and protection of the environment was put under the responsibility of the seventeen autonomous regions and in certain areas has become extremely active. These regional organizations are known as the Agencia de Medio Ambiente (AMA) and are all under the administration of Dirección General del Medio Ambiente in Madrid.

Vast amounts of money and effort are being spent in developing the Natural Parks which these autonomies manage. Large and extensive reception and information centres are being built, which help to make the general public aware of the importance of preserving and protecting the countryside. The guides and staff at these centres are always extremely helpful and knowledgeable, and are often available to take parties on organized tours of the reserves.

There are many factors which are rapidly changing the ecology of the key areas. Overgrazing by sheep and goats does an enormous amount of damage, turning large expanses of natural grassland into steppe land devoid of much vegetation. The formation of reservoirs (embalses) drowns large areas of river basins, destroying much of the local habitat. The formation of hydro-electric stations at the base of these embalses also produces problems due to disfigurement of the countryside by power cables, which in addition destroy a large number of birds by entanglement. Tourism coupled with urbanization has a detrimental effect, destroying habitats and lowering water tables.

Disturbance of endangered species, which in many cases is critical, has to a certain extent been taken care of by designating some areas Integral Reserves of Scientific Interest. These are usually within an existing reserve and access is completely prohibited to the public to safeguard the nesting rare birds, breeding mammals or rare plants.

Effluent from whatever source has a detrimental effect on the environment. Pesticides and insecticides from rice production have killed many thousands of birds in the Coto Doñana, Albufera de Valencia and the Ebro Delta. Discharges from the industrial port of Huelva into the river have also done harm. The opencast copper mine at Río Tinto destroys habitat as well as discharging chemicals derived from copper and sulphur into the Río Tinto itself, turning the water blue and yellow in some places and killing aquatic vegetation.

New afforestation with exotic Eucalyptus is very dangerous as the natural vegetation is completely destroyed and takes many years to regenerate, if it ever does. Monoculture like this and intensive vegetable growing can have an adverse effect on the wildlife. In Almería near Roquetas de Mar there are hundreds of hectares completely covered with plastic houses for early vegetable

Effluent from the Río Tinto copper mine killing vegetation and fish in the river and turning the water bright green and yellowish. Pollution like this still goes on despite the great work being carried out by ICONA and the regional conservation organizations to try to maintain the wilder areas of Spain.

cultivation. From a distance these areas look like huge lakes, yet in reality they are devoid of wildlife.

Fire can be a serious problem, destroying many hectares of woodland and scrub each year. These are started either accidently by cigarettes carelessly thrown out of vehicle windows onto the tinder-dry roadsides or by a piece of glass left by campers or picnickers. Occasionally arson is the cause. Recently seventy helicopters have been contracted to help during some of the summer months in some of the more important areas for wildlife. They rapidly extinguish any fires within their particular regions.

Over 1,250,000 licences for shooting are issued each year, and inevitably, despite considerable restrictions, private and restricted shooting areas and the majority of birds being totally protected, a lot of illegal shooting takes place.

In many species the decline in numbers appears to have ceased and in many cases numbers are actually increasing. For example, Wild Boar and Red Deer have bred so successfully in some areas that they now have to be culled. On the whole the measures taken since 1985 seem to be having an effect, but only time will tell.

TRAVEL TIPS

Finally, here are a few tips for the traveller to Spain. In brochures, Spain is always depicted as a land of sun and sand along its Mediterranean coastline. There is much more than this, and it must be remembered that being a high-altitude country there is also snow and frost. With this in mind the best times to visit must be chosen accordingly.

If you want to see overwintering birds, ducks, geese and Cranes in particular, the southern regions are much milder with little or no snow. The weather on the inland plains can be severe in winter with substantial snowfall but they are well worth a visit. The spring is superb for migrating birds, especially in the environs of Gibraltar where birds pass in their thousands over the narrow Straits. Equally, April and May are the best times for flowers along the coastal strip and for land below 1500m (4920 feet), particularly in Andalucía.

The summer months are perfect almost anywhere: the high Alpine meadows are at their best, the butterflies are a riot of colour and the summer visiting birds are at their peak. The plains can be extremely hot and the mountains delightfully cool. The

Many square kilometres of plastic-covered structures for early vegetable production destroy natural habitat in southern Spain.

autumn with its deciduous trees, especially in the north, the grape harvest and the autumn migration completes a year full of interest. At all times of the year, even in summer, there can be a large temperature drop at dusk, and therefore a warm garment may be needed for evenings.

The major trunk roads between the main centres of population are very good with some toll roads which can be avoided. Be careful to respect the speed limits as there can be heavy on-the-spot fines for speeding; seat belts are obligatory. As the roads often by-pass the towns, petrol stations can be few and far between unless you go deliberately into a town. Toilets at the larger petrol stations are usually spotless, but sometimes the 'Ladies' is locked, in which case you have to ask the attendant for the key.

There are generally plenty of cafés and restaurants of all grades. The larger transport cafés are reasonably cheap and clean, but of course not five star. Within the main tourist areas there are excellent camping sites but many, except for the larger ones, are closed outside the main tourist season. Wild camping is not encouraged, but many of the reserves have camping areas within their boundaries, equipped with water and grills. Charcoal may be used on these but fires are not allowed. Hiking is permissible, but do not enter restricted areas which are adequately signed or fenced off, as there may be fighting bulls grazing within!

Hotels and hostels are numerous. As map references in this book have been based on the Michelin map co-ordinates, I would suggest their *Red Guide* as a sleeping and eating reference, as places mentioned in it are underlined on the maps.

For photographers it is always advisable to take plenty of film as this can be expensive in Spain. Remember that the light is very much stronger than in Britain, especially in the south, so any photographs taken in the middle of the day may look over-exposed and washed out. Under recent legislation, it is forbidden to carry extra-long telephoto lenses, telescopes and binoculars in some of the key areas, in theory to prevent nest robbing and disturbance of rare nesting birds.

It is sensible to carry a first-aid kit, but in many villages and certainly all towns there are very well-marked first-aid posts. These are well equipped to deal with minor injuries. Chemist shops (farmacias) can also be very helpful. Snakes and scorpions are around, but the possibility of being bitten or stung is very slight. There is a European Black Widow spider which can cause a minor problem and medical advice should be sought if you are bitten as some irritation and pain can result. I hasten to add that in over twenty years of living in the Iberian Peninsula I have only heard of two or three cases! Lastly, on some beaches the Scorpion Fish can inflict painful stings and in such cases the nearest first-aid post should be sought.

SECTION II.
SITE GUIDE

In the pages that follow, 150 of the best sites to see wildlife in Spain are described. The sites have been divided into eleven convenient regions, each of which begins with a map showing the main towns, roads, rivers, and positions of the sites. The map on page 26 shows the eleven regions as a whole.

Every site begins with a summary box which gives the location and main features of the site at a glance. The sub-headings in the summary boxes are fairly self-explanatory but mean the following:

Grid reference: the reference on the Michelin maps, scale 1/400,000 for Spain;
Location: the general position of the site relative to the nearest town or city;
Access: how easy or difficult the site is to reach with comments on any restrictions to access;
Season: the best time of year to visit;
Terrain: the habitat and general topography;

Comments: any useful advice, such as need for heavy footwear or insect repellent;
Specialities: unusual, rare or exciting species for which the site is renowned which should enthuse the naturalist to visit the site;
Subsidiary: other interesting sites nearby which may or may not be of a similar habitat.

The main text for each site describes how to get there, what to expect at the site in terms of scenery and habitat, and what particular species to look out for.

Throughout the section, species of particular interest in the region are highlighted in *Special Species Boxes.* The measurements given in these boxes relate to length (L) or width (W) and are given in centimetres.

The table beginning on page 228 gives a summary of all the sites and indicates which sites are best for birds, mammals, reptiles, amphibians, butterflies and flowers.

Opposite: *the fantastic futuristic rock formations at El Torqual de Antequera (see Site 117).*

Right: *the Silver-studded Blue (Plebejus argus) is a common butterfly throughout much of Spain.*

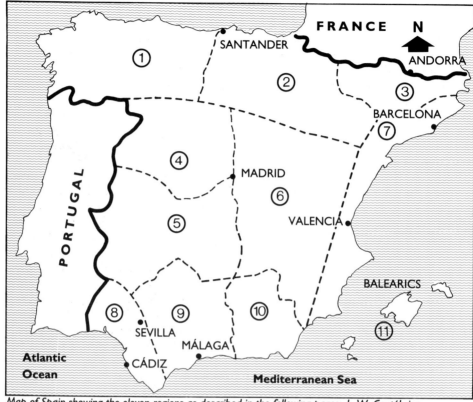

Map of Spain showing the eleven regions as described in the following pages. 1. W. Cantábrica; 2. E. Cantábrica; 3. Pyrenees; 4. N. Meseta; 5 Extremadura; 6. Iberian Mountains; 7. Mediterranean; 8. W. Andalucía; 9. Central Andalucía; 10. E. Andalucía; 11. Balearics.

1. WEST CANTÁBRICA

INTRODUCTION

This area forms the north-west of Spain. The western and northern limits are bounded by the sea, from the Portuguese frontier in the south-west to Santander in the north-east. The southern boundary follows the northern Portuguese frontier as far as the Sierra de la Culebra, then through Benavente to Palencia and finally north to Santander.

Its coastline receives the full force of the Atlantic storms which drive in from the west across the Bay of Biscay. These have eroded the softer rocks and created fiords running many kilometres inland. The northern coastline has a very fertile narrow strip before the land rises steeply to the mountains. Here cattle and sheep feed on the lush pastures which are divided into small-holdings. These are very characteristic of the area. Many of the sea cliffs are rugged and awesome in size.

Beyond the fertile strip is the high backbone of the Cantábrican mountains with many peaks over 2000m (6560 feet).

These gradually slope towards the south to create the large plateau which forms a large part of Spain's land area.

The mountains in the west are composed of Cambrian and Silurian rocks and are much older geologically than the high carboniferous limestone of the Picos de Europa in the east.

This is the wettest region of Spain. The barrier of the Cantábrican mountains induces depressions to deposit their moisture on the northern slopes either as rain in summer or snow in winter. The south side of the range is considerably drier.

On the coast the climate is equable, but humid, seldom reaching freezing in winter and rarely exceeding 30°C in summer. The mountains can become very cold with frequent snowfalls between October and May.

Wild and remote, West Cantábrica is important as a stronghold for a number of rare mammals, birds and reptiles and for many endemic plants and butterflies. In this area of small and very hilly pasture-lands, the more primitive methods of agriculture have been and still are practised, largely due to the region's inaccessibility. Artificial fertilizers and pesticides have not been used with the result that the meadows and pastures remain botanically rich and full of butterflies. There are, for example, many varieties of narcissi which in early spring cover the lower pastures. As the snow recedes, crocuses and gentians appear with large numbers of orchids and a wealth of other plants which turn the mountainsides into a paintbox of colour. Following the flowers the butterflies appear in profusion with a number of rare subspecies in isolated communities: Almond-eyed Ringlet, Scarce Swallowtail, Spanish Argus and subspecies of the Gavarnie Blue and Chapman's Ringlet.

Rare birds also have their strongholds in these mountains, such as Wallcreeper, Black Woodpecker and Middle Spotted Woodpecker which can be found here and in the

FIFTY INTERESTING SPECIES TO LOOK FOR

Cory's Shearwater	Middle Spotted	Chamois	Dog's-tooth Violet
British Storm-	Woodpecker	Swallowtail	Large-flowered
petrel	Snow Finch	Large Tortoiseshell	Butterwort
Black-necked	Alpine Accentor	Apollo	Green Hellebore
Grebe	Alpine Chough	Clouded Yellow	Narcissus asturiensis
Golden Eagle	Fire Salamander	Cleopatra	Narcissus triandrus
Peregrine	Iberian Wall Lizard	Almond-eyed	Peony
Griffon Vulture	Bocage's Wall	Ringlet	Pyramidal
Capercaillie	Lizard	Ringlet	Saxifrage
Grey Partridge	Brown Bear	Blue-spot	Pyrenean Lily
(Spanish race)	Wolf	Hairstreak	Sea Daffodil
Iberian Guillemot	Asturcón Horse	Gavarnie Blue	Black Vanilla
Eagle Owl	Pyrenean Desman	Chalk-hill Blue	Orchid
Black Woodpecker	Wild Boar	Fritillaria hispanica	Lizard Orchid
Wallcreeper	Roe Deer	Horned Violet	Man Orchid

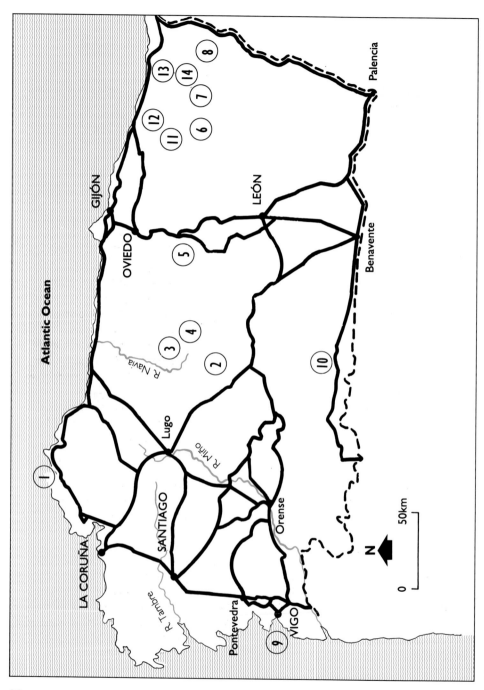

Spectacular scenery at the most north-western point of Spain. Atlantic storms have attacked the softer rocks to produce a rugged coastline of spectacular cliffs and fiord-like inlets. Seabirds are a feature of the area.

Pyrenees. The western coast boasts some of the last examples of the Iberian race of the Guillemot in Spain. The Capercaillie and Grey Partridge, due to isolation, have evolved distinct races here.

Amphibians and reptiles can be found in good numbers in rivers and low-lying areas with snakes in the scrub. Fire Salamander, Stripe-necked Terrapin, Marsh Frog, Iberian Wall Lizard, Common Toad, Bocage's Wall Lizard and Grass Snake are all present.

Brown Bears, Wolves, Chamois and the Pyrenean Desman are almost holding their own in this scenically stunning part of Spain.

Habitats vary from large Alpine and sub-alpine areas in the Cordillera Cantábrica to coniferous forests and deciduous broad-leaved woods scattered in the valleys, and steppe land in the southern dry plateau. Sea cliffs are a dominant feature of the coastline. Several small rivers have their sources and mouths in this mountainous region.

The grid references used in the following site descriptions relate to Michelin map number 441.

Opposite: map of West Cantábrica. The sites are numbered as in the text. Only main roads and the major rivers of the region are shown.

I ORTIGUEIRA ESTUARY	
Grid reference:	A 6
Location:	At Ortigueira
Access:	Excellent
Season:	All year round
Terrain:	Tidal mudflats
Comments:	Maybe Atlantic storms
Specialities:	Puffin, Wigeon, Pintail, Kentish Plover, Bar-tailed Godwit
Subsidiary:	Ribadeo Estuary, B 8

This estuary is situated on the northern coast on the C 642 between Cabo Ortegal and Punta de la Estaca de Bares. It is a wide tidal estuary with extensive mudflats which provide a feeding and resting ground for a large range of migrant birds. The mudflats are covered at high tide, but there is a wide belt of vegetation at the river edge of mainly *Salicornia* where migrating warblers rest.

This part of Galicia is characterized by deep fiord-like inlets and high rocky cliffs. They are continually subjected to massive Atlantic rollers and storms that bring considerable rainfall. The rain in turn waters the green pastures for which the area is noted.

During the winter vast numbers of ducks

29

Mudflats on the Ortigueira Estuary are an excellent feeding ground for ducks and waders, especially during winter and the migration periods. Commoner species to see here include Wigeon, Teal, Pochard, Mallard, Pintail, Grey Plover, Kentish Plover, Bar-tailed Godwit and Sanderling.

feed on the estuary including Wigeon, Teal, Pochard, Mallard, Pintail and Shoveler. Waders on passage, such as Grey Plover, Bar-tailed Godwit, Turnstone, Oystercatcher, Kentish Plover and Sanderling, rest in large numbers on the sandy shores.

Razorbill, Guillemot, Puffin and Kittiwake breed on the rocky headlands, while offshore Manx, Cory's and Great Shearwaters skim the waves. Gannets pass in their thousands on their migration routes. Some British Storm-petrels may be seen as there is a large breeding colony to the east.

2 RESERVA NACIONAL DE LOS ANCARES LEONESES	
Grid reference:	D 9/10
Location:	NW of Ponferrada
Access:	Very small winding roads
Season:	Late spring, summer and early autumn
Terrain:	Mountains with forests and maquis scrub
Comments:	Can be snowbound
Specialities:	Short-toed Eagle, Red Squirrel, Wild Boar, Lizard Orchid, Green Hellebore

This reserve is reached from Ponferrada by joining the LE 711 north of the town then continuing on the LE 712 (both small roads). This is a remote, sparsely populated area on the western spur of the Cantábrican mountains. The northern slopes contain large forests of deciduous oak, Silver Birch and Spanish Chestnut. The southern slopes are dry and covered with maquis scrub consisting of Sage-leaved and Narrow-leaved Cistus, Heather and Gorse.

The area is full of mammal life, including Wild Boar, Genet, Beech Marten, Wild Cat and the Red Squirrel, which in the northern part of Spain is considerably darker in colour than its southern counterpart.

The bird population is notable for the large numbers of Capercaillie, the large black bird like a cross between a turkey and a Black Grouse! Look for the Short-toed Eagle, the summer visitor which feeds mainly on the snakes and amphibians which inhabit the river valleys. When hunting, this eagle hovers with a slow flapping of the wings, its legs dangling and its head looking downwards.

Plants are both plentiful and well worth looking out for. Species which may be seen include *Narcissus nobilis*, Green Hellebore and the Lizard Orchid amongst other varieties. The unusual Tongue Orchid is very common in this area.

A typical corn store or 'hórreo', raised up on stone 'mushrooms' as a protection from vermin.

3 COTO NACIONAL DE MUNIELLOS

Grid reference:	C/D 9/10
Location:	S of Cangas de Narcea
Access:	By small roads, winding in the last part
Season:	Late spring, summer and early autumn
Terrain:	Deciduous woods, mountainous
Comments:	Sensible walking shoes
Specialities:	Black Woodpecker, Capercaillie, Wolf, Beech Woods, Man Orchid
Subsidiary:	Puerto de Rañadoiro, D 10

Angel's Tears Narcissus *Narcissus triandrus*

This is one of the most distinctive narcissi found in northern Spain. It is not particularly rare, being found from sea level up to and on occasion exceeding 2000m (6560 feet) in the Cordillera Cantábrica. It is a very variable species ranging from white to deep yellow. There is still some confusion in its classification regarding the possible formation of subspecies according to flower colour.

Up to four flowers on a 40cm (16 inches) stem open from March through to May according to the height at which they are growing. They have recurved petals giving an unmistakable appearance, and are usually found on acid soil with plenty of moisture during the growing season, preferably on the north-facing aspect.

Situated south of Cangas de Narcea, the site is reached by first taking the O 734 to Venta Nueva then turning west onto the O 701. The forest of Muniellos is an EEC Special Protection Area covering 2975ha. It is composed of deciduous Pedunculate and Sessile Oak as well as a good stand of European Beech. It is therefore one of the best preserved areas of natural deciduous forest in Spain.

It is a mountainous area, rising to a height of 1685m (5528 feet) at La Bobia de Teleyerba and 1680m (5512 feet) at Candanosa. It is formed of slate and quartzite and is therefore much older geologically than the higher Picos de Europa, further to the east, which are of carboniferous limestone.

Because it is a highly protected area it is a haven for the more uncommon mammals; Brown Bears find refuge, especially amongst the Beech trees, Wolves roam through the forest, and Wild Boar forage in the undergrowth for tubers and roots.

This is a recognized breeding site for a large number of Capercaillie and the Black Woodpecker. Another unusual bird found in these remote forests is the Middle Spotted Woodpecker, which is mainly found in south-east Europe.

Many plants are to be found, in particular the Man Orchid and the Angel's Tears Narcissus (*see* box on previous page).

4 RESERVA NACIONAL DE DEGAÑA	
Grid reference:	D 10
Location:	N of Ponferrada
Access:	Small roads, quite good
Season:	Avoid the winter months
Terrain:	Mountainous with Beech woods
Specialities:	Capercaillie, Brown Bear, Chamois, *Narcissus asturiensis*, Angel's Tears Narcissus
Subsidiary:	Sierra de Gistreo, D 10

This reserve is approached from Ponferrada northwards or southwards from Cangas de Narcea on the C 631. At Caboalles de Abajo turn onto the LE 733 which goes over the Puerto de Cerrado (1359m; 4459 feet) and across the reserve. It is a mountainous area, well covered with Beech woods, which benefit from the heavy rain which falls when the Atlantic depressions drive in from the Bay of Biscay. Within the Beech forests, Common Hazel often grows, as well as fine stands of Spanish Chestnuts, both of which produce commercially important nuts.

Patches of pasture-land are grazed by cattle, sheep and goats and many extremely good local cheeses can be obtained. This is another stronghold of the Brown Bear, whose favourite habitat is within Beech forests like this. Unfortunately, these animals

Brown Bear *Ursus arctos* L to 213

At the beginning of this century there were estimated to be at least 1000 Brown Bears living in Spain. Now ninety years later the population is down to approximately 100, with the main stronghold in the Cordillera Cantábrica in the Asturias province, and scattered groups in the Pyrenees.

Continued persecution and destruction of habitat has brought this fine animal to the brink of extinction in Iberia. Now, however, it may survive and even prosper, if the latest conservation laws are upheld. These impose a fine of 1,000,000 pesetas with possibly a year's imprisonment for killing one. Equally, should bear damage be proven, compensation is available to farmers.

Brown Bears are basically nocturnal. They are omnivorous in their eating habits, catching fish (preferring salmon!), eating berries, robbing bee hives and grubbing for roots. When fully mature, at four years old, they weigh 200kg. Their life span is in the region of thirty years.

are becoming very scarce and are on the endangered species list, partly due to habitat destruction (*see* box). Chamois are common on the higher ground, while Roe Deer are plentiful within the woods. Wild Boar and Wolves may be seen. Capercaillie are frequent as is a subspecies of the Grey Partridge restricted to the northern part of Iberia.

During spring look for species of narcissus, as this northern area holds some very interesting species, such as *Narcissus nobilis*, a great trumpet daffodil, *N. asturiensis*, Angel's Tears Narcissus · and varieties of Hoop Petticoat Narcissus. Moist meadows where the snow has melted are the best localities to find this group. Butterflies abound in these meadows too.

5 RESERVA NACIONAL DE SOMIEDO

Grid reference:	C 11/12
Location:	SW of Oviedo
Access:	Winding secondary roads
Season:	Late spring, summer and early autumn
Terrain:	Mountain and lakes
Comments:	Roads can be inaccessible during winter
Specialities:	Black Woodpecker, Middle Spotted Woodpecker, Large-flowered Butterwort, *Teesdaliopsis conferta*, Dog's-tooth Violet
Subsidiary:	Puerto de Pajares, D 12; Desfiladero del Teverga, C 11

This site is approached by the N 634 from Oviedo westwards, turning south onto the O 424. It is a large mountainous area containing old Palaeozoic rocks rising up to 2417m (7930 feet), with many deep gorges, well-wooded slopes with oak and Beech, fertile river basins and Alpine pasture. High

in the centre of the reserve are the lakes of Saliencia, which lie in a glaciated valley.

The area is rich in both plant and animal life, especially in the high meadows, where after the snow recedes gentians are common, along with *Narcissus asturiensis*, *Fritillaria hispanica*, the insectivorous Large-flowered Butterwort, the endemic *Teesdaliopsis conferta*, and the beautiful Dog's-tooth Violet which can cover large areas with its pink-violet flowers. Very many varieties of butterflies, especially Small Copper, Escher's Blue, Brown Argus and Clouded Yellow, are found in these flowery pastures.

In the beech woods, Brown Bears are present, unfortunately a diminishing population, but they are heavily protected as are the Wolves which also roam these woods.

Birds are numerous, with many Capercaillie and Grey Partridge of the Spanish race. Black and Middle Spotted Woodpeckers are found throughout most of the woodlands in the reserve.

Dog's-tooth Violet (Erythronium dens-canis) found in many of the woodland areas in northern Spain.

6 RESERVA NACIONAL DE RIAÑO	
Grid reference:	C 14/15
Location:	S from Cangas de Onis
Access:	Winding but good
Season:	Late spring, summer, early autumn
Terrain:	High mountainous area
Comments:	Can be snow-covered in winter
Specialities:	Black Woodpecker, Capercaillie, Brown Bear, Apollo, Blue-spot Hairstreak
Subsidiary:	Reserva nacional de Fuentes Carrionas, D 15/16; Reserva nacional de Mampodre, C/D 13/14

This is a very high mountainous area rising up to 2140m (7021 feet), generally sloping towards the south and with the Picos de Europa lying to the north. It is easily accessible from the northern Costa Verde by good but winding roads, either from the south from Cangas de Onis on the C 637 or from the north-east on the N 621.

Riaño village was known as the most beautiful in the whole of the Cantábrican area, but it is now submerged under 50m of water within the Embalse de Riaño. Deforestation has also taken place to provide new pasture-land. Even with so much destruction of the natural habitat, it is still a wonderful place to visit, with meadows full of *Narcissus nobilis* and flower-filled pastoral mountainsides which are a haven for butterflies. Chalk-hill Blue, a form of the Blue-spot Hairstreak, Adonis and Common Blues, Ringlet, Large Tortoiseshell, a variety of fritillaries, Apollo, Silver-spotted Skipper and Large Skipper are just some to be seen.

Large areas of deciduous oak and Beech hold a small number of Brown Bears, a large concentration of Capercaillie, Black Woodpecker, Middle Spotted Woodpecker and in summer Short-toed Eagles.

7 RESERVA NACIONAL DE SAJA	
Grid reference:	C 15/16
Location:	S of San Vicente de la Barquera
Access:	By three different routes
Season:	Late spring, summer and early autumn
Terrain:	High mountains and valleys
Comments:	Can be a lot of snow in winter
Specialities:	Wolf, Red Fox, *Crocus nudiflorus,* Lizard Orchid, Black Vanilla Orchid
Subsidiary:	Cuevas de Altamira, B 17 (with museums and caves)

This is reasonably easy to reach from the Costa Verde by a series of different routes. Travel southwards either on the N 621 from Panes or the S 224 from Bielba or the C 625 from Cabezón de la Sal. It is one of the largest reserves in Spain, situated on the eastern end of the Picos de Europa, just north of the Picos de Tres Mares. It is mountainous with some huge limestone ridges rising to 2046m (6713 feet). Two rivers, the Saja and Nansa, run through the centre.

The valleys are very lush, with abundant grassland extending up to the base of the limestone cliffs. Woodlands consist of Beech, deciduous oak and Silver Birch, with an undergrowth of Bracken, Tree Heather and Holly. By the roadside and on rocky outcrops, various species of *Sedum,* scabious,

Looking towards the Reserva nacional de Saja with a salmon-fishing river bordered by Poplars (Populus alba) in the foreground. The pastures in the valleys of the reserve are good for wild flowers and butterflies; the high mountains are the haunt of birds of prey, such as Griffon Vulture (Gyps fulvus) and Golden Eagle (Aquila chrysaetos).

Lithospermum, heather and *Pulsatilla* can be found. In spring, orchids come up in quantity in the pasture-land; the spectacular Lizard Orchid is plentiful, as is the Black Vanilla Orchid. In autumn these same pastures are covered with *Crocus nudiflorus*.

Birds of prey are numerous, with Griffon Vulture and Golden Eagle on the high crags, and Buzzard, Kestrel and Raven hunting in the lower slopes. In the woods there are Jay, woodpeckers, Blackbird, Robin and Wren, and Wolves and Foxes may also be seen.

8 ALTO CAMPOO	
Grid reference:	C 16/17
Location:	S of San Vincente de la Barquera
Access:	Fairly easy
Season:	Late spring, summer and early autumn
Terrain:	Mountain and valley
Comments:	Sensible walking shoes
Specialities:	Almond-eyed Ringlet, Horned Violet, Pyrenean Lily, Lizard Orchid, *Narcissus nobilis*
Subsidiary:	Embalse del Ebro, C/D 17/18

Reasonably easy to reach from the Costa Verde coast by the N 634, travelling east to Cabezón de la Sal then south on the C 625 to Espinilla and west from there on the C 628. A very high mountainous area to the east of the Picos de Europa incorporating the Picos de Tres Mares, rising up to 2175m (7136 feet) and giving birth to rivers which flow into three seas. The great Río Ebro flows into the huge freshwater lake, the Embalse del Ebro, and then continues south-east to the Mediterranean. The rivers Saja and Nansa flow north to the Bay of Biscay, while the Areños and Pisuerga flow south to join the Duero and enter the Atlantic at Oporto.

The valleys of Alto Campóo leading up to the snowy heights of the Pico are covered with Pyrenean Oak where Brown Bears and Wolves still shelter. Higher up the valleys the woodlands give way to Alpine pastures that produce a wealth of flowers. In springtime the grasslands can be carpeted with *Narcissus nobilis* in company with Cowslips and Horned Violets. Orchids are numerous with the Lizard Orchid further down the valley, where you can also see, with luck, the Yellow Pyrenean Lily.

Of the many butterflies found in the pastures, the Almond-eyed Ringlet is the most

SECTION II: SITE GUIDE

interesting as it is found here and nowhere else in Spain. Iolas and Baton Blues, Silky and Large Ringlets, Meadow and Heath Fritillaries, maybe the Swallowtail, and in early spring the Cleopatra are all to be seen.

The mountain birds usual to this region are present with the addition of the occasional Booted Eagle.

9 ISLAS CIES NATURAL PARK	
Grid reference:	F 3
Location:	W of Vigo
Access:	By ferry from Vigo
Season:	Spring, summer and autumn
Terrain:	Islands, steep cliffs and sand dunes
Comments:	Campsite, no other accommodation
Specialities:	Guillemot, Fire Salamander, Iberian Wall Lizard, Bocage's Wall Lizard, *Corema album*
Subsidiary:	Inland Natural Park of Monte Alhoya, F 3/4

These two small islands off the west coast of Spain can only be approached by ferry from Vigo. They cover an area of 430ha, but are very important for breeding seabirds, Shags in particular, which nest in the caves and on rocky ledges. They are, however, more important perhaps for the Iberian Guillemot as only about 150 pairs remain, all on these islands. The islands are virtually uninhabited, with a few fishermen living there during the winter and some tourists enjoying the beaches and campsite during the summer.

They are mainly grass covered, but there are a few small plantations of pine and Eucalyptus. On the beaches in summer the highly scented Sea Daffodil grows with the

Sea Daffodil (Pancratium maritimum) *grows on stony and sandy beaches. It is very highly scented.*

rare shrub *Corema album* with its sweet white mistletoe-shaped fruit.

The brilliantly coloured black-and-yellow Fire Salamander is found in moist areas, but is nocturnal. During the day the Iberian Wall Lizard and Bocage's Wall Lizard can be seen sunning themselves on the rocks.

There are two bird observatories for which you need a license to visit. These can be obtained from ICONA, Michelina 1, Pontevedra, Spain.

10 SIERRA DE LA CABRERA AND VALLE DE SANABRIA	
Grid reference:	F 9/10
Location:	Immediately N of Puebla de Sanabria
Access:	Good, by a series of small roads
Season:	Late spring, summer and early autumn
Terrain:	Alpine meadows and woodlands
Comments:	Good walking shoes
Specialities:	Golden Eagle, Grey Partridge, *Hispidella hispanica, Narcissus rupicola*, Black-veined White
Subsidiary:	Montes de León, E 10/11

A series of small roads running to the north from Puebla de Sanabria give access to this region. The lake of Sanabria is situated within the natural park at 1028m (3373 feet), with the rounded mountain tops of the Sierra de la Cabrera rising to 2124m (6969 feet) further to the north, where snow can lie for much of the year. These mountains are composed of Cambrian and Silurian rocks with outcrops of granite, therefore producing an acid soil where Heather predominates.

In the valley by the lake, there are Spanish Chestnut and Pyrenean Oak. By the roadsides an attractive hawkbit-like plant *Hispidella hispanica* is showy with its yellow flowers. In some of the side valleys interesting flowers can be found: Martagon Lily with deep orange recurved flowers, the colourful Peony and also species of saxifrage and geranium. On the high plateau, growing in the short grass and Heather, *Narcissus rupicola* and the yellow-flowered Mountain Pansy can be found.

There are numerous butterflies to be seen, including fritillaries, Meadow Brown, Wood White, Black-veined White, Clouded Yellow and Swallowtail.

Birds of prey, such as Golden Eagle and Kestrel, nest in the rocky sites; Magpies are numerous; Grey Herons fish in the rivers; and Griffon Vultures nest on the cliffs, especially in the Barranco de Fornillo. In summer, Short-toed Eagles can be seen hunting for snakes, lizards and frogs.

PICOS DE EUROPA

This is an area situated on the watershed of the Cordillera Cantábrica, within easy reach of the Costa Verde on the Bay of Biscay coastline (grid reference C 14/15/16). The region is dominated by huge precipitous limestone crags rising to 2648m (8688 feet) at La Torre Cerredo.

Covadonga, Spain's first national park, was created in 1918 and provides a refuge and protection for a large number of endangered species. There is a wealth of butterflies, plants, mammals and birds within this whole area. Three great gorges, cut into the mountains by the rivers Deva, Cares and Sella, are spectacular with cliffs rising 500m (1650 feet) almost vertically from the river beds. Small plants cling to the rocks and where the mountains are not as steep there are woods of Beech where Brown Bears still exist.

The Alpine meadows are of great botanical importance. Forty species of orchid can be found here including a large number of the 'insect' or *Ophrys* species. As the snow recedes the pastures come alive with flowering plants such as crocuses, Dog's-tooth Violet, narcissi and gentians.

On the pastures sheep graze, producing milk from which the famous 'Cabrales' blue-veined cheese is made. A few of the wild Asturcón (Garrano) Horses are found, especially near the glacial lakes at Vega de Enol, and Chamois inhabit the higher zones and can easily be seen. At the beginning of this century they were rare, but with careful conservation they are now safeguarded and are relatively abundant.

Lower down in the valleys, by the streams, lives the very rare Pyrenean Desman, a relative of the Mole but brown with a long snout, round tail and flattened spade-like hind feet. Sadly their numbers have been greatly diminished by habitat destruction as they need very pure water for breeding.

Birds are a very great feature of the 'Picos' with a large number of them rarely found elsewhere in Spain. The Wallcreeper with red and black wings can occasionally be seen

37

Early morning above the clouds in the Picos de Europa. This wonderfully unspoilt region is home to many rare animals and plants.

searching for insects on the cliff sides. Chough and Alpine Chough can be observed higher up and Griffon Vultures fly around the peaks. In the woods Black Woodpecker, Capercaillie and Eagle Owl can be found.

Butterflies are plentiful, especially in the high Alpine meadows: Scarce Swallowtail, Swallowtail, Gavarnie Blue and Spanish Argus are notable examples.

Salmon fishing is available within this area, with some wide, good, shallow rivers. Permits have to be obtained and enquiries should be made at the local tourist office.

This area is generally very wet climatically, catching the full force of depressions coming in from the Atlantic. During winter, heavy snowfalls occur and there is much fog, but during the summer it can be warm with clear skies.

11 DESFILADERO DE LOS BEYOS

Grid reference:	C 14
Location:	S of Cangas de Onis, N of Riaño
Access:	Good
Season:	Spring, summer and autumn
Terrain:	Deep spectacular gorge
Comments:	Can be snow-bound in winter
Specialities:	Wallcreeper, Snow Finch, Giant Orchid, *Antirrhinum braun-blanquetti*, Angel's Tears Narcissus

South of Cangas de Onis on the C 637 at the western end of the Picos de Europa massif is a deep spectacular gorge, cut by the Río Sella.

In some places it is only a few metres wide whereas in others it is wide enough to contain a small village.

The plants growing in this gorge are very interesting and in a wide variety. At the high pass of Puerto del Pontón (1290m; 4232 feet) there are some meadows full of orchid species, including the spectacular Giant Orchid, while on the rocks the Pyramidal Saxifrage grows, which is similar to the Pyrenean Saxifrage but has broader strap-shaped leaves. Further down the gorge the high cliffs have large plants of *Antirrhinum braun-blanquetti* with big yellow-and-cream flowers. Also look for the blue *Aquilegia* species and Angel's Tears Narcissus.

Birds are numerous with Griffon Vultures gliding on the thermals and Golden Eagles on the rocks, but look on the cliffs within the gorge and you may see Wallcreeper, Alpine Accentor and the Snow Finch.

The Spectacular 80cm-high Giant Orchid (Barlia robertiana) in the Desfiladero de los Beyos. The basal leaves are enormous.

12 COVADONGA

Grid reference:	C 14
Location:	SE of Cangas de Onis
Access:	Good
Season:	Spring, summer and autumn
Terrain:	High mountains
Comments:	Higher roads impassable in winter; information centre open in summer
Specialities:	Middle Spotted Woodpecker, Eagle Owl, Chamois, Gavarnie Blue, Dog's-tooth Violet

Leave Cangas de Onis eastwards on the C 6312, shortly turning south onto the C 220. Historically, here in about 722AD Pelayo defeated the Muslims and was proclaimed King of Asturias. In this way the area became the cradle of the Spanish monarchy and to this day its monuments are of national cultural significance.

Ecologically, this is an EEC Special Protection Area comprising 16,925ha. It is a site full of rarities and is scenically beautiful. Covadonga is surrounded by large Beech woods full of birds: Black and Great, Middle and Lesser Spotted Woodpeckers, Nuthatch, Short-toed Treecreeper, Pied Flycatcher, Robin and Wren, while in the evening you may hear the low hoot of the Eagle Owl.

Higher up the mountainside the woods give way to Alpine pasture where sheep graze and wild horses roam. Here there are two glacial lakes, Lagos de Enol and de la Ercina.

The area is a paradise for flowers, butterflies, birds and mammals. The exotic Dog's-tooth Violet, which is not in any way related

Sheep grazing in a lower pasture-land of Covadonga. This site became Spain's first national park in 1918.

13 DESFILADERO DE LA HERMIDA	
Grid reference:	C 16
Location:	SW of San Vicente de la Barquera
Access:	Good
Season:	Spring, summer and autumn
Terrain:	Deep spectacular gorge
Comments:	Fine salmon-fishing river
Specialities:	Griffon Vulture, Alpine Chough, Chapman's Ringlet, Lizard Orchid, *Narcissus asturiensis*

to the violet, but refers to the colour of the beautiful flower, may be found as may Bee, Fly and Woodcock Orchids early in the season. The Tongue Orchid opens its unusual flowers later on.

Many of the skippers, including Small and Lulworth, should be seen and also the Gavarnie Blue. Chamois are present on the mountain tops, and Wolves and Brown Bears are around but are becoming increasingly rare.

There are many fine walks within the mountains with dramatic views of the tall 'Picos' limestone pinnacles. This truly magnificent site well deserves the privilege of having been Spain's first national park

Situated on the N 621, this is the easternmost gorge in the Picos de Europa. Leave San Vicente de la Barquera westwards on the N 634 and after 12km turn south onto the N 621 towards Potes. The Río Deva cuts through the hard limestone rock making a narrow defile just wide enough to take the road.

The cliffsides have many small plants securing a hold in the crevices. On the narrow roadsides *Linaria*, iris, *Ajuga*, *Dianthus* and Foxglove grow amongst the Bracken which seems to be everywhere where there is moisture and shade. As the snow recedes, the delightful *Narcissus asturiensis* appears. Lizard Orchids are found along the roadsides where there is plenty of moisture.

Near the village of Panes the valley suddenly opens out, with Beech woods and pasture-land. High overhead, birds of prey circle: Griffon Vulture, Golden Eagle, and Booted Eagle with a Peregrine suddenly diving down from its craggy perch to capture some small bird. Both Chough and Alpine Chough can be found.

Butterflies include the rare Chapman's Ringlet, Long-tailed Blue and the Apollo which is now becoming rarer.

Entering the deep moist gorge of Desfiladero de la Hermida. The area is excellent for mountain flowers and good for birds, mammals and butterflies. There is also good salmon-fishing in the river which runs through the gorge.

14 POTES	
Grid reference:	C 16
Location:	E end of Picos de Europa
Access:	Easy on the N 621
Season:	Spring, summer and autumn
Terrain:	Mountain valley
Comments:	Micro-climate in Alpine valley
Specialities:	Capercaillie, Black Woodpecker, Apollo, *Narcissus nobilis*, Lizard Orchid

Potes is a small village on the eastern fringe of the Picos de Europa, which is easily accessible on the N 621. There are facilities for Jeep hire and horse riding here.

It is situated in the valley of the Río Deva, one of the best known rivers in the area for salmon fishing. Licences and information can be obtained at local tourist offices.

This is a good point from which to explore the eastern slopes of the Picos de Europa. As Potes is sheltered from the north-west by the Picos de Europa it has a climate protected from the more severe weather.

Flowers abound on the mountain pastures, with *Narcissus nobilis* abundant in wet pasture-land and orchids such as Lizard, Giant and several *Ophrys* species. Many butterflies are also to be seen: the Queen of Spain Fritillary, Common Blue, Essex Skipper and the large colourful Apollo may be found.

Golden Eagles and Griffon Vultures are found on the highest peaks with Black Woodpecker and Capercaillie in the woods.

Narcissus nobilis grows in very moist meadows. It is one of the largest of the wild narcissi.

2. EAST CANTÁBRICA AND THE RÍO EBRO WATERSHED

INTRODUCTION

This is the north-central region of Spain. Its western edge runs from Santander on the Atlantic coast to Palencia, the southern border from there to Alcañiz, then north-east to Lérida, up to Puerto de Somport in the Pyrenees and along the French frontier to the Bay of Biscay. It is bounded in the north by the Bay of Biscay and rises steeply in the north and west to the mountains of the Basque and the eastern Cantábrican range. Most of the region is relatively high with many mountains over 1500m (4920 feet).

Two great rivers pass through this region: the Río Duero which rises in the Sierra de la Demanda to exit into the Atlantic at Oporto; and the Río Ebro which rises near Reinosa and passes right through the centre of the region, gathering rainfall from the eastern Cantábrican mountains and the southern watershed of the Pyrenees, providing perfect conditions for the wine lands of Rioja. The latter exits into the Mediterranean.

Along the northern coastline the steep mountains are sufficiently high to cause a climatic barrier. The north-facing slopes get copious rainfall and a generally mild winter. Inland where the mountains occur heavy snowfall can be experienced during the colder months. The moist climate produces lush pastures to feed dairy cows and swell the apple orchards and maize crops.

The summers are pleasantly warm and can be hot inland. On the south-facing slopes and in the Ebro valley the climate can be extreme. Rainfall is very light as it has been deposited on the northern slopes. Frost is experienced in winter while in the summer temperatures exceeding 35°C are common.

Floristically there is much diversity. With the relatively warm moist climate experienced along the border of the Bay of Biscay, deciduous Beech and Pyrenean Oak are common, but in the harsh climate of the

A typical Basque village showing small stone-walled fields. The village consists mainly of smallholdings. Cattle, sheep and goats are kept to produce dairy products which provide the villagers with their main source of income.

Opposite: *map of East Cantábrica. The sites are numbered as in the text. Only main roads and the major rivers of the region are shown.*

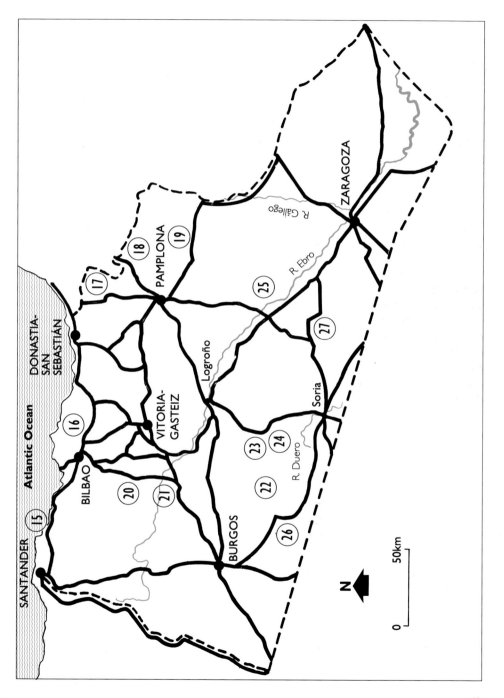

mountains Scots Pines are the dominant feature. In the Alpine meadows, narcissi and orchids give a blaze of colour in late spring. The high Alpine zone produces numerous gems: Pyrenean Saxifrage, *Saxifraga moncayensis* and *Erodium paui* are all endemic. The woods can also produce a few surprises: the Lady's Slipper Orchid, so rare in Britain, can be found here.

The bird life is just as varied and interesting: there are cliffs with huge colonies of nesting Griffon Vultures; the majestic Bearded Vulture (Lammergeier) can be found in the region; and a host of small birds pass this way on their migrations. The dry Ebro valley holds breeding populations of Dupont's Lark and the Great Bustard still nests in the area.

The ubiquitous Wild Boar is present in the woods and the shy and rare Pyrenean Desman can sometimes be seen in the rivers. Dark-coloured Red Squirrels are common within the woods.

Butterflies are abundant in the meadows and include Swallowtail, Scarce Swallowtail, Cleopatra, Chequered Skipper, Long-tailed Blue, Apollo, and many others.

Most habitats are represented in the region. There are coniferous forests and Alpine zones adjoined by large areas of maquis scrub on some of the higher mountains, and broad-leaved deciduous forests dominate the lower land. Steppe is common in the Ebro valley and there are a number of freshwater lakes and embalses along the river valleys. Cliffs are frequent, both coastal and inland, and there are a few salt- and freshwater marshes by the coast.

Many of the major arterial roadways from northern Europe pass through this beautiful region. There are numerous interesting places where you can stay *en route* to explore the fabulous countryside.

The grid references used in the following site descriptions relate to Michelin maps numbers 442 and 443.

FIFTY INTERESTING SPECIES TO LOOK FOR

Honey Buzzard	Golden Oriole	Pyrenean Brook	*Ranunculus*
Lesser Kestrel	White-backed	Salamander	*gregarius*
Hen Harrier	Woodpecker	Scarce Swallowtail	Rock Rose
Bearded Vulture	Black Woodpecker	Chequered Skipper	Pyrenean Saxifrage
Razorbill	Crag Martin	Woodland Brown	*Saxifraga cuneata*
Puffin	Crested Tit	*Catanache caerulea*	*Saxifraga*
Pochard	Treecreeper	Columbine	*moncayensis*
Avocet	Dupont's Lark	Dog's-tooth Violet	Mistletoe
Kentish Plover	Lesser Short-toed	*Erodium paui*	*Tulipa australis*
Dotterel	Lark	Hoop Petticoat	*Viola cornuta*
Spoonbill	Blue Rock Thrush	Narcissus	*Viola montcaunica*
Woodcock	Rock Thrush	Kermes Oak	Lady's Slipper
Grey Partridge	Black Wheatear	Large Flowered	Orchid
(Spanish race)	Pyrenean Desman	Butterwort	Burnt Orchid
Roller	Wild Boar	Martagon Lily	

Ria de Gernika: a favourite wintering haunt for ducks and waders.

15 LAS MARISMAS DE SANTOÑA	
Grid reference:	B 19
Location:	E of Santander
Access:	Excellent
Season:	All year round
Terrain:	Natural harbour and marshland
Specialities:	Puffin, Razorbill, Avocet, Shelduck, Spoonbill

The site is very easily accessible by travelling east from Santander on the N 634/E 70 turning northwards at Gama and proceeding towards Santoña on the C 629. There you will find a large marshland and natural harbour sheltered by the huge Monte Buciero promontory. This promontory is almost bare at the top, but near the base there are evergreen oak and Strawberry Trees. Fish caught in the Bay of Biscay make Santoña a very busy fishing port. There is also a thriving shellfish industry. Along the narrow coastal strip small dairy farms provide produce for nearby Santander.

Like many other river estuaries and marshes in northern Spain, this area attracts large numbers of migratory and wintering birds. One of the specialities is the Spoonbill which stops over to feed on its way to the Coto Doñana. Other waders which can be seen are Avocet, Greenshank, Curlew, Grey Plover, Redshank and Kentish Plover.

Unexpected birds may appear here, such as Red-breasted Merganser and Shelduck. This is one of the very few sites in Spain where Shelduck breed. Ducks like Mallard, Teal, Shoveler, Wigeon, Pochard and Pintail winter in large numbers in the sheltered bay, and in the vegetated area Grey Heron, Snipe and Coot may all be found.On the sea cliffs, Puffin, Guillemot, Razorbill and several species of gull breed.

Long-tailed Blue
Lampides boeticus W 30–36mm
The range of this exquisite butterfly is almost worldwide within warm countries. It is strongly migratory, with many finding their way to England and northern Europe from the Mediterranean countries in August and September. It is a strong and fast flier and is therefore difficult to see.

The upper wing in the male is a beautiful violet-blue with two black spots at the base of the 'tail'. The female is brown but with some violet in the forewing. The underside in both sexes is 'marbled' in shades of buff and white, and the two spots at the base of the tail are orange and blue.

The caterpillar can sometimes become a serious pest as it feeds inside the pods of leguminous plants.

16 RIA DE GERNIKA	
Grid reference:	B 21
Location:	NE of Bilbao
Access:	Good
Season:	All year round
Terrain:	Marshy river estuary
Specialities:	Razorbill, Shag, Greenshank, Bar-tailed Godwit, Mistletoe

This estuary is easily accessible from Bilbao via Amorebieta on the N 634. It is best to avoid the motorway from Bilbao. From the town of Gernika (remembered for the 1937 massacre during the Civil War) the river widens into a very large muddy estuary with extensive marshes and sandbanks which are uncovered at low tide.

This is a major site for waders and gulls. Many Cormorants winter in the estuary with Redshank, Greenshank, Dunlin, Sanderling, Bar-tailed and Black-tailed Godwits, and Turnstone, and a large number of species stop on passage, particularly the Spoonbill.

There is a small island and some cliffs near the entrance to the estuary, holding an assortment of gulls, Shags and Razorbills.

A variety of broad-leaved trees with a few pines dot the pastoral landscape, which is divided into small fields for dairy cattle and vegetable growing. Red peppers are a great favourite locally and when ripe are threaded on strings and hung from balconies, making a colourful sight. Poplar trees are grown in the valleys and are often heavily adorned with the parasitic Mistletoe.

17 MONTE GORRAMAKIL	
Grid reference:	C 25
Location:	NE of Pamplona
Access:	Easy by winding roads
Season:	Spring, summer and autumn
Terrain:	Mountain and valley
Comments:	Snow in winter
Specialities:	Griffon Vulture, Peregrine, Buzzard, Primrose, Rock Rose

Take the N 121 north from Pamplona and turn right onto the NA 254 just past Almandoz. After approximately 25km turn right and follow the road to the summit of Pico Gorramakil. This is the most northerly point of the Pyrenees where the mountain range suddenly drops down to the Bay of Biscay. The Pico Gorramakil rises to 1090m (3576 feet) and there are fantastic panoramic views from the top. To the north the land falls away rapidly towards Biarritz in France, and to the south and east are the snow-capped peaks of the Pyrenees.

This is a high rainfall area and therefore there are a lot of wet meadowlands. Small rushing streams have cut deeply into the hard bedrock forming ravines with a few awesome

Part of the vast mixed forests of Beech and Silver Fir around Roncesvalles.

cliffs which form nesting ledges for a large colony of Griffon Vultures. Peregrine and Buzzard are also present.

The valleys are well wooded with Beech but amongst the rocks and boulders Heather and Broom flourish with Common Rock Rose. In the wet meadows orchids are plentiful with anemones and Primroses.

Numerous butterflies feed on the flowers. The Painted Lady and Long-tailed Blue (*see box*), pass through on migration. Look also for the Silver-studded Blue. The countryside in the lower lands is highly cultivated in small fields: grassland for dairy and sheep grazing, rotated with maize and vegetables.

18 RONCESVALLES	
Grid reference:	C/D 25/26
Location:	Around Roncesvalles, NE of Pamplona
Access:	Good
Season:	Late spring, summer and early autumn
Terrain:	Mountain and woodland
Comments:	Snow in winter
Specialities:	White-backed Wood pecker, Black Wood pecker, Crested Tit, *Viola cumuta*, Martagon Lily
Subsidiary:	Coto nacional Quinta Real, C 25

This is a mountainous area through which the important C 135 road passes into France. Roncesvalles is on this road, about 50km north-east of Pamplona. It is the site where in 778AD the rear-guard of Charlemagne's army was massacred by the Basques on their retreat into France.

From the naturalist's point of view the interest is in the enormous Beech and Silver Fir forest at Irati, slightly to the east, which is the largest Beech forest in Iberia. It is a high region with heavy snowfall during winter, the highest peak, Onzanzurieta, rising to 1570m (5151 feet). In these woods are found the beautiful Black and White-backed Woodpeckers. The latter is a rare bird and one which is fast retreating in range due to loss of habitat, as it must have a large number of rather old rotten Beech and conifer trees from which to feed. Other birds which inhabit the woods include Crested, Long-tailed and Great Tits, Jay and Magpie.

Bracken grows between the trees in many of these deciduous woods but in some of the grasslands there is an abundance of flowers. Narcissus species are common with Martagon Lily, *Fritillaria* spp., Primulas and *Viola cornuta*.

There are many butterflies including the Silver-washed and Dark Green Fritillaries, and the Long-tailed Blue on migration.

19 SIERRA DE LEYRE	
Grid reference:	D/E 26
Location:	SE of Pamplona
Access:	Easy
Season:	Spring, summer and autumn
Terrain:	Woods, valleys and gorges
Specialities:	Bearded Vulture, Pyrenean Desman, Pyrenean Brook Salamander, *Catananche caerulea*, Pyrenean Saxifrage

From Pamplona, the N 240 leads south-east to the sierra. After 32km turn north onto the NA 211 which wends its way into the sierra. This is a small range of mountains rising to 1356m (4449 feet) with a very picturesque

The Embalse de Yesa showing one of the deserted villages.

road climbing to the summit. Here there is a fine panoramic view overlooking the huge man-made Embalse de Yesa. This is an area where there are a number of deserted or semi-deserted villages. The younger people have moved away to local industrial centres.

Within the region there are a number of spectacular gorges leading up to two botanically very interesting valleys, Valle de Roncal and Valle de Salazar. There are enormous rosettes of Pyrenean Saxifrage on the sides of the gorges as well as *Dianthus hispanicus*, a woody perennial with bright pink flowers and widely spaced petals. By the road *Catananche caerulea*, a strange blue everlasting flower, is common. There are woods in the valleys, evergreen oak on the south-facing slopes and Scots Pine on the moister and cooler north-facing ones.

The impressive Bearded Vulture can be seen in the valleys and there is a large colony of Griffon Vultures.

In the woodlands there are a few Wild Boar and in the streams the very rare Pyrenean Desman can sometimes be seen. The Pyrenean Brook Salamander is often plentiful but only in trout-free streams, for obvious reasons!

The Swallowtail, Clouded Yellow and Cleopatra butterflies should all be seen.

*The Chequered Skipper (*Carterocephalus palaemon*) is mainly a central European species. This is possibly its most westerly location.*

This pass is situated approximately 40km south of Bilbao on the N 625. It is a pass at 900m (2953 feet) at the very eastern end of the Cordillera Cantábrica. The surrounding land to the south of the pass is gently undulating pasture with young pine plantations. The older woodland consists of deciduous and evergreen oak, and Beech.

There are large tracts of limestone 'pavement' with grass, Box, Dog Rose and Hawthorn growing in between. At the top of the pass high limestone crags and cliffs form an escarpment, the land falling away northwards towards the highly industrial city of Bilbao in the distance and the Bay of Biscay.

There are large colonies of birds nesting on the cliffs, particularly Griffon Vulture and Chough.

Many varieties of butterflies are seen, including the Scarce Swallowtail and two interesting species which inhabit the scattered woodland, the Woodland Brown and the Chequered Skipper.

In spring and early summer, plants colour the area. Do look out for many of the bulbous varieties, Muscari, Tulips, orchids and narcissi, especially in the meadowlands where large flocks of sheep graze. Intensive dairy farming is also carried out.

20 PUERTO DE ORDUÑA	
Grid reference:	D 20
Location:	S of Bilbao
Access:	Excellent
Season:	Most of the year
Terrain:	Pasture and woodlands
Specialities:	Griffon Vulture, Chough, Woodland Brown, Chequered Skipper, Scarce Swallowtail
Subsidiary:	Sierra Salvada, D 20

Grid reference:	E 20
Location:	W of Miranda de Ebro
Access:	Very easy
Season:	All year round
Terrain:	Limestone gorge
Specialities:	Griffon Vulture, Raven, Blue Rock Thrush, Black Redstart, Stonechat

A favourite haunt of the Griffon Vulture (Gyps fulvus), high on the crags overlooking Pancorbo.

Access is by the N 1 approximately 15km west of Miranda de Ebro and not by the motorway. A dramatic gorge cutting through hard limestone mountains provides a pass through which the fast motorway has been constructed connecting Burgos, Vitoria-Gasteiz and Bilbao. Historically this pass was where Napoleon made a last stand when being pursued by Wellington during the Peninsula wars. A notable feature of Pancorbo village is the fascinating array of low-pitched tiled roofs when seen from above.

Even though heavy traffic continually passes along the road at the bottom of the gorge Griffon Vultures nest happily on the ledges higher up and can usually be seen gliding on the thermals. Ravens are also in evidence as are Blue Rock Thrush, Black Redstart and Stonechat amongst the rocks.

Away from the gorge the surrounding land is used for cereal production and there are extensive vineyards. Sheep graze the hillsides and shepherds will certainly not be forgotten as there is a large statue of a shepherd with a sheep dominating a hillside site slightly to the north. This is in memory of a shepherd killed by a sudden thunderstorm in the mountains in 1959 while he was guarding his flock against Wolves, which are now probably extinct in this area.

22 SIERRA DE LA DEMANDA	
Grid reference:	F 20/21
Location:	SE of Burgos
Access:	Good but by small roads
Season:	Spring, summer and autumn
Terrain:	Mountain and Alpine pastures
Comments:	Can be snow in winter
Specialities:	Hen Harrier, Marsh Tit, Woodcock, Hoop Petticoat Narcissus, Columbine
Subsidiary:	Montes de Oca, E 19/20

Access is fairly easy by a series of small roads leading south off the N 120 east of Burgos. It is a high mountainous area rising in many places to over 2000m (6560 feet). There are two national game reserves, La Demanda and Ezcaray, which in effect means that shooting is restricted to specific species and therefore the rarer wildlife should not get depleted. There are some deciduous forests comprising Pyrenean Oak and Beech, but in the past much of the ancient forest was felled and is now scrub and Alpine pasture-land. Some re-afforestation with Scots Pine is taking place on the hillsides. There is still sufficient Beech forest in the area to support important furniture making and wood turning industries in the small villages and towns. On the lower slopes of the sierra, dairy farming and market gardening help supply the nearby towns of Burgos and Vitoria-Gasteiz with some of their needs. During the winter months, winter sports are a favourite pastime of the local population.

Many interesting plants can be found. These belong primarily to the Cantábrican floral list rather than to that of the Pyrenees which is only a short distance to the east. Meadows are covered with Hoop Petticoat Narcissus, *Tulipa australis* and Columbine, and later, in early summer, orchids make their appearance. In the maquis scrub there is a dominance of Heather and Gorse.

Honey Buzzard, Booted Eagle and Hen Harrier breed in this zone. It is also interesting to note that the population of Short-toed Treecreeper here overlaps with the more northerly population of Treecreeper. Woodcock and Marsh Tit also breed, well south of their usual breeding range.

Amongst the butterflies Cleopatra, Long-tailed and Common Blue, and the Apollo should all be seen.

The large and colourful Apollo butterfly (Parnassius apollo) is relatively common on the high mountains and Alpine ranges from 1–2000m. It is easily identified by its large wingspan of up to 85mm and rather heavy flapping flight. The caterpillar feeds on species of Sedum and Sempervivum.

23 RESERVA NACIONAL DE CAMEROS	
Grid reference:	F 21/22
Location:	Midway between Logroño and Soria, to the west
Access:	Comparatively easy
Season:	Spring, summer and autumn
Terrain:	Wood and scrubland
Comments:	Snow in winter
Specialities:	Golden Oriole, Woodpigeon, Large Flowered Butterwort, Early Purple Orchid, Burnt Orchid
Subsidiary:	Valle de Iregua, F 22

Bumble Bee Orchid (Ophrys fusca), one of the many orchids to be seen in Reserva nacional de Cameros.

Easily accessible from the main N 111 joining Logroño with Soria. It is on the eastern slopes of the Sierra de la Demanda rising to 2164m (7100 feet). The lower levels have large forests of Beech and Pyrenean Oak, with Scots Pine higher up. The oak and Beech provide good timber for the furniture industry which is important in this area.

There are large zones of scrub which are very rich in orchids, such as Bumble Bee, Late Spider, Burnt, Early Purple and many others. The main constituents of the scrub are species of Heather and *Genista*. In some of the damp areas the ground can be covered with Hoop Petticoat Narcissus and Large Flowered Butterwort during June. In some of the acidic boggy areas the insectivorous sundew may be found.

In the valleys, woodland birds like Great Spotted Woodpecker, Jay, Great Tit and Crested Tit, and in summer Golden Oriole can be seen. The autumn migration can be spectacular as many thousands of Woodpigeons and smaller migrants pass through the Santa Inés and Sancho Leza valleys on their way south.

Amongst the butterflies which should be seen are the Swallowtail, Cardinal, Marbled Fritillary and Marbled White.

24 LAGUNA NEGRA DE URBION	
Grid reference:	F/G 21
Location:	NW of Soria
Access:	By small roads
Season:	Spring, summer and autumn
Terrain:	Mountain lake and Alpine meadows
Comments:	Snow in winter
Specialities:	Hen Harrier, Honey Buzzard, Hoop Petticoat Narcissus, *Erodium paui*, Dog's-tooth Violet

In spring, Hoop Petticoat Narcissi (Narcissus bulbocodium) cover the moist meadows around Laguna Negra de Urbión.

This small mountain lake is reached by taking either the SO 810 or the SO 840 to join the SO 830 off the N 234 to the north-west of Soria, passing the Embalse de la Cuerda del Pozo on the way. It is a deep glacial trout lake situated at 1700m (5577 feet) in the centre of the Sierra de Urbión. The surrounding woods are composed of Scots Pine, Beech and Pyrenean Oak with an undergrowth of Heather.

As the rocks in these mountains are both acidic and calcareous a very diverse flora occurs. In the nearby Alpine meadows there is a cascade of colour in May and June with carpets of Columbine, yellow *Tulipa australis*, violet-and-yellow Wild Pansy, purple-spotted-leaved Dog's-tooth Violet and the deep-yellow Hoop Petticoat Narcissus. The endemic *Viola montcaunica* is found here and

in neighbouring Moncayo to the east. In the rocky crevices *Sempervivum* spp. grow and another rarity, the endemic *Erodium paui*, is found only on this mountain.

With all these flowers there is a wealth of butterflies, including Apollo, Common and Escher's Blues and Brown Argus.

There are many streams and waterfalls when the snow is melting, and it is here that the great Río Duero starts its long journey to flow into the Atlantic at Oporto in Portugal.

Grey Partridge, Honey Buzzard, Hen Harrier, Booted Eagle and large numbers of smaller birds passing through on migration can all be seen.

25 BARDENAS REALES	
Grid reference:	F 25
Location:	N of Tudela
Access:	By very small roads
Season:	All year round
Terrain:	Steppe land
Comments:	Can be very bleak in winter
Specialities:	Dupont's Lark, Lesser Short-toed Lark, Pin-tailed Sandgrouse, Little Bustard, Rosemary
Subsidiary:	Nuevo Gallipienzo, E 25

Reasonably easily reached from Tudela by taking the N 121 northwards for about 15km and then one of several small roads to the east. Bárdenas Reales is a large dry steppe area in the Río Ebro valley composed mainly of gypsum and clay. The gypsum has been eroded into a very desert-like scene with a large number of ravines and cliffs leading up to flat-topped plateaux. These have a very sparse vegetation comprised of Thyme, Lavender, Rosemary and the holly-like Kermes Oak. Where cultivation is possible, dry-land cereal growing is practised and on the sparse grasslands sheep are grazed. There are a few small woods of Aleppo Pine.

Many steppe birds are present with Black-bellied and Pin-tailed Sandgrouse, a large population of Dupont's Lark and also Lesser Short-toed Lark. A small number of Great and Little Bustards are here as are the usual birds of prey nesting on the cliffs within the ravines.

This region can be very cold with snow during the winter, but frequently has temperatures of up to 35°C in summer.

26 SANTO DOMINGO DE SILOS	
Grid reference:	G 19
Location:	SE of Burgos
Access:	Very good
Season:	Spring, summer and autumn
Terrain:	Valleys and gorges
Comments:	Can be snow in winter; sensible walking shoes
Specialities:	Lesser Kestrel, Roller, Crag Martin, *Silene boryi*, *Matthiola fruticulosa*
Subsidiary:	Covarrubias, F19

From Burgos take the N 234 for 52km to Salas de los Infantes. 4.5km past this town turn west onto the BU 903. A further 13km will bring you to an historical monastery built in the eleventh century and used by pilgrims on their way to Santiago de Compostela. It is particularly noted for the fantastic series of capitals in the cloister which depict animal and bird motifs. It is picturesquely situated in a moist valley with Poplars, which hold Serin, Woodchat Shrike, and Roller. Amongst the buildings Lesser Kestrel can be seen and White Storks nest in the towers.

A short distance along the road to the south the Río Yecla has cut a 3km-long gorge through the limestone rock, in places more than 100m deep and only 2m wide. The road goes through a tunnel but there is a pathway cut into the side of the gorge where you can walk looking down to the river. Here in the shade the interesting flora includes *Silene boryi* with bright pink flowers, *Dianthus furcatus*, *Saxifraga cuneata* and *Matthiola fruticulosa*.

On the high ground Black Redstart, Black Wheatear, Rock Sparrow, Spotless Starling, Crag Martin and Rock Thrush are all found.

27 PARQUE NATURAL DE LA DEHESA DEL MONCAYO	
Grid reference:	G 24
Location:	S of Tarazona
Access:	From a series of very minor roads
Season:	Late spring, summer and early autumn
Terrain:	Alpine mountain
Comments:	Snow in winter
Specialities:	Sparrowhawk, Lady's Slipper Orchid, *Digitalis parviflora*, *Viola montcaunica*, *Saxifraga moncayensis*
Subsidiary:	Sierra de Alcarama, F/G 23

This park is reached by a series of small roads due south of Tarazona. It is an interesting and rather isolated mountain east of Soria which rises to 2313m (7589 feet). The summit is covered with snow for up to nine months of the year but by July most of this has gone and the screes and loose boulders make the mountain look inhospitable. However, it is here that an interesting Alpine flora grows. The endemic *Saxifraga moncayensis* flourishes in crevices as do *Silene ciliata, Ranunculus gregarius* and *Viola montcaunica.*

Butterflies are plentiful and the Marbled White, Clouded Yellow and Blue-spot Hairstreak should all be seen.

Below the Alpine zone there is scrubland of mainly Heather and Juniper, and an area of Alpine meadows where sheep graze during the summer months. During the summer months, these sheep are taken to the lower grounds. The ewes are milked twice daily and the milk makes delicious cheeses.

Lower in altitude, Pyrenean Oak and Beech woods form large tracts of deciduous forest. Within the Beech woods the canopy of leaves is so thick that very little will grow, but in areas where oak predominates there is a fine flora with *Digitalis parviflora,* the white-flowered St Bruno's Lily and the very rare Lady's Slipper Orchid.

Birds of prey are common here with Griffon Vultures on the mountain tops, and Sparrowhawks and Buzzards lower down in the wooded valleys.

28 BELCHITE

Grid reference:	I 27
Location:	SE of Zaragoza
Access:	Very easy
Season:	All year round
Terrain:	Dry flat plains
Comments:	Extremely hot in summer and cold in winter
Specialities:	Stone Curlew, Black-bellied Sandgrouse, Dupont's Lark, Lesser Short-toed Lark, Dotterel
Subsidiary:	Villanueva del Huerva, H 26

Situated south-east of Zaragoza, the site is easily accessible by taking the N 232 for approximately 20km, then turning south onto the C 222. This road travels across typical steppe habitat. It is one of the driest parts of Spain, and also has one of the most extreme ranges of temperature, from very cold sub-zero temperatures with occasional snow to torrid heat and day-time highs frequently reaching 37°C.

It is basically flat land in the plains of the Río Ebro with a few hills rising to 700m (2297 feet). Dry-land farming with extensive wheat and barley is practised. The villages in the area are few and far between and the population is diminishing, the younger people preferring the more sophisticated amenities and more comfortable living conditions of town life in preference to the harsh climate and spartan living conditions that their forebears have endured for centuries.

Recently, irrigation schemes have been started to try to bring some of this arid land into more productive cultivation. The water comes from the Río Ebro.

This is one of the best sites in Spain for steppe birds. Stone Curlew are frequent and up to 1000 pairs of Black-bellied Sandgrouse breed locally. The very rare Dupont's Lark, with up to 800 pairs in the vicinity, can also be found in this part of the Ebro basin. This is a species usually confined to the steppe lands of Africa. It is extremely difficult to find and hours of patient watching of suitable habitat may be required if you are to find one. It keeps well hidden in grass and scrub and is not easily flushed.

In addition, there is also a large population of Lesser Short-toed Lark nesting here. During the winter a large number of birds migrate down this depression, with Dotterel moving from its arctic breeding grounds to Africa one of the specialities.

3. THE PYRENEES

INTRODUCTION

The high Pyrenean range forms a natural boundary between Spain and France, from the Mediterranean at Portbou to the Bay of Biscay, and reaching 3404m (11,168 feet) at Aneto in the Benasque Reserve. It creates a barrier to depressions from the north with the consequence that most rain falls on the French side leaving the southern Spanish slopes much drier.

Snow lies on the highest peaks for most of the year, and a number of passes can be closed for short periods. The heaviest rainfall is during the summer when violent thunderstorms may occur suddenly. The foothills, especially near the Ebro valley, can become very hot with maximum daytime temperatures over 30°C. In winter these areas are subjected to hard frosts.

The rare Bearded Vulture (Gypaetus barbatus) is one of the specialities of the Pyrenees, and may be seen with luck.

The whole region is a treasure house for plant enthusiasts, with many endemics, the Pyrenean Gentian, Columbine, *Ramonda myconi*, Martagon Lily, Honeysuckle and species of saxifrage, *Ranunculus, Fritillaria, Geranium,* bellflower, hyacinth and many, many more.

Equally animal life is full of surprises: a few Brown Bears remain in some of the remote areas; Chamois are numerous and can often be seen leaping from rock to rock or grazing quietly in the Alpine pastures; the Pyrenean Desman, the most odd European creature, lives in lonely Alpine streams; and the endemic Pyrenean Brook Salamander and the Fire Salamander can be seen.

Butterflies in quantity visit the Alpine meadows, ablaze with flowers once the snow has retreated. Gavarnie, Spanish Chalkhill and Glandon Blues, Spanish Purple Hairstreak, Mountain Clouded Yellow and Apollo are just a few that can be seen.

Bird life is excellent here: the rare Bearded Vulture or Lammergeier, the shy Wallcreeper and Alpine Chough grace the cliffs, and the woodlands conceal Black and White-backed Woodpeckers, Capercaillie and Eagle Owl.

Many habitats are represented within this region: Alpine and subalpine areas are found everywhere above the treeline; coniferous forests cover the mountainsides; lower down there are mixed deciduous broad-leaved forests of Beech and Pyrenean Oaks; there are Poplars by the rivers and man-made lakes; and maquis scrub and steppe occur lower still in the dry hills leading to the Ebro valley.

This region is used for livestock grazing, the milk being made into very fine cheeses. Forestry is also of economic importance.

The grid references used in the following site descriptions relate to Michelin map number 443.

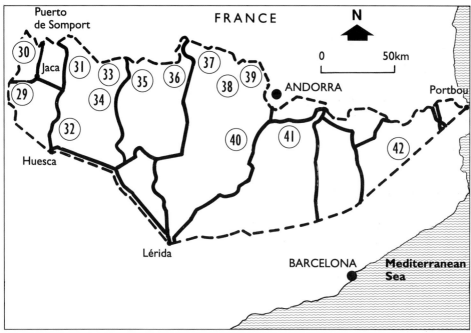

Map of the Pyrenees. The sites are numbered as in the text. Only main
roads of the region are shown.

FIFTY INTERESTING SPECIES TO LOOK FOR

Lesser Kestrel	Fire Salamander	Silvery Argus	Moss Campion
Bearded Vulture	Pyrenean Brook	Alpine Grizzled	Pyrenean
Tengmalm's Owl	Salamander	Skipper	Columbine
Ptarmigan	Painted Frog	Chequered Skipper	*Gentiana burseri*
Capercaillie	Asp Viper	Alpine Anenome	Pyrenean Gentian
Black Woodpecker	Beech Marten	*Androsace carnea*	Pyrenean Saxifrage
White-backed	Pyrenean Desman	*Arenaria*	*Ramonda myconi*
Woodpecker	Alpine Marmot	*purpurascens*	*Ranunculus*
Red-backed Shrike	Otter	Cobweb	*pyrenaeus*
Wallcreeper	Brown Bear	Houseleek	Red Alpine
Rock Sparrow	Wild Cat	Edelweiss	Primrose
Snow Finch	Chamois	*Fritillaria pyrenaica*	*Viola cornuta*
Citril Finch	Clouded Apollo	Green Hellebore	Martagon Lily
Alpine Chough	Long-tailed Blue	Pale Lent Lily	Black Vanilla
Marbled Newt	Spanish Argus	Narcissus	Orchid

This typifies much of the scenery of the Pyrenees: flat fertile valleys, steep wooded cliffs and high snow-capped peaks. This is the cirque of the Parque nacional de Ordesa showing Monte Perdido rising to 3555m (11,663 feet). It forms the southern part of the well-known Cirque de Gavarnie which is in France. Both cirques are renowned for butterflies, birds and plants.

29 SAN JUAN DE LA PEÑA

Grid reference:	E 27/28
Location:	SW of Jaca
Access:	Very easy
Season:	Spring, summer and autumn
Terrain:	Low mountain and pasture
Comments:	Sensible walking shoes
Specialities:	Red-backed Shrike, Rock Sparrow, Rock Bunting, Ortolan Bunting, Martagon Lily
Subsidiary:	Coto nacional de la Acumuer, E 28

Leave Jaca southwards on the C 125 over the Puerto del Oreol and continue along the HU 230. This forgotten mountain, 1552m (5092 feet) high, lies on the southern slopes of the Pyrenees. There are many pine plantations at the base but as the road winds upwards they give way to evergreen oak and maquis scrub, with Box and areas of Lavender and Thyme. There are some open pasture-lands and in late spring these are alive with the colour of narcissi, orchids in variety, Martagon Lily and Spanish Iris, while in the autumn *Merendera montana* colours the hillsides (*see* box). The rainfall in this area is slightly higher than might be expected and gives rise to a lush vegetation.

Griffon and Egyptian Vultures nest in the rocks near the high summit and lower down the Lesser Kestrel hawks for insects like a large swift. These small gregarious falcons nest on cliffs and around castle battlements. Within the woods and scrub areas Woodchat and Red-backed Shrikes, Rock, Ortolan and Cirl Buntings, Rock Sparrow, Hoopoe and Golden Oriole can be found, and overhead Black and Red Kites can often be seen.

The famous monastery built in 922AD must not be missed. Built within the mountainside and hewn out of solid rock, it is very impressive. From here the view looking over the forests to the snow-capped mountains in the background is breathtaking.

In springtime, within this floral wonderland unharmed by pesticides and protected by its very isolation, there are many of the northern Iberian species of butterflies to look out for. Species such as Mountain Clouded Yellow, Gavarnie Blue and the Pearl-bordered Fritillary can be seen.

Merendera montana

The dry pastures have been grazed down to the soil and the relentless sun has baked the ground hard during the long summer until it is beginning to crack. After one good autumn thunderstorm the soil soaks up the life-giving rain like a sponge and this parched land suddenly becomes alive.

One of the first plants to appear is *Merendera montana*, pushing its seemingly naked body through the hard earth to expand into a beautiful pink star-shaped flower, fully 3cm across and covering whole hillsides in a delicate shade of pink.

The flower is very short, looking like a crocus, but it has no perianth tube. The leaves appear after the flowers have died and can be confused with a crocus.

The Spanish name for this exquisite plant is 'Espanta Pastores', which means that when the flowers appear, it is time for the shepherds to take their flocks down from the mountain pastures. The plant foretells the coming of winter and the need to take the flocks to safety.

30 PUERTO DE SOMPORT	
Grid reference:	D 28
Location:	N of Jaca
Access:	Very good
Season:	Late spring, summer and early autumn
Terrain:	High mountain pass
Comments:	Snow in winter
Specialities:	Alpine Chough, Ring Ouzel, Fire Salamander, Pyrenean Saxifrage, *Dianthus hispanicus*
Subsidiary:	Reserva nacional de los Valles Vissaurin, D 27/28; Coto nacional del Anayet, D 28

This pass over the Pyrenees is 32km north of Jaca and is a continuation of the N 330. It is one of the major passes in the higher part of the western Pyrenees, originally built by the Romans, trodden by the pilgrims on their journey to Santiago de Compostela and finally made suitable for fast modern transport in the present century.

High mountains tower on both sides of the road to 2670m (8760 feet). In the valley there is a small, fast-flowing river fed by the glacial lakes on the French frontier. There are some woods of Beech here while higher up on the mountainside Silver Fir, Scots and Mountain Pine predominate. By the roadside *Dianthus hispanicus* is common and on the rocky mountain crags Pyrenean Saxifrage produces huge rosettes almost as large as dinner plates.

Butterflies include the Small Copper, Silver-studded Blue and Grizzled Skipper amongst others.

Interesting birds are abundant: Chough and the rarer Alpine Chough, and in the high

*Pyrenean Saxifrage (*Saxifraga longifolia*) is one of the spectacular plants of the Pyrenees. It can attain 35cm in diameter and produce flower sprays over 60cm long.*

Alpine pastures Snow Finch and Ptarmigan. Ring Ouzels are found in the valleys well west of their normal range.

Brown Bears are still believed to breed here and Wild Boar are found in the valleys. In moist areas the nocturnal Fire Salamander may be found with its striking appearance of bright yellow or orange stripes or spots on a black background.

31 RESERVA NACIONAL DE VIÑAMALA	
Grid reference:	D/E 29
Location:	NE of Biescas
Access:	Fairly good
Season:	Late spring, summer and early autumn
Terrain:	High peaks and gorges, with Alpine meadows
Comments:	Can be snow-bound much of the year
Specialities:	Ptarmigan, Chamois, Edelweiss, *Ramonda myconi*, Great Yellow Gentian

This large reserve is just north-east of Biescas and is accessible from bordering roads, such

Arenaria tetraquetra

For eight months of the year this plant is dormant under a thick blanket of snow. As soon as the covering has melted, the warmth of the sun rapidly brings it to life. The tiny leaves expand and in a very short time it is covered with white flowers, each 1cm in diameter looking like a patch of snow.

It is very low growing, only about 2cm high, but forms a tight cushion up to 25cm in diameter. The leaves are 1–5mm long and form minute quadrangular rosettes. It grows in scree or in cracks and crevices at high altitudes, usually from 2000m (6560 feet) upwards. It is found in the Sierra Nevada, Pyrenees, Cantábrican mountains, Montes Universales, Sierra de Gredos and Sierra de Guadarrama, areas well separated from one another. Therefore it is reasonable to believe that these isolated populations were left behind after the last ice age retreated.

as the N 260 and C 136, for roadside viewing and walking. The C 136 runs from Biescas north along a high and beautiful valley leading up to the French frontier at Puerto del Pourtalet. Peaks rise to 3076m (10,092 feet) and are snow-covered for much of the year. A number of small glaciated valleys, which hold several lakes fed from the melting snow, occur in the reserve.

In the Alpine meadows *Gentiana burseri* and *G. brachyphylla*, Great Yellow Gentian,

Red Alpine Primrose, *Ranunculus pyrenaeus*, Alpine Anemone, the Pale Lent Lily Narcissus and *Erigeron uniflorus* are abundant. High on the mountain tops, tight small plants cling to the crevices, such as Cobweb Houseleek, *Arenaria purpurascens*, *A. tetraquetra* (*see* box), Edelweiss and Fringed Pink, which are all well worth seeking. The valleys have woods of pine and pasture-land.

The Garganta del Escalar is a spectacular gorge, 14km north of Biescas, the sides covered with *Ramonda myconi*, *Lonicera pyrenaica* and *Antirrhinum sempervirens*.

Ptarmigan and Grey Partridge are found on the higher slopes and the Golden Eagle and rare Bearded Vulture may also be seen. Chamois are common in the high mountains during the summer, coming down to the woods and more sheltered areas during the winter.

populations of birds of prey. Red Kites should always be seen as about twenty pairs breed within this area. Griffon Vultures have extensive breeding colonies dominating the heights with up to 200 breeding pairs. Their young usually migrate annually to Africa until they are about four years old when they are mature and become sedentary. Golden Eagle, Short-toed Eagle, Honey Buzzard and Bearded Vulture are all found within this sierra.

Many small isolated villages have now been abandoned and are falling into decay. A few evergreen oaks remain but large tracts of previous pasture-land are degenerating into maquis scrub: coniferous plantations are being developed.

Wild Boar are common in the scrub and Roe Deer may be seen. Many typical Alpine flowers and butterflies can be found.

32 SIERRA DE GUARA	
Grid reference:	F 29
Location:	NE of Huesca
Access:	By small roads
Season:	Late spring, summer and early autumn
Terrain:	Mountain and Alpine pastures
Comments:	Snow in winter; good walking shoes
Specialities:	Bearded Vulture, Honey Buzzard, Golden Eagle, Red Kite, Roe Deer

33 PARQUE NACIONAL DE ORDESA	
Grid reference:	D/E 29/30
Location:	E of Torla
Access:	Fairly easy
Season:	Late spring, summer and early autumn
Terrain:	Cliffs and Alpine meadows
Comments:	Summer information centre, just outside Torla on the HU 360; good walking shoes
Specialities:	Wallcreeper, White-backed Woodpecker, Otter, Asp Viper, Edelweiss

Situated north-east of Huesca and reached by several small roads, such as the HU 330, from the N 240, this is a large and rather isolated dominating mountain rising up to 2077m (6814 feet) on the southern slopes of the Pyrenees. It is a limestone massif through which numerous small rivers have cut deep gorges which provide nesting ledges for large

This large and very important reserve was designated in 1918 less than a month after Covadonga in the Picos de Europa. It is reached by taking the HU 360 north from Torla about 9km.

Peña Montañesa (2291m; 7516 feet), one of the many jagged outcrops seen within the Parque nacional de Ordesa. This is the haunt of the Bearded Vulture.

The high cirque of Monte Perdido (3355m; 11,007 feet) is the Spanish edge of the French Cirque de Gavarnie, so well known amongst Alpine plant enthusiasts. The huge dramatic cliffs in varying shades of brown, white and red form an impressive backdrop to this naturalist's paradise.

The Valle de Ordesa, covered with Beech, Scots Pine and Mountain Pine, has a number of lush meadows grazed by sheep and cattle which in springtime become a kaleidoscope of colour. Martagon Lily and its yellow Pyrenean form, various species of geranium and narcissus, Spanish Iris and many orchids grow in profusion. Above the treeline, grow Spring, Pyrenean and Trumpet Gentians and Edelweiss with its grey tufted felt-like flowers poking out from between the rocks.

Pyrenean Saxifrage and *Ramonda myconi* can be found on most moist cliffs.

Butterflies abound including Gavarnie, Common, Spanish Chalk-hill amd Glandon Blues and also the Dryad.

There is an abundance of bird life and rarities like the Bearded Vulture and the elusive Wallcreeper, flashing its red wings as it climbs up the rocks, may be seen. Snow and Citril Finches, are found here, apparently far out of their normal range, as is the White-backed Woodpecker which is usually found in eastern Europe, but has a small nucleus in the Pyrenees.

Wild Boar may be seen in the woods, and Otters live in the river. Spanish Ibex, once common, are now rare. The Asp Viper can be found amongst the rocks, and the rare Spanish Argus butterfly completes the fascinating wildlife found in this magnificent site.

There are many very well-marked walks in the area.

34 RIO VELLOS	
Grid reference:	E 30
Location:	N of Ainsa
Access:	Fair
Season:	Late spring, summer and early autumn
Terrain:	River and gorge
Comments:	Can be snow-bound in winter; very narrow road
Specialities:	Alpine Accentor, *Ramonda myconi*, Pyrenean Saxifrage, Pyrenean Columbine, Green Hellebore

Travel approximately 11km north from Ainsa on the HU 640 as far as the village of Escalona. Then turn left onto the HU 631. This is a wonderful narrow valley at the eastern end of the Parque nacional de Ordesa, which is so narrow in parts that there is only room for the single track road and the river, which rushes along many metres below. Passing points have been constructed!

After a wooded area of Pyrenean Oak, pines and Poplars the gorge begins. *Ramonda myconi* covers vast areas of the cliff face

The Chamois (Rupicapra rupicapra) is a very agile goat-like creature, common in parts of the high mountains of northern Spain.

wherever it can get a hold, and Pyrenean Saxifrage, with huge sprays of white flowers, is prolific, in some favourable localities reaching 35cm in diameter. Pyrenean Columbine and Green Hellebore are common by the roadside. Purple Saxifrage is a wonderful sight in spring.

Although high in altitude, many northern European birds are common: Robins, Great Tits, Chaffinches, and Blackbirds are everywhere and the confiding Alpine Accentor is often seen. High above the gorge Golden Eagles soar, Chough and Alpine Chough are easily visible and if you are lucky a Bearded Vulture may come into view.

35 RESERVA NACIONAL DE LOS CIRCOS	
Grid reference:	D/E 30/31
Location:	N of Bielsa
Access:	Fairly easy
Season:	Late spring, summer and early autumn
Terrain:	Mountains and valleys
Comments:	Good walking shoes; can be snow-bound in winter
Specialities:	Ptarmigan, Alpine Marmot, Mountain Clouded Yellow, Pyrenean Hyacinth, Pyrenean Bellflower

The reserve is easily accessible just north of Bielsa off the HU 640. It is a long high range of mountain peaks, many rising to over 3000m (9840 feet), bordering France on the northern edge. At Bielsa there is a road which goes west to a hotel (parador) at the end of the Valle de Pineta and follows the Río Cinca, which rises in La Munia lake.

It is a beautiful valley full of Alpine gems, such as *Ramonda myconi* clinging to crevices,

Reserva nacional de los Circos taken from the eastern approaches to the Parque nacional de Ordesa. This particularly beautiful valley is typical of many in this area of the Pyrenees, which take the melting snows down into the plains. The snow-capped mountains in the distance are still in the grip of winter.

Pyrenean Bellflower, *Campanula cochleariifolia* and Pyrenean Hyacinth in the lower ground, with Martagon Lily and Spanish Iris. Butterflies are numerous and include Apollo, Mountain Clouded Yellow and the Long-tailed Blue during its migration.

Wild Boar and Hares are common in the wooded valley, Alpine Marmots being found higher up. There is also a breeding pair of Brown Bears, now very rare in the Pyrenees.

Typical high altitude birds are seen, for example Golden Eagle, Ptarmigan and Bearded Vulture.

36 RESERVA NACIONAL DE BENASQUE	
Grid reference:	E 31
Location:	N of Benasque
Access:	Small roads
Season:	Late spring, summer and early autumn
Terrain:	Mountains and Alpine pastures
Comments:	Sensible walking shoes
Specialities:	Alpine Marmot, Alpine Grizzled Skipper, Birds-eye Primrose, *Saxifraga aretioides*, Spring Gentian

Small roads from Benasque give access to this reserve. It is a dramatic site right in the middle of the highest mountains of the Pyrenees, with the Aneto the highest peak rising to 3404m (11,168 feet) and the Pico de la Maladeta just 100m (330 feet) lower. The coniferous woods soon give way to Alpine pastures which become a mass of flowers immediately the snow melts in late spring. Pink Cuckoo Flowers, golden-yellow Globe Flowers and the white-leaved, pink-flowered Birds-eye Primrose are found in the meadows, and higher up Spring and Trumpet Gentians add brilliant shades of blue. Between the rocks the beautiful Moss Campion forms huge mounds covered with pink flowers and *Arenaria tetraquetra* forms dense hard pads with white flowers protruding from the top of the four-angled shoots. *Saxifraga aretioides* clings to cracks in the rocks producing yellow flowers from its tight clusters of leaves.

In this zone, Alpine Marmots have their burrows. They can easily be seen at a distance but soon vanish if approached. Chamois are common on the higher mountainsides. In the woods Capercaillie can be seen as well as Black Woodpecker, Jay and the usual small woodland birds.

Butterflies are seen all over the Alpine meadows and include the rare Alpine Grizzled Skipper, only found in three locations in the Pyrenees.

37 VALL D'ARAN	
Grid reference:	D 32
Location:	N of Vielha
Access:	Very good
Season:	Late spring, summer and early autumn
Terrain:	Valley and high mountain pastures
Comments:	Sensible walking shoes
Specialities:	Alpine Chough, Alpine Marmot, Chequered Skipper, Clouded Apollo, *Primula intricata*

Access is from Vielha on any of the small roads which go north from the N 230. This is a very high mountain range lying along the French border. Until 1948 when the Túnel de Vielha was built, the area was frequently isolated for six months annually. The wide fertile Río Garona valley through which the N 230 runs supports cattle and sheep.

High Alpine pastures, rich with flowers, make this a haven for butterflies. The Alpine Grizzled Skipper and the rarer Chequered Skipper may be found. The Clouded Apollo, lacking the red spots of the other Apollo species, has formed a subspecies *republicanus* here in the Pyrenees. Another rarity in the valley is the Silvery Argus, the male having blue wings and the female brown.

Chamois are seen on the higher ground, as is an occasional shy Alpine Marmot.

Plants are a speciality with an amazing number of narcissus species, such as *Narcissus bicolor*, *N. pallidiflorus*, *N. abscissus* and *N. poeticus* in drifts, colouring the meadows. Higher up the valley are *Aquilegia pyrenaica*,

Viola cornuta, *Fritillaria pyrenaica*, *Gentiana acaulis*, *Primula intricata* and many more.

Birds are numerous in the valley: Ring Ouzel, Alpine Chough, Chough, Capercaillie, Ptarmigan, Black Woodpecker and three pairs of breeding Bearded Vultures.

38 PARQUE NACIONAL DE AIGÜES TORTES AND ESTANY DE SANT MAURICI	
Grid reference:	E 32/33
Location:	W of Espot, SE of Vielha
Access:	By very small roads
Season:	Late spring, summer and early autumn
Terrain:	Mountain with Alpine meadows
Comments:	Sensible walking shoes; information centre open during the summer months; Estany is the local name for reservoirs and lakes
Specialities:	Bearded Vulture, Ptarmigan, Alpine Snowbell, *Androsace carnea*, Spring Gentian

From Vielha take the C 142 and then the C 147 for 52km. Turn right to Espot where there is a well-marked summer information centre, and access to the park is a few kilometres further on.

This national park is scenically one of the most beautiful parts of the Pyrenees, designated a national park in 1988 This was unfortunately after considerable damage had been caused by the construction of hydroelectric works and dams. Now, by law, it is being restored to its former glory.

A huge mountain rises to 2982m (9783 feet) in the park. The valleys are pasture-lands with woodlands of Mountain

A tranquil scene within the Parque nacional Aigües Tortes and Estany de Sant Maurici. A superb walking area.

With such a mass of flowers, butterflies are everywhere, with the Long-tailed and Adonis Blues in evidence, and also Mountain Clouded Yellow, Apollo, Mountain Fritillary and several skippers. Overhead soar Griffon Vulture, Golden Eagle and the rare Bearded Vulture, and on the ground Ptarmigan run to hide amongst the rocks.

It is not advisable to visit between October and May as the site is snow covered.

39 RESERVA NACIONAL DE ALTO PALLARS-ARAN	
Grid reference:	D/E 33/34
Location:	E of Vielha
Access:	Easy but long distances between roads which enter reserve
Season:	Late spring, summer and early autumn
Terrain:	Mountains and pasture
Comments:	Sensible walking shoes; snow-bound in winter
Specialities:	Alpine Accentor, Otter, Pyrenean Brook Salamander, Grass Frog, *Arenaria tetraquetra*

Pine and Silver Fir, and occasional plantings of Silver Birch. Among the trees, Black Woodpecker, Jay, Magpie, Capercaillie and Tengmalm's Owl occur; also Chamois come down for shelter in the winter.

Alpine plant enthusiasts will find this a paradise. There are some high meadows on a plateau containing the main lakes and here grow Pyrenean, Spring and Great Yellow Gentian, *Gentiana alpina*, Spring and Alpine Anemones, *Pinguicula grandiflora* and St Bruno's Lily, while higher up in the rocks and scree, mounds of *Androsace argentea* and *A. carnea*, Alpine Snowbell and Purple Saxifrage grow with a range of other Alpines in profusion.

Situated north of the C 147 Tremp to Vielha road. From Llavorsí northwards there are several roads which wend their way into the reserve. The reserve is a very high mountain range which borders France on the northern side, Andorra on the east and the Vall d'Aran to the west. The highest point is Monteixo at 2905m (9531 feet). The C 147 passes over the crest of the Pyrenees at Puerto de la Bonaigua (2072m; 6798 feet) which is frequently impassible in winter. The Garonne river rises in this mountain range to exit at Bordeaux in France.

In the Garonne Valley the reptile and amphibian population is interesting. The

Fertile valley with Poplar trees and the Reserva nacional de Pallars-Aran in the background. The valleys in this area are becoming highly popular for winter sports from November until May. When the snow recedes, the pastures become full of flowers.

Otter (Lutra lutra) feeding on trout. Although endangered over much of Europe, the Otter's population is stable in Spain.

Pyrenean Brook Salamander is found in streams, under rocks and in damp places up to 2000m (6560 feet). The Common or Grass Frog is found here at the extreme western edge of its distribution and the Asp Viper is sometimes found in the scrubland sunning itself on rocks. It is a rather timid snake but should be left alone!

On the grassland at the high pass in June, when the snow has finally melted, you may find *Ranunculus pyrenaeus, Androsace carnea,* Purple Crocus, and in the rocks by the roadside *Arenaria tetraquetra.* Butterflies are numerous and exciting and are similar to those found in the neighbouring Vall d'Aran.

Chamois are common in the mountains

and woods, Wild Boar and Wild Cat live in the valleys, and Otters may be seen in the rivers. The usual mountain birds are here, but do look for the Alpine Chough, Alpine Accentor and the rare Bearded Vulture .

40 SIERRA DEL BOUMORT	
Grid reference:	F 33
Location:	S of Sort, NE of Tremp
Access:	By very small roads
Season:	Late spring, summer and early autumn
Terrain:	Alpine pastures and mountain
Comments:	Sensible walking shoes
Specialities:	Tengmalm's Owl, Pyrenean Brook Sala mander, Pale Lent Lily Narcissus, Black Vanilla Orchid, *Viola bubanii*
Subsidiary:	Desfiladero de Collegats, F 33

North-east of Tremp and south of Sort there are several small roads from the N 260 which give access to the area. This is a mountain range in the lower southern part of the Pyrenees. The highest of the limestone crags is the Boumort peak at 2070m (6791 feet).

Winter wonderland: a frozen waterfall typical of some of the higher areas of the Pyrenees during the winter months.

Later in the season many species of orchid, such as Black Vanilla, Elder-flowered, Musk and Small White should all be found. Naturally many species of butterflies can be seen within these pastures so rich in flowers, one especially being Forster's Furry Blue.

In the valleys near the streams the Pyrenean Brook Salamander can be observed hiding under stones at the edge of the water.

41 SIERRA DEL CADI	
Grid reference:	F 34/35
Location:	SE of La Seu d'Urgell
Access:	By small roads
Season:	Late spring, summer and early autumn
Terrain:	Alpine pastures
Comments:	Walking shoes; snow-bound in winter
Specialities:	Tengmalm's Owl, Black Woodpecker, Apollo, Pyrenean Gentian, *Ramonda myconi*
Subsidiary:	Reserva nacional Cerdanya, E 34/35

Pine woodlands, mainly Scots Pine, Black Pine and Mountain Pine, cover the lower slopes and these give cover for Capercaillie, Grey Partridge and Black Woodpecker, this being the latter's southern limit. Teng-malm's Owl and the Eagle Owl, both very rare, are found here and there is a very large colony of Griffon Vultures, possibly the largest in Cataluña: Raven, Chough and maybe Alpine Chough are also present.

Interesting flowers on the lower slopes include saxifrages and species of *Aquilegia*, *Helleborus* and *Viola*, including *Viola cornuta*, Mountain Pansy and on the cliff faces *V. bubanii*. In the Alpine pastures grazed by sheep and cattle, narcissi are prolific, particularly forms of Pale Lent Lily Narcissus.

Travelling south from La Seu d'Urgell on the N 260 and then the C 1313 there are several small roads which head east into the area. This is a long high range of mountains south of Andorra rising to 2913m (9557 feet), the peaks snow-covered for most of the year.

It is a very wild area with many tracks to follow and a few small villages on the lower slopes. The valleys leading up to Andorra are relatively wide with Alpine pasture-land grazed by woolly Swiss brown cows and sheep. The sheep's milk is used for making the delicious 'Cadi' cheese.

On the higher meadows there is a wealth of plant life. The Yellow Pyrenean Lily grows in moist areas with *Aquilegia pyrenaica* showing its blue and white flowers. The very rare

Narcissus alpestris can also be found. It is the true Alpine flora for which this site is famous, with large mounds of *Androsace villosa* and *Silene acaulis*, drifts of *Primula integrifolia* and *P. viscosa*, Pyrenean Gentian and *Gentiana alpina* giving a dazzling display of vivid blue. Clinging to the rocks species of saxifrage throw out their sprays of sparkling white flowers, while nearby *Ramonda myconi* opens its violet flowers.

There are many, many varieties of butterflies including the colourful Apollo, and you may be lucky enough to see the Turquoise, Ripart's Anomalous or even the Forster's Furry Blue as they have been recorded here. Chamois live on the Alpine crags and Roe and Red Deer inhabit the Pine woods. They all come down to the lower lands during the severe winter.

Golden Eagle, Short-toed Eagle and if you are lucky the Bearded Vulture may be seen in the mountains, and in the woods Black Woodpecker and the rare Tengmalm's Owl can be found.

42 PARQUE NATURAL DE LA ZONA VOLCANICA DE LA GARROTXA	
Grid reference:	F 37
Location:	NW of Gerona
Access:	Very good
Season:	All year round
Terrain:	Cultivated valleys with wooded hills
Comments:	Sensible shoes; information centres
Specialities:	Hawfinch, Three-toed Skink, Marbled Newt, Palmate Newt, Painted Frog
Subsidiary:	Santa Pau, F 37; Castellfollit de la Roca, a village on basalt outcrop, F 37

This site is approximately 40km north-west of Gerona, and is easily accessible from the C 150/N 260. It is an area of 120km², unmarked on the Michelin map, but well marked on entering the area. It is basically within the triangle created by Olot, Santa Pau and Castellfollit de la Roca. An information centre in Santa Pau and another along the road towards Olot can supply maps of the area. The latter centre also has horse-drawn wagons with drivers to tour the Beech woods. It is a beautiful area with heavily cultivated valleys and well-wooded hills.

Geologically speaking, there was recent volcanic activity in the area (11,000 years ago) and there are at least thirty volcanic cones with distinct craters. A typical one is Santa Margarida, west of Santa Pau, which has a crater 450m in diameter and 75m high. It is sign-posted from the OE 524 between Santa Pau and Olot. Here, a well-defined volcanic ash pathway through deciduous woods of Beech and Pyrenean Oak, some ivy-covered, leads to the top where you overlook a saucer-shaped, grass-covered crater with an ancient hermitage in the centre (dated 1428).

A large number of rare reptiles and amphibians inhabit the moist woodlands. There is the Three-toed Skink, like a small silvery snake with rudimentary legs, and in the wetter areas Marbled Newt, Palmate Newt and the rare Painted Frog.

Long-tailed Tit, Nuthatch, Great Spotted Woodpecker and if you are lucky Wryneck and the heavy-billed Hawfinch may all be seen in the woods, while on higher ground Egyptian Vultures soar overhead.

The Garden Dormouse and the Beech Marten also inhabit this area.

This is a fascinating and unusual site, the medieval villages of the area exuding a sense of tranquility.

4. NORTH MESETA

INTRODUCTION

This is the north-central region of Spain and is bordered by Portugal's north-eastern frontier in the west, the Cantábrican region in the north, the Basque–Rioja region to the east and Extremadura westwards from Madrid in the south. It is a region dominated by the high mountain range along its southern edge of the Sierra de Gredos and the Sierra de Guadarrama, which rise up to 2592m (8504 feet) at the Pico Almanzor. To the north there are wide open plains and the basin of the Río Duero. The climate is harsh in winter, with freezing temperatures and snow, and hot and dry but cool in the mountains in summer.

Male Little Bustard (Otis tetrax) stamping on its display ground. This is a typical bird of the dry steppe lands of North Meseta.

The birds are interesting as there are many mountain species, in particular Golden Eagle, Griffon and Egyptian Vultures, Chough and Alpine Accentor. In the woods Magpie, woodpeckers, finches, flycatchers and warblers are plentiful. The Río Duero basin has some of the largest breeding colonies of herons in the north of Spain and around the small lakes near Zamora the only known Iberian wintering area for the Bean Goose is located. In the corn-growing plains between Valladolid and Salamanca typical steppe birds, for example Great and Little Bustards, Pin-tailed and Black-bellied Sandgrouse, and Dupont's Lark, breed.

No less interesting is the flora. The high Alpine meadows of the Sierra de Gredos and Sierra de Guadarrama become alive with flowers as soon as the snow retreats in May. Crocuses, narcissi, especially *N. rupicola* in Navacerrada, *Fritillaria* spp. and of course the 'hedgehog' plants, *Cytisus purgans, Echinospartum lusitanicum* and *Genista hystrix.*

In the valleys, heavily wooded with Scots Pine and Pyrenean Oak, there is also a wealth of plant life, which is at its best in May and June: orchids grow in profusion, cistus and Lavender dominate the maquis scrub and Foxgloves and lupins light up the roadside.

With the abundance of flowers, butterflies are numerous with many of the woodland species present including the Great Banded Grayling and the Southern Hermit. One notable moth is the spectacular Spanish Moon Moth found in the pine forests.

The most impressive mammal of the region is the Spanish Ibex which has a stronghold on the mountain tops of the Sierra de Gredos.

Opposite: map of North Meseta. The sites are numbered as in the text. Only main roads and the major rivers of the region are shown.

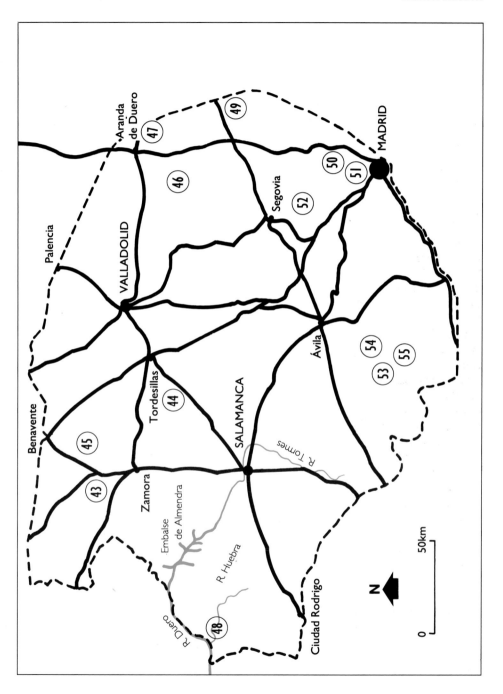

FIFTY INTERESTING SPECIES TO LOOK FOR

Booted Eagle	Dupont's Lark	Scarce Swallowtail	*Aquilegia dichroa*
Spanish Imperial	Bluethroat	Cardinal	*Cistus psilosepalus*
Eagle	Black-eared	Queen of Spain	*Crocus carpetanus*
Peregrine	Wheatear	Fritillary	Greater Broomrape
Marsh Harrier	Fan-tailed Warbler	Heath Fritillary	Hoop Petticoat
Red-crested	Alpine Accentor	Marsh Fritillary	Narcissus
Pochard	Great Grey Shrike	Clouded Yellow	*Linaria elegans*
Greylag Goose	Hoopoe	Great Banded	*Merendera montana*
Bean Goose	Spotless Starling	Grayling	*Narcissus rupicola*
Night Heron	Parsley Frog	Long-tailed Blue	Spanish Oyster
Purple Heron	Marsh Frog	Spanish Chalk-hill	Plant
Spoonbill	Red Squirrel	Blue	Round-leaved
Greenshank	Wolf	Silver-studded Blue	Sundew
Great Bustard	Wild Boar	Brown Argus	Broad-leaved
Crested Tit	Spanish Ibex	Alpine Anemone	Helleborine

Most habitats exist here: Alpine in the high mountains, freshwater in the river basin, coniferous forest in the high mountains, broad-leaved forest in the lower regions and extensive steppe land in the north-east and centre.

The grid references used on the following site descriptions relate to Michelin maps numbers 441 and 442.

43 SALINAS DE VILLAFAFILA AND EMBALSE DEL ESLA DE RICOBAYO

Grid reference:	G/H 12/13
Location:	N of Zamora and S of Benavente
Access:	Very good
Season:	All year round
Terrain:	Freshwater reservoir and saltwater lakes
Specialities:	Bean Goose, Greylag Goose, Spoonbill, Pochard, Wigeon

Both these sites are easily accessible from the N 630, which runs from Benavente south to Zamora. The salinas are to the east of the ZA 701 and the embalse is to the west.

The Río Esla rises in the Picos de Europa and joins the Duero just west of Zamora. A dam across the river has produced a long basin with very little vegetation along the edges. This is a roosting site for the only wintering population of the Bean Goose in Spain. This species should not be confused with the Greylag Goose which is paler in colour and has pink feet and legs.

A few kilometres to the north-east are three small saltwater lakes which tend to dry up in the summer months. These are noted for wintering Wigeon, Mallard, Shoveler, Teal, Pintail and Pochard and also a large concentration of Greylag Geese which roost here, moving into the cereals and pastures by day to feed. Spoonbills rest here during migration as do a mass of waders, all passing on their way to the Coto Doñana marismas.

The landscape is gently undulating,

mainly treeless grainland and grassland, but near the river irrigation schemes are used for sunflower and sugar-beet cultivation.

44 CASTRONUÑO

Grid reference:	H 14
Location:	W of Tordesillas
Access:	Good
Season:	All year round
Terrain:	Freshwater marshes
Comments:	Can be bleak in winter
Specialities:	Black Kite, Night Heron, Kingfisher, Fan-tailed Warbler, Great Reed Warbler

This spot is to the west of Tordesillas and is easily accessible by travelling south on the N 620/E 80 and then taking the VA 600 to the west for 18km to Castronuño. Here the Río Duero has been dammed to produce the relatively shallow and small Embalse de San José. This has extensive freshwater marshes and alluvial woods composed of willow, Poplar and elm. These woods contain the largest heronry in Castille y León which includes a number of Night Herons as well as the more common Grey Heron.

In the *Phragmites*-fringed edge of the embalse, Fan-tailed, Cetti's, Savi's, Reed and Great Reed Warblers can usually be seen during the breeding season. On the water, Moorhen, Great-crested and Little Grebes, and Mallard are common. Kingfishers may be seen sitting on overhanging branches while overhead Black Kites hunt for fish.

The surrounding land is well irrigated and is used for cereal and sugar-beet production. There are also large areas of lucerne which is cut while green for dairy cattle. Further out from the river on the dry cereal lands Great and Little Bustards and Black-bellied Sandgrouse are typical.

45 VILLAFAFILA PLAIN

Grid reference:	G 13
Location:	N of Zamora and S of Benavente
Access:	Good
Season:	All year round
Terrain:	Pasture-land and cereals
Comments:	Can be very hot in summer
Specialities:	Great Bustard, Little Bustard, Black-bellied Sandgrouse, Marsh Harrier, Parsley Frog

This plain is easily accessible and is situated on both sides of the N 630 between Zamora and Benavente. It is a dry arid plain just east of where the Río Esla widens into the

The Great Reed Warbler (Acrocephalus arundinaceus) *breeds throughout Spain wherever there are large expanses of reeds.*

Embalse del Esla de Ricobayo. Dry grassland and intensive cereal production provide ideal habitat for good numbers of typical steppe birds.

This is possibly one of the best areas in Iberia for the endangered Great Bustard, with an estimated 500 pairs breeding here. During spring you may be lucky to see heads poking out of the corn while others are busy feeding. They are huge birds (adult males weighing up to 18kg) with a brown, grey and white plumage, and moustache-like feathers on the face. Little Bustard and Black-bellied Sandgrouse are both common in this area. The best time of day to see them is in the early morning when they fly to their feeding grounds.

Down near the river, Marsh and Montagu's Harriers, and Black and Red Kites can be seen. In and around the river there are storks and herons, and you may also discover Marsh and Parsley Frogs.

46 CAÑON DEL DURATON

Grid reference:	H 18
Location:	SW of Aranda de Duero
Access:	By small roads
Season:	All year round
Terrain:	River and dry land
Specialities:	Dupont's Lark, Short-toed Lark, Cardinal, Brown Argus, Silver-studded Blue

Just south of Aranda de Duero take the C 603 for approximately 35km to the Río Duratón. The river has eroded a deep canyon through the limestone hills at this point. There are Poplar and willow plantations along the riversides. The Poplar is used for the timber industry and match making, while the willow is pollarded and used for basket making.

Swallowtail *Papilio machaon* W 6.4–10cm

Look particularly amongst the foliage and stems of fennel during spring and summer and you may find the beautiful caterpillar of the Swallowtail butterfly. When fully grown it is a magnificent and handsome creature up to about 40mm long. The basic ground colour is pale green with black bands around each segment. The band in the centre of each segment is wider, black with orange spots giving a very striking appearance.

The butterfly itself is unmistakable and highly coloured with yellow, red, black and blue. It flies strongly from flower to flower in search of nectar. It can be found throughout most of Spain, but is more plentiful along the southern coast.

The sides of the canyon have scrub vegetation with Spanish Juniper and evergreen oak, but also large areas of Lavender and Thyme much favoured by the large quantity of butterflies seen in the area. Thyme in particular is a favourite with fritillaries and blues, especially the Cardinal, Queen of Spain Fritillary, Heath Fritillary, Marsh Fritillary, Silver-studded Blue and Brown Argus. Look for the Swallowtail, especially near the river banks (*see* box).

Beyond the canyon and riverside there are extensive grasslands used for sheep grazing. These hold Little Bustard, Black-bellied Sandgrouse, the elusive Dupont's Lark, Crested Lark and during the summer the Short-toed Lark. Within the canyon, there is a large colony of Griffon Vultures, a smaller one of Egyptian Vultures and a large number of Choughs.

The Spanish Oyster Plant (Scolymus hispanicus) is colourful, prickly and thistle-like. The habitat in which it grows is typical of much of Spain.

47 MONTEJO DE LA VEGA	
Grid reference:	H 19
Location:	S of Aranda de Duero
Access:	By small roads
Season:	All year round
Terrain:	River and scrubland
Specialities:	Hoopoe, Woodchat Shrike, Dupont's Lark, Spotless Starling, Spanish Oyster Plant

Take one of several small roads east of the N 1/E 5 south of Aranda de Duero. The area is classified as a game refuge which at least gives some protection to the local fauna.

Near the Río Riaza large plantations of Poplars are grown for normal timber use and also for the match-making industry, for which Poplar is very suitable, being fast growing and easily split. Within the woods Magpie, Green and Great Spotted Woodpeckers, Jay, Great Grey and Woodchat Shrikes, Golden Oriole, Spotless Starling, Hoopoe and Little Owl can be seen. A limestone canyon by the river holds large colonies of both Griffon and Egyptian Vultures.

Away from the river the main habitat is of grassland and scrub, with Lavender and Thyme predominating, and here can be found Dupont's Lark, a bird more often associated with the semi-deserts of North Africa. A small local industry producing honey is common where Lavender and Thyme are found.

In this dry area irises, asphodels and various species of thistle thrive. The Spanish Oyster Plant in particular is colourful with masses of yellow flowers in August.

75

48 RIO HUEBRA	
Grid reference:	1 9
Location:	N of Ciudad Rodrigo
Access:	Comparatively easy
Season:	All year round
Terrain:	Undulating land
Specialities:	Black Stork, Eagle Owl, Wolf, Wild Boar, *Merendera montana*

This is a very remote area where the Río Huebra joins the Río Duero at the Portuguese frontier. It is reached by taking the SA 324 north from Ciudad Rodrigo to Lumbrales, and then picking up the SA 330 for a further 25km to reach the point where the rivers meet. When the Río Huebra reaches Portugal it has become a formidable force and has carved a channel through hard granite rocks, forming high cliffs at the point where the two rivers meet.

The surrounding zone is of undulating corn-growing land, grassland for grazing large herds of cattle and sheep, and extensive areas of scrubland with scattered evergreen oaks which have an undergrowth of cistus and Juniper. This gives cover for Wild Boar, Red Foxes and in the more dense thickets a few Wolves.

Where the grassland has been extensively grazed, *Merendera montana* forms carpets of pink crocus-like flowers in late summer and autumn, usually just after the first rainfall of the season. Its leaves appear much later on.

The cliff edges by the river provide ideal nesting sites for an impressive variety of birds of prey. There are large colonies of Griffon and Egyptian Vultures, some Golden and Bonelli's Eagles and a very large colony of Choughs. A few spectacular Eagle Owls and a number of the rare Black Stork all breed within this locality.

49 RESERVA NACIONAL DE SONSAZ	
Grid reference:	I/J 19/20
Location:	NE of Madrid
Access:	Difficult, by small roads
Season:	Spring, summer and autumn
Terrain:	Woodland and maquis scrub
Comments:	Snow during winter
Specialities:	Golden Eagle, Honey Buzzard, Great Grey Shrike, Crested Lark, Short-toed Treecreeper
Subsidiary:	Sierra de Ayllón, I 19

Access is by the N 1/E 5 about 80km northeast of Madrid. Several small roads leave the main trunk road and head into the area, an extension of the Sierra de Guadarrama, rising to 2273m (7457 feet) at the Pico del Lobo and containing the important Beech woods of the Natural Park of Hayedo de Tejera Negra in the north around Cantalojas.

This very extensive site has been subjected to erosion. The grassland has degenerated and cistus maquis scrub has become a dominant feature. Livestock grazing has declined and a number of villages have been abandoned. There are a number of small woods of Pyrenean Oak and Beech and recently large forests of Scots Pine have been planted.

Birds found in the mountains include a large number of breeding Golden Eagles, as well as Bonelli's Eagle, Peregrine, Honey Buzzard and Griffon Vulture in smaller numbers. Within the woods there is the nocturnal Eagle Owl and many small woodland birds including Short-toed Treecreeper, Great Tit, Blue Tit, Greenfinch, Chaffinch and various woodpeckers. In the more open

Embalse de Santillana viewed from the Parque Regional de Pedriza. This is a large man-made reservoir, which is a notable resting place for vast numbers of migrating birds, in particular the White Stork (Ciconia ciconia).

areas Goldfinch, Spotted Flycatcher, Crested Lark, Great Grey Shrike, Little Owl and Stonechat can be found.

From the name of the highest point, Pico del Lobo, Wolves must have inhabited the area in the past. Now it is a grazing ground for sheep and goats although there are Rabbits, Red Fox and Wild Boar in the scrublands.

50 EMBALSE DE SANTILLANA	
Grid reference:	J 18
Location:	N of Madrid
Access:	Very good
Season:	All year round
Terrain:	Lake with reed beds
Comments:	Information centre just outside Manzanares el Real
Specialities:	White Stork, Purple Heron, Little Egret, Black-tailed Godwit, Greenshank
Subsidiary:	Embalse de El Vellón, J 18/19

Access is very good by taking the M 607 for about 50km from Madrid and then turning north onto the M 612 to Manzanares el

Real. There is an information centre just outside this town towards the Parque Regional de La Pedriza (*see also* Site 51).

This large embalse is one of the most important resting places for migrant birds passing through central Spain. During autumn up to 900 White Storks have been counted at one time on the gently sloping banks. There are one or two small islands and a shallow shoreline which provide ideal habitat for large numbers of ducks and waders, many of which overwinter here. Mallard, Shoveler, Wigeon, Teal, Pintail, Pochard and the occasional Red-crested Pochard can be counted amongst the ducks, and waders are just as numerous, with Redshank, Greenshank, Bar- and Black-tailed Godwits all seen. There are a number of reed-beds where Coot, Moorhen, Little Grebe and Great-crested Grebe breed, and Grey and Purple Herons shelter. Cattle Egrets feed in quantity on the grasslands along some of the lake edges and Little Egrets wade and catch fish in the shallow water.

The surrounding area is mainly un-dulating corn-growing land, but along the northern edge is the town of Manzanares with the huge rocky mountains of the Sierra de Guadarrama in the background.

There are two well-positioned hides at the northern end of the embalse, for which permits are needed from the information centre, but plenty can be seen away from the hides.

51 PARQUE REGIONAL DE LA PEDRIZA DE PARQUE REGIONAL DE LA CUENCA ALTA DEL MANZANARES	
Grid reference:	J/K 18/19
Location:	N of Madrid
Access:	Comparatively easy
Season:	All year round
Terrain:	Enormous boulders and pasture
Comments:	Information centre just outside Manzanares el Real
Specialities:	Short-toed Treecreeper, Bee-eater, Spanish Ibex, Wild Boar, Round-leaved Sundew

This particular region of the larger park is situated at the northern end and is approached from Manzanares el Real about 50km north of Madrid (*see* previous site). The whole area is administered by AMA with a new reception and information centre opened in 1990 just outside Manzanares, which gives a good description of the local ecology. It is a truly amazing site with vast cliffs and massive boulder-type rocks piled one upon the other like some giant's playground! Many of the huge rocks have been given fanciful names. One of the most spectacular is Yelmo, which looks like a huge helmet rising straight up for 150m. Its rounded summit can be seen from Madrid.

Spanish Ibex have been introduced from Sierra de Gredos and Monfragüe. These are animals which have been bred in captivity and after careful rehabilitation released into the wild. Wild Boar also inhabit the park and in the evenings make their way down to the river to drink.

The lower part of the reserve is heavily forested with pines and evergreen oak, and a colourful undergrowth of *Cistus psilosepalus*, Lavender, Thyme and Heather, with Round-leaved Sundew, irises, narcissi and orchids all producing nectar for the numerous butterflies, such as Swallowtail, Painted Lady, Scarce Copper, Green and Spanish Hairstreaks, and Spanish Chalk-hill Blue.

Birds of prey nest in the rocky buttresses.

The high peak in the right of the picture is in the Parque Regional La Pedriza. It is known as Yelmo (the Helmet) and can be seen from Madrid. There are camping facilities in the park, but camping in general is strictly controlled. It is very popular with the local Spaniards who come out from Madrid which is comparatively close.

Red-legged Partridge, Jay, Magpie, wood-peckers, Short-toed Treecreeper, Bee-eater and many warblers can all be seen.

52 SIERRA DE GUADARRAMA	
Grid reference:	I/J/K 17/18
Location:	SE of Segovia, NW of Madrid
Access:	Very good
Season:	Late spring, summer and early autumn
Terrain:	Mountain, forest and Alpine meadows
Comments:	Snow in winter; watch out for cattle on the sides of the main road
Specialities:	Egyptian Vulture, Alpine Accentor, *Cistus psilosepalus*, *Merendera montana*, Round-leaved Sundew
Subsidiary:	Mirador (viewpoint) de las Robledos near El Paular, J 18

These mountains are within easy reach of both Madrid and Segovia and are therefore used extensively for skiing. They are accessible by either the N VI/A 6 or the A 1/E 5 roads from Madrid via a number of well-marked inner roads. The tallest peak rises to 2429m (7969 feet) which is slightly lower than the neighbouring Sierra de Gredos; the mountains are also more rounded. There are widespread Scots Pine forests on both sides up to almost 2000m (6560 feet).

At the head of the Puerto de Navacerrada, a mountain pass at 1860m (6102 feet) *Narcissus rupicola* is found growing freely, and earlier in the year, just after the snow has receded, *Crocus carpetanus* appears. *C. asturicus* flowers here in autumn. During the summer when the ski runs are clear of snow a very interesting flora emerges. In the wet zones Sundew is sometimes so prolific that some patches shine red. Small Hairbells and Toadflax appear amongst the short grass.

In the river valleys there is scrub, with *Cistus psilosepalus*, Lavender and Juniper predominating and *Merendera montana* growing underneath in the autumn.

Birds of prey like Golden and Spanish Imperial Eagles, and Black, Griffon and Egyptian Vultures nest on the rocky summits. The Alpine Accentor nests here too and Pied Flycatchers can be seen on migration.

A quiet backwater amongst the pine trees, so typical of the Sierra de Guadarrama. This sierra is easily accessible from Madrid.

In the bare patches at the side of this icy-cold water, carpets of the pink Merendera montana appear in autumn.

53 SIERRA DE GREDOS, NORTHERN SLOPES	
Grid reference:	L 14
Location:	SW of Avila
Access:	Good
Season:	Spring, summer and autumn
Terrain:	Alpine pastures and mountains
Comments:	Good walking shoes
Specialities:	Black Kite, Spanish Ibex, Long-tailed Blue, Alpine Anemone, *Aquilegia dichroa*
Subsidiary:	Woods at Hoyocasero, K 15; Embalse de Burguillo, K 16

Situated south-west of Ávila, it is best to take the N 403 southwards, turning on to the C 500 after 26km. Follow this road until just beyond Barajas, and then turn south onto the AV 931. Continue to the large parking area at the end. This brings you into the Reserva nacional de Gredos.

The northern slopes are a complete contrast to the southern side; here they are more rounded and do not fall away in steep cliffs and screes. The lower slopes are almost treeless, with just a few woods of Scots Pine, very reminiscent of parts of Scotland.

This is the stronghold of the Spanish Ibex (*see* box) and near Laguna Grande de Gredos, approached by a track from the parking area, you will usually see them climbing almost impossible precipices or balancing on the tops of rocky pinnacles. Although they are true wild animals, it is very rewarding to see them at this locality, as here they are quite confiding.

Flowers, such as Hoop Petticoat Narcissus and *Narcissus rupicola*, cover the turf in

Spanish Ibex *Capra hircus pyrenaica* L 119–148

At the end of the nineteenth century the Spanish Ibex became almost extinct, with only twenty thought to exist in the wild. A strict hunting ban was imposed and the result is the present population of over 10,000. Some from the Sierra de Gredos have now been introduced into other mountain areas, notably Sierra de Cazorla.

The Ibex is a goat-like animal weighing 70kg, the male sporting two enormous horns, the female smaller with short horns. They have the ability to climb almost vertical cliff faces.

A good area to see them is by parking at El Refugio on the northern slopes of the Sierra de Gredos, beneath the towering 2592m (8504 feet) of Pico Almanzor and following the track up to Laguna Grande de Gredos.

May, and in the woods *Fritillaria hispanica*, *Aquilegia dichroa*, Alpine Anemone and two species of peony can be seen.

With the abundance of flowers there are numerous butterflies including Clouded Yellow, Spanish Chalk-hill Blue, Common Blue, Long-tailed Blue, Swallowtail, skippers and fritillaries.

Black and Red Kites are always present, wheeling in the air looking for food, as are Chough and Raven, with Black-eared Wheatear hopping around the rocks.

The Heath Fritillary (Mellicta athalia) is one of the more widespread and variable fritillaries.

The Roman road leading over the pass at Puerto de Pico remains in a state of good preservation.

54 PUERTO DEL PICO, GREDOS	
Grid reference:	L 14
Location:	NE of Arenas de San Pedro
Access:	Fairly easy
Season:	Spring, summer and autumn
Terrain:	Mountain and forest
Comments:	Can be snowbound
Specialities:	Egyptian Vulture, Booted Eagle, Red Squirrel, Great Banded Grayling, *Linaria elegans*
Subsidiary:	Cuevas del Aguila, L 14

This mountain pass is reached by travelling north-east from Arenas de San Pedro on the AV 923 for about 14km. This is the pass from the rugged southern slopes of Sierra de Gredos to the northern more rounded area and follows the old Roman road. Today there is a fast modern highway, but from the top of the pass at 1352m (4436 feet) you can see the road built almost 2000 years ago, winding down the mountainside, in most places in a perfect state of repair! This Roman road still has its uses, as in autumn sheep are taken down from the high mountain pastures using this road on their way to their wintering quarters. This keeps them away from the new major highway.

White Spanish Broom and yellow *Cytisus*

striatus cover the mountainsides, and the mauve *Linaria elegans* can be seen on the roadsides. Woods of Scots Pine cover the lower slopes and here the Red Squirrel may be seen, bright red in colour, differing from the almost black variety found further north.

Birds of prey are common: Black and Red Kites, Honey Buzzard and Golden and Booted Eagles are regularly seen, and with luck the Spanish Imperial Eagle and Black Vulture; Griffon and Egyptian Vultures are almost certain to be seen.

Butterflies are everywhere during spring and summertime and in particular the Great Banded Grayling should be seen in the woods.

55 GUISANDO, SIERRA DE GREDOS

Grid reference:	L 14
Location:	N of Arenas de San Pedro
Access:	Good but twisting
Season:	Spring, summer and autumn
Terrain:	Mountain with extensive woodland
Comments:	Can be very cold in winter
Specialities:	Bluethroat, Pied Flycatcher, Spanish Ibex, Great Banded Grayling, Broad-leaved Helleborine
Subsidiary:	There are very many well-marked forest tracks to superb sites in this area: Río Cantos, El Hornillo, La Francisca, Domingo Fernando and Collado de la Casa

A good but twisting road leads about 6km from Arenas de San Pedro to the stunningly beautiful southern slopes of the Sierra de Gredos mountain range. The area is heavily wooded with Pyrenean Oak, Scots Pine and Maritime Pine, and the steep sides to the hills are terraced and planted with vegetables, peach and cherry trees, and, near the villages, vines. Lower down where the land levels out towards the Río Tiétar, large commercial areas of tobacco, cayenne peppers and asparagus are grown.

From all points on the southern slopes of Gredos, the jagged, often snow-clad peaks appear above the pine forests. In the valleys sparkling clear water splashes down over huge weathered granite boulders, giving spectacular scenery and effects unlike anywhere else in Spain.

The Alpine meadows below the peaks are full of flowers, with specialities like the Jersey Orchid with magenta-coloured blooms and the plainer Broad-leaved Helleborine. The Greater Broomrape, an odd-looking parasite 80cm tall, *Verbascum* and various species of Heather, cistus and Broom complete the colourful picture.

The sierras are full of birds: the usual Chaffinch, Jay, Pied Flycatcher, Green Woodpecker, Great and Crested Tits, and Short-toed Treecreeper, but also nesting Bluethroat. Birds of prey are abundant, with Red and Black Kites most numerous.

Butterflies are plentiful: Swallowtail, Scarce Swallowtail, blues and skippers, and in the woods Great Banded Grayling.

At the end of the metalled road at Nogal del Barranca is a great statue of the 'Macho de Cabra Montes', the male Spanish Ibex.

Opposite: *a 'garganta' or rock-strewn bed, with well water-eroded rocks at Guisando in the Sierra de Gredos.*

5. EXTREMADURA

INTRODUCTION

This central western region of Spain joins Portugal on its west side, Andalucía in the south, the high plateau of La Mancha to the east and Sierra de Gredos on its northern boundary. The whole region is in reality a high plateau, within which there are the isolated mountainous areas of Sierra de Gata, Sierra de la Peña de Francia, Montes de Toledo and Sierra Morena. It is sheltered from cold northerly winds by the high Sierra de Gredos to the north, but snow can be experienced. In general, rainfall is fairly light and mainly during the winter and early spring. The summers are hot and dry, baking the land hard.

The Great Spotted Cuckoo (Clamator glandarius) is large, with a long tail and distinct crest. It is often seen hopping along the ground Magpie-like.

Much of the countryside is devoted to cereal growing and stock grazing, mainly on very large estates. Pasture-land with scattered evergreen oaks stretches as far as the eye can see and is grazed by sheep, goats, cattle and herds of black pigs.

Two major rivers cross the region: the Río Tajo and the Río Guadiana. The river basins have deep rich soil where various specialized crops are grown, such as soya bean, tobacco, cayenne peppers and asparagus.

In the main the wildlife of the region lives in the mountains: the Pardel Lynx has a refuge in the extensive Monfragüe Reserve; the Egyptian Mongoose can often be seen crossing a road, sometimes in family groups, and disappearing into the undergrowth; and Red and Roe Deer, Wolves, Foxes, Rabbits, Hares and Wild Boar are all present.

Flowers cover the mountainsides in spring and early summer; cistus, Thyme, Lavender and Gorse colour the valleys which abound with butterflies; and in the cool woods and meadows there is a profusion of orchids.

The cool mountains contain a wealth of bird life and it is in this region that the Black Vulture and the Black Stork have their major nesting areas, especially in the Monfragüe Reserve. The plains with extensive grain land have Great and Little Bustards, Black-eared Wheatear, Pintailed and Black-bellied Sandgrouse, Great Spotted Cuckoo, and Crested and Thekla Larks. In winter Cranes, Lapwing and Golden Plover feed amongst the emerging wheat. The Tablas de Daimiel Reserve is a haven for water birds and a stronghold of the Bearded Tit.

Most inland habitat ecosystems are found within the region. There are some Alpine areas on the highest mountain tops of the Peña de Francia and Sierra de Gata.

Opposite: *map of Extremadura. The sites are numbered as in the text. Only main roads and the major rivers of the region are shown.*

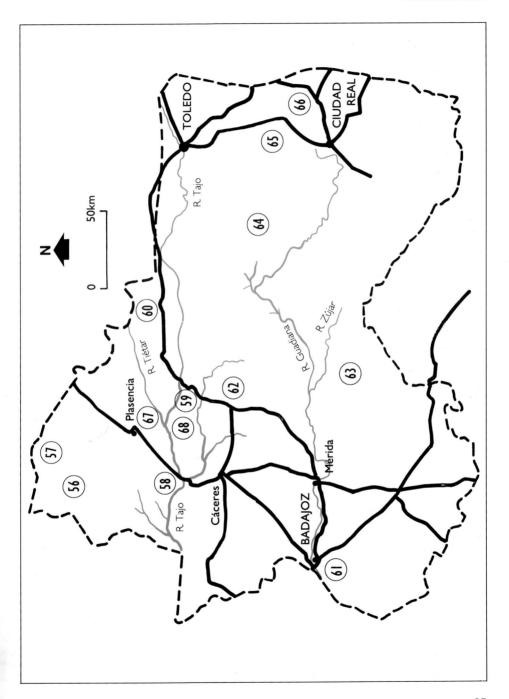

EXTREMADURA

85

A bull-fighting ranch with breeding stock amongst the Cork Trees.

56 SIERRA DE GATA

Grid reference:	K/L 10
Location:	S of Ciudad Rodrigo
Access:	Not very easy, by small roads from the C 526
Season:	Most of the year
Terrain:	Low mountain, pasture and forest
Specialities:	Black-winged Kite, Honey Buzzard, Booted Eagle, Wild Boar, Pardel Lynx

Coniferous and broad-leaved deciduous forests are found in most of the mountainous areas, with some as commercial forests and others as natural woodlands. Steppe and maquis scrub are confined to the higher hills of the central plateau and there is much open lowland mixed forest in the river basins.

The grid references used in the following site descriptions relate to Michelin maps numbers 441 and 444.

This site is situated about 35km south of Ciudad Rodrigo and is reached by taking the C 526, then one of the small unnumbered roads. This is a range of relatively low mountains near the Portuguese border, only reaching to 1367m (4485 feet). There are considerable Maritime Pine forests and some small villages. On the lower land both deciduous and evergreen oaks are scattered

FIFTY INTERESTING SPECIES TO LOOK FOR

Black-winged Kite	Bearded Tit	Azure-winged	Roe Deer
Lesser Kestrel	Black-eared	Magpie	Swallowtail
Spanish Imperial	Wheatear	Golden Oriole	Death's Head
Eagle	Cetti's Warbler	Stripe-necked	Hawk Moth
Honey Buzzard	Red-rumped	Terrapin	Emperor Moth
Montagu's Harrier	Swallow	Painted Frog	Beautiful
Black Vulture	Serin	Midwife Toad	Demoiselle
Eagle Owl	Crossbill	Viperine Snake	*Trithemis annulata*
Ferruginous Duck	Bluethroat	Wolf	*Cistus crispus*
Black Stork	Spanish Sparrow	Red Fox	*Cytinus ruber*
Purple Heron	Great Spotted	Pardel Lynx	*Digitalis thapsi*
Black-winged Stilt	Cuckoo	Wild Cat	*Narcissus rupicola*
Crane	Bee-eater	Egyptian	Sawfly Orchid
Great Bustard	Spotless Starling	Mongoose	Pyramidal Orchid
Firecrest	Hoopoe	Wild Boar	

within pasture-land used for grazing. Near the River Arrago to the south, where there is adequate irrigation, orchards dominate.

Pardel Lynx are present in small numbers in these mountains and in the valleys Wild Boar are plentiful. On the craggy hills, Black Vulture, Honey Buzzard, Booted Eagle and the occasional Spanish Imperial Eagle breed.

On the southern end of the Sierra is the Embalse de Borbollón. Within this embalse is a small island which is managed as an ornithological reserve. It is an extremely important breeding site for a very large colony of Cattle Egrets (over 1000 pairs) and for over fifty pairs of Black Kites. Many waders winter at the lake, most notably thousands of Black-tailed Godwit. In the cultivated grain lands a large number of Cranes overwinter.

One of the specialities of the region is the Black-winged Kite, which is about the same size as a Kestrel, but pale dove-grey with black wing-tips and shoulders. It often hovers when hunting. This kite's range was very restricted in Spain but is now expanding.

Black-winged Kite (Elanus caeruleus). In Europe, this kite is only found in south-west Iberia.

57 SIERRA DE LA PEÑA DE FRANCIA	
Grid reference:	K 11/12
Location:	NW of Béjar
Access:	Excellent
Season:	Spring, summer and autumn
Terrain:	Mountain, woodland and scrub
Comments:	Snow in winter
Specialities:	Black Vulture, Griffon Vulture, Pardel Lynx, Wolf, Roe Deer
Subsidiary:	Las Hurdes, a river area, K/L 11

Situated north-west of Béjar and easily accessible from the N 630/E 803 main road via the C 515 which continues through to Ciudad Rodrigo. This is a remote mountainous area of western Spain, the hard crystalline rock culminating in the pyramidal summit of Peña de Francia at 1723m (5653 feet). Small medieval-style villages cluster in the valleys where only recently metal surfaced roads have brought modern technology to the area.

The slopes of the mountain are covered with evergreen and deciduous oak, with a thick undergrowth of cistus, Broom, Thyme and in the wetter parts Bracken which represents the old original woodland cover. The peaks are bare of vegetation except for little pockets of soil between rocks where *Narcissus rupicola* flowers after the snow has receded. Near the villages in the valleys, there is extensive terracing on which cherry, peach and apricot orchards have been planted.

This is another stronghold of the endangered Black Vulture, of which there are an estimated thirty pairs nesting within the area in the tall trees. Griffon Vultures nest on ledges in the craggy heights. The Black Vulture is larger than the Griffon, darker in colour and the wings are more 'square' with a straight trailing edge.

Pardel Lynx, Wolves, Roe Deer and Wild Boar are present, although the Roe Deer is the only one likely to be seen.

58 EMBALSE DE ALCANTARA	
Grid reference:	M 10
Location:	N of Cáceres
Access:	Very easy
Season:	All year round
Terrain:	Very large man-made lake
Specialities:	Great Bustard, Stone Curlew, Bonelli's Eagle, Great Crested Grebe, *Trithemis annulata*
Subsidiary:	Embalse de Talaván, M 11

About 25km north of Cáceres, off the N 630/E 803, there are small roads leading across to Alcántara village, either north or south of the reservoir. Embalse de Alcántara is a very large lake on the Río Tajo which has inundated a vast amount of land between the

Sierra de la Peña de Francia, a fairly high rainfall area with lush vegetation.

village of Alcántara and the Puente Romano de Alconétar.

The surrounding land is dry grassland with scattered trees and many ponds. This type of habitat is ideal for arid country or steppe birds and there are large numbers of Great Bustard, Stone Curlew, and Black-bellied and Pin-tailed Sandgrouse, all of which breed here. Near the embalse the vegetation changes to maquis scrub dominated by the small holly-like Kermes Oak and Gum Cistus.

The embalse edges are steep with a few cliffs, which make excellent nesting places for Griffon and Egyptian Vultures, and Bonelli's Eagles. White Storks nest in the vicinity on any tall structure, such as trees, on electricity pylons, chimneys or church towers.

Trithemis annulata

This is a strikingly beautiful dragonfly. It is relatively common at the edges of slow-flowing rivers, resting on stones or riverside vegetation. It is medium sized and clear winged, with the base of the rear wing having a large amber spot. The thorax of the male is red and covered with a blue pruinescence (powder), which gives it a striking metallic-violet colour. The female is a dull yellow.

Large numbers of dragonflies and damselflies are found within Iberia wherever there is water: mountain pools, slow and fast-flowing rivers, salt and freshwater marshes, with the best habitat of all being a stagnant river surrounded by vegetation. Although dragonflies are found almost anywhere, and even migrate vast distances, most will be found where the water conditions are correct for them to breed.

As with most embalses, ducks are absent due to the water being too deep. In shallower areas, where a small amount of *Phragmites* grows, Little and Great Crested Grebes breed. Large groups of Cranes and Cormorants overwinter here.

This is a good area for dragonflies and damselflies, including the spectacular *Trithemis annulata* (*see* box).

59 RIO TAJO (NEAR ALMARAZ)

Grid reference:	M 12
Location:	S of Navalmoral de la Mata
Access:	Excellent
Season:	All year round
Terrain:	River banks and Poplars
Comments:	Car parking very easy
Specialities:	Crane, Great Spotted Cuckoo, Azure-winged Magpie, Beautiful Demoiselle, *Trithemis annulata*
Subsidiary:	Small lake about 3km along C 511 (M 13); rubbish tip about 5km along C 511 (M 13); both situated on the left travelling from the N V/E 90 towards Plasencia, the tip just before crossing the railway line

This site is easily accessible, approximately 20km south of Navalmoral de la Mata on the N V/E 90. It is a quiet stretch of water where the river widens before being joined by the Río Tiétar a few kilometres downstream in the Monfragüe Reserve. The banks are lined with Poplars and a few willows, and the hillsides are devoted to Eucalyptus plantations and pines.

Up-river is an area of pasture and cereal-growing land which is well watered from the Tajo and Tiétar, where many hundreds of Cranes overwinter. In summer there is a wealth of dragonflies here, the most spectacular being *Trithemis annulata*. A striking damselfly is the Beautiful Demoiselle, which has a dark metallic-blue abdomen and almost all-black wings.

Kingfisher and Azure-winged Magpie, with Great Spotted Cuckoo, Bee-eater and Golden Oriole in the summer, can all be seen, as well as the ubiquitous Black and Red Kites. Its close proximity to the Monfragüe Reserve means Black Vulture and Black Stork may be seen.

60 CORCHUELA ROAD	
Grid reference:	L/M 14
Location:	N of Oropesa
Access:	Fairly easy
Season:	All year round
Terrain:	River, woods and pasture
Comments:	Fly repellent may be necessary
Specialities:	Spanish Sparrow, Azure-winged Magpie, White Stork, Red Kite, Red Deer
Subsidiary:	Embalse de Navalcán, L 14

Immediately west of Oropesa turn north onto the TO 910, but be careful just after leaving the main road, to bear right. Shortly on the right side you come to the municipal rubbish dump. All rubbish dumps are worth investigating as they attract a large number of birds of many species and this one is no exception. White Storks are always present in large numbers, with Ravens, Magpies, Cattle Egrets and many small birds. Black and Red Kites, and Buzzards are regular scavengers with the occasional Griffon Vulture.

Further along the road the surroundings change from flat grain-growing land to scattered trees and pasture (dehesa). The woods contain Red Deer, many Rabbits which burrow into the sand, and Foxes. Azure-winged Magpie, Spotted Flycatcher, Great Grey and Woodchat Shrikes, Turtle Dove, Great

Spotted Woodpecker, Black-eared Wheatear, Firecrest, Crested Tit, Crossbill and Serin can all be commonly seen.

Near the river further along the road Spanish Imperial Eagle nest and there is a well-known tree near the road where one used to breed. Golden Oriole, Spotless Starling, Cetti's Warbler and Bee-eater all nest in the area, the Bee-eaters burrowing into the river banks. This is one of the sites where one is likely to see the rare Spanish Sparrow.

61 BADAJOZ, RIO GUADIANA	
Grid reference:	P 9
Location:	River E of Badajoz
Access:	Excellent
Season:	All year round
Terrain:	River valley with undulating grain land
Specialities:	Black-winged Stilt, Bluethroat, Cetti's Warbler, Savi's Warbler, Viperine Snake
Subsidiary:	Río Zapatón, O/P 9

It is best to take the C 537 westwards from Mérida or east from Badajoz. Several small roads lead to the river. The wide valley of the Río Guadiana is heavily cultivated, water being taken from the river to irrigate fields of sunflower, sugar-beet, asparagus, tomatoes, potatoes, cotton and maize, as well as large orchards. On all hillsides there are extensive vineyards and beyond them dry cereal-growing land and grassland.

With adequate water in the river and in stretches of lush vegetation many water-birds can be seen. Black-winged Stilt, Little Egret, Purple and Grey Herons wading in the shallower water, and Great Reed, Fan-tailed, Reed, Cetti's and Savi's Warblers in the *Phragmites* and vegetation at the river edge.

Red-rumped Swallows are common in

Typical wild country in the environs of Trujillo. The town of Trujillo has great historical interest as the home of many of the conquistadores who 'opened up' the Americas. They returned with great wealth and one even came back with an Inca princess for a mistress.

the summer, usually nesting under bridges, building unusual flask-shaped nests with a short entrance tube. Bee-eaters are common nesting in the soft sandy river banks like Kingfishers. Other birds which should be seen include Bluethroat, Crested Lark, the blue-headed race of the Yellow Wagtail, Grey Wagtail, Woodchat and Great Grey Shrikes, and Hoopoe.

In the slower flowing parts of the river, snakes, such as Viperine and Grass Snakes, may be seen swimming and seeking fish. Stripe-necked Terrapins may be seen basking in the sun on the river banks.

Look out for the Death's Head Hawk Moth and the Emperor Moth on potato-growing areas with orchards.

62 TRUJILLO AND ENVIRONS	
Grid reference:	N 12
Location:	Just off the N V/E 90 from Trujillo
Access:	Excellent
Season:	All year round
Terrain:	Undulating plains
Specialities:	Lesser Kestrel, Montagu's Harrier, Great Bustard, Black-bellied Sandgrouse, Azure-winged Magpie

This undulating plain is very easily reached by various roads, such as the C 524, to the west of the main N V/E 90 trunk road. It is a large cereal-growing area which in some places is dotted with huge granite rocks. There are also woods of evergreen oak, often with herds of black pigs feeding on the fallen acorns.

It is a rather desolate landscape but is magnificent for steppe birds. Large numbers of Little Bustard and many Great Bustard feed in the cornfields, and Pin-tailed and Black-bellied Sandgrouse are present but are best looked for in the early morning or evening when they go to water to drink. Stone Curlew can also be found but are very shy and difficult to see.

Within the woods both Magpies and Azure-winged Magpies are present in large numbers as well as Jay, Great Spotted Woodpecker and Great Spotted Cuckoo. During winter Cranes feed in the cornfields and in summer large numbers of Montagu's Harriers breed within the area. White Storks nest on all suitable chimneys and church towers, and there is a large colony of Lesser Kestrels breeding on the old buildings within Trujillo. The town itself is noted for its medieval monuments.

63 LA SERENA

Grid reference:	P 13
Location:	SE of Trujillo, E of Mérida
Access:	Relatively easy, but a good map is necessary
Season:	All year round
Terrain:	Slightly undulating with xerophytic grassland
Comments:	Summer can be very hot; take a picnic
Specialities:	Black-winged Kite, Great Bustard, Crane, Black-bellied Sandgrouse, Pin-tailed Sandgrouse
Subsidiary:	Sierra de Siruela, P 14/15; Reserva Nacional de Cijara, O 15

La Serena is situated 90km east of Mérida and slightly further south-east of Trujillo. From the N V/E 90 take the N 430 eastwards, just north of Torrefresnada. After 9km turn south onto the C 520 to Villanueva de la Serena, then continue along the C 420 to Castuera and turn north on the C 413. This is an extremely vast desolate area of xerophytic grassland with few trees; it is very sparsely populated. The land is slightly undulating with the distant mountain ranges of Montes de Toledo and Sierra de Guadalupe to the north. This is an area of vast horizons, where the sky never seems to end, and magnificent sunsets touch the distant mountain tops.

It is a region devoted almost entirely to sheep grazing with occasional areas of dry cereal-growing land, and is one of the most important areas in Spain for breeding steppe birds. Hundreds of Black-bellied Sandgrouse, Great Bustards and Montagu's Harriers and thousands of Pin-tailed Sandgrouse, Stone Curlews and Little Bustards nest in the region. Thousands of Cranes and many thousands of Golden Plovers winter here. Around the Zújar reservoir small numbers of Black Storks congregate in summer after breeding in nearby Monfragüe and are joined by hundreds of White Storks. Many birds of prey, especially Black and Red Kites, and some Black-winged Kites nearer to the Sierra de Siruela, may be seen.

Due to the lack of habitation it is advisable to take a picnic!

A male Great Bustard (Otis tarda). This is a typical species of the grain-growing plains.

64 SIERRA DEL CHORITO

Grid reference:	N 16
Location:	SW of Las Ventas con Peña Aguilera
Access:	Series of small roads
Season:	All year round
Terrain:	Sparsely populated plains
Specialities:	Black Vulture, Black Stork, Black-winged Kite, Spanish Imperial Eagle, Eagle Owl
Subsidiary:	Embalse Torre de Abraham, N 17

Situated south-west of Ventas con Peña Aguilera and reached by taking the C 403

The Embalse de Torre de Abraham, with the Montes de Toledo in the background. This is a resting place for migrant birds, especially ducks, which move on to the nearby wintering grounds of the Tablas de Daimiel.

just beyond El Milagro, then turning right onto the CR 700 and at Retuerta del Bullaque turning left. These are the plains at the southern end of the Montes de Toledo. They are very sparsely populated and divided into huge estates.

The terrain is mainly extensive areas of evergreen oak and grazing land which is the ideal habitat for the Black Vulture. This is the second most important site in Spain for this species with an estimated seventy pairs; the most important area is not very far away to the north-west in the park of Monfragüe. Other interesting breeding birds here are White Storks, which are fairly numerous nesting on church towers, tops of chimneys, in tall trees or even on electricity pylons. Black Stork, Black-winged Kite and Spanish Imperial Eagle can also be seen, but it takes time to locate the Eagle Owl which also breeds in this sierra. It is most easily located at dawn and dusk by listening for its powerful call, *hooo*, which can be heard up to 5km away. During migration, flocks of birds can be seen moving over this area.

On the hillsides there are patches of maquis scrub with cistus predominating, mainly Gum Cistus, and in spring various species of narcissus can be found.

65 COTO NACIONAL DE LOS QUINTOS DE MORA

Grid reference:	N 17
Location:	S of Toledo
Access:	By very small roads
Season:	Spring, summer and autumn
Terrain:	Grassland with scattered trees
Comments:	Very bleak in winter
Specialities:	Black Vulture, Golden Eagle, Eagle Owl, Pardel Lynx, *Cytinus ruber*
Subsidiary:	Sierra del Robledo, N 18; Sierra de los Yébenes, N 18; Sierra del Pocito, N 17

This national park is within the long range of the Montes de Toledo. To reach the park, head south-east from Toledo on the N 401, and soon afterwards turn south-west remaining on the N 401. After 50km turn onto a small road to the right. At El Rodedillo turn right again. The area rises up to 1309m (4295 feet) and is composed of large estates used mainly for cattle and sheep grazing. Scattered trees of evergreen and deciduous oak with maquis scrub on the hillsides make this an ideal habitat for breeding birds of prey. Black Vultures, while not numerous, can be seen (*see* box). Golden Eagle and the now very rare Spanish Imperial Eagle may also be seen. The large Eagle Owl is present in the area but is difficult to find as it only appears to hunt at night.

The maquis scrub is composed of Gum Cistus and Strawberry Trees. In some of the

---

Black Vulture *Aegypius monachus*
L 100–110, W 235–275

This is a bird very much on the endangered list; but now, due to strict conservation measures, the numbers are slowly increasing. The areas where they are most numerous are open regions with scattered trees (typical dehesa) where they build their nests. Although there is a good population of thirty pairs in the Sierra de la Peña de Francia, they are most plentiful in the Monfragüe Reserve and the Montes de Toledo.

It is the largest bird of prey in Europe with the female weighing up to 12kg. Broad wings enable them to remain almost motionless 'riding the thermals', often in the company of Griffon Vultures.

They are carrion eaters and take precedence over Griffon Vultures who in turn feed before the waiting Egyptian Vultures, with Ravens cleaning up any remains.

---

rocky places *Cistus crispus* grows and underneath this the strange parasite *Cytinus ruber* can be found emerging out of the ground, only showing its red and white waxy flowers. In some of the grassy spaces narcissus species make a fine show in springtime.

The Pardel Lynx can also be found but it is rarely seen as it is basically nocturnal.

---

66 TABLAS DE DAIMIEL	
Grid reference:	O 18/19
Location:	NE of Ciudad Real
Access:	Good
Season:	All year round
Terrain:	Fresh marshland with *Phragmites*
Comments:	Sensible walking shoes; insect repellent may be necessary; information centre – closed Monday–Tuesday
Specialities:	Bearded Tit, Ferruginous Duck, Garganey, Red-crested Pochard, Stripe-necked Terrapin
Subsidiary:	Lakes around Alcázar de San Juan, N 20; Lakes around Pedro Muñoz N 21

This site is easily located by a well-marked small road north of Daimiel from the N 420-430. This important park has national status under the management of ICONA. A large car-park with a comprehensive information centre is open from 9am to 9pm in summer and 10am to 6pm in winter, but is closed on Mondays and Tuesdays.

It is a marshy area within the vast La Mancha plain, fed by the Río Guadiana, and surrounded by vineyards, with maize and cereals rotated with sugar-beet. These crops are irrigated from the river and in conse-

The impressive Phragmites-covered marshland of the Daimiel Reserve, a haunt of Bearded Tits (Panurus biarmicus) and also Reed Warblers (Acrocephalus scirpaceus) on migration. In the open expanses between the Phragmites marshland, thousands of ducks spend the winter and can easily be seen.

quence most of the wetland in this 1500ha park has been drained. Concern about this threat to such a valuable habitat has lead to remedial processes being put into effect, which should, with care, restore the area to its former importance.

There are well signposted paths to the various hides and observation points, situated on small raised islands overlooking the large expanse of *Phragmites* and tamarisk interspersed with clear lagoons. Here, during winter, Bearded Tits may be seen with a large number of ducks: Red-crested Pochard, Shoveler, Garganey, Gadwall and Ferruginous Duck. One hide overlooks a fenced-in pool where pinioned ducks are kept for breeding and then release. During summer Wild Boar may wallow in the muddy marsh getting cool, while Stripe-necked Terrapins sun themselves on the banks.

MONFRAGÜE NATURAL PARK

This exceptionally important park also has an Integral Park completely out of bounds to the public. The only accessible area of the park by road is via the C 524 which runs through the park. From Plasencia take the N 630/E 803 south and turn onto the C 524. From Trujillo take the C 524 north.

The northern side is bounded by the Sierra de Serrejón and the south by the Sierra de Piatones and the Corchuela ridge. The central valley contains the Río Tajo joined by the Río Tiétar which form the reservoirs Torrejón–Tiétar and Torrejón–Tajo. The area is heavily wooded with evergreen Ilex and Cork Oaks on the higher slopes interspersed with cistus scrub. The lower slopes are of dehesa for cultivation and stock grazing. Higher up, Penfalcōn and Corchuela are huge rocky outcrops almost devoid of vegetation. There are areas of Eucalyptus, but further planting has been restricted.

The park is superb for birds with in particular Black Stork (*see* box overleaf)), Griffon and Egyptian Vultures nesting on the crags, while in the woodland Black Vulture, Spanish Imperial, Booted and Short-toed Eagles, Black-winged Kite, Azure-winged Magpie, Golden Oriole, Hoopoe, and Great Grey and Woodchat Shrikes can be seen; Bee-eaters nest in the sandy banks.

Pardel Lynx, Egyptian Mongoose, Wild Cat, Wild Boar, Red Fox, deer and many bat species all breed within this Reserve. Reptiles

Black Stork *Ciconia nigra* L 100, W 155

This is another bird which had diminished drastically in previous years, but now due to conservation measures its decline has been eliminated and in some areas it is actually increasing. Its stronghold is in the Monfragüe Reserve where a few can be seen nesting on the Penfalcōn crag and in the tall oak trees in the woods.

Its migration pattern is the same as its near relative, the White Stork, moving to central Africa in October and returning in early March. However, some adults remain on their breeding ground throughout the year. They are smaller than the White Stork, and are glossy black except for white underparts. They are not gregarious and tend to be shy birds, preferring marshy tracts among coniferous forests.

Griffon Vultures (Gyps fulvus) on a breeding cliff in the Monfragüe Natural Park.

and amphibians can also be found here in good variety: the Midwife Toad (the male of which carries the eggs on it's back), Marbled and Painted Frog, Marbled Newt, the unusual Bedriaga's Skink (a very short-limbed lizard with five toes, which gives birth to live young) and several snakes and salamanders.

There is an information centre at the tiny hamlet of Villarreal de San Carlos situated behind Monfragüe Bar. It is open during the morning and late afternoon and gives out maps suggesting interesting walks of 5–7km.

67 THE TAJO TIÉTAR, MONFRAGÜE	
Grid reference:	M 11/12
Location:	S of Plasencia
Access:	Good
Season:	All year round
Terrain:	Rivers, valleys and mountain
Comments:	Information centre
Specialities:	Black Stork, Black-winged Kite, Spanish Imperial Eagle, Pardel Lynx, Midwife Toad

This is the accessible north part of the park. It is an area of woodland and scrub with the

A view of the rivers Tajo and Tiétar with the famous Penfalcōn cliff to the left. This is one of the major nesting sites of the Black Stork (Ciconia nigra) in Spain. The area is very vulnerable to forest fires during the hot and dry summer months.

rivers in view. From here you can see many birds. Do look out for the three vultures and eagles; also check any hovering bird as the Black-winged Kite hovers like a Kestrel.

The woodlands produce Great Tit and Great Spotted Woodpecker and a large number of Azure-winged Magpie, while the wetter lands have Black Stork, White Stork and heron species. The latter area also produces many dragonflies including the Beautiful Demoiselle, with almost black wings and metallic-blue body, and *Trithemis annulata*, the male with its violet-red appearance and the less impressive yellowish female. This a truly beautiful area with plenty to interest the naturalist.

68 SANTUARIO DE MONFRAGÜE	
Grid reference:	M I I
Location:	S of Plasencia
Access:	Steep poor road
Season:	All year round
Terrain:	Heavily wooded hillside
Comments:	Magnificent views
Specialities:	Black Vulture, Azure-winged Magpie, Red-rumped Swallow, Egyptian Mongoose, *Digitalis thapsi*

This is easily located from the southern side of the park and is signposted from the C 524 via an extremely steep road. It is a twelfth century building 465m (1526 feet) above sea level and affords breathtaking views over Monfragüe, the confluence of the Tiétar with the Tajo and in particular Penfalcōn peak.

The scrubland around consists of cistus, *Daphne*, Broom, Heather and French Lavender. Look out for the pink-flowered *Digitalis thapsi*.

Most of the mammals within the site and its environs are nocturnal, but you may see with luck the Egyptian Mongoose with its 'bottle-brush' tail hunting in the undergrowth, or a female taking her young on a hunting expedition, usually in single file. This species is thought to have been brought over by either the Romans or the Moors, either as a pet or as a killer of vermin, especially snakes.

From the Santuario you should see a number of birds, such as Black-winged Kite, Short-toed Eagle, Griffon Vulture and in particular the Black Vulture. In the scrub are Sardinian Warbler, Crested Lark and Azure-winged Magpie. Red-rumped Swallows soar overhead and are easily distinguished from the more common Swallows by their pale creamy-pink rumps.

6. IBERIAN MOUNTAINS

INTRODUCTION

This east-central region of Spain is bounded in the west by Extremadura and North Meseta, in the north by East Cantábrica and the Río Ebro watershed, in the east by the Mediterranean region and in the south by East Andalucía. It is a region which could have been divided into two geographically: in the south is the flat highland plain of La Mancha which rises up to the Serranía de Cuenca in the north. It is hot and dry in summer but can be cold with snow in winter, especially in the mountains. Rainfall is fairly high in the mountains, but the high plateau in the southern region is relatively arid.

The La Mancha region is devoted to grain and vine growing, the latter around Valdepeñas. Wide vistas over large estates with windmills on every high point dominate the bleak landscape. In contrast, the mountains although no less dramatic are clothed in pine woods used for forestry products. Sheep raising is carried out in La Mancha and the mountains.

Deep canyons cut into the hard limestone rock are a dominating feature of the region. In places extraordinary futuristic rock formations have been eroded, as in the Enchanted Village near Cuenca (*see* Site 80). It is a sparsely populated region and an incredibly beautiful one. However, it is rarely visited by the tourist.

Floristically the best time to visit the region is in April, May and June, as it is then that the large numbers of orchid species are at their best.

This is renowned as being one of the most rewarding areas in Spain for the butterfly enthusiast. The two eminent lepidopterists, Manley and Allcard, spent many weeks over a number of years based in Teruel and made an exhaustive study. Three rarities are found here, the Large Blue, Iolas Blue and the Spring Ringlet, but there are an enormous number of species to be seen.

The best place to see the Spanish mammal life is at the Hosquillo Research Station. This is run by ICONA and permission to visit must be obtained in Cuenca. Here Brown Bears, Wolves, Red, Fallow and Roe Deer, Spanish Ibex, Mouflon and Wild Boar are bred for study and for re-introduction into the wild where necessary.

Because of the diversity of habitat within the zone there is a large variety of bird life. In the forests and gorges of the mountainous areas there are the usual woodland birds and also a large number of birds of prey. One notable huge red limestone cliff contains an enormous colony of Griffon Vultures, noticed from afar by the white streaks of guano adhering to the red cliff face! On this same cliff a large number of Chough also breed. In winter at Gallocanta many thousands of Cranes can be seen in the company of a multitude of ducks. The plains contain the steppe birds, Great and Little Bustards, Black-bellied and Pin-tailed Sandgrouse, and Stone Curlew. In the depressions where water lies during the winter, duck are also present.

The grid references used in the following site descriptions relate to Michelin maps numbers 444 and 445.

Opposite: *map of the Iberian Mountains. The sites are numbered as in the text. Only main roads and the major rivers of the region are shown.*

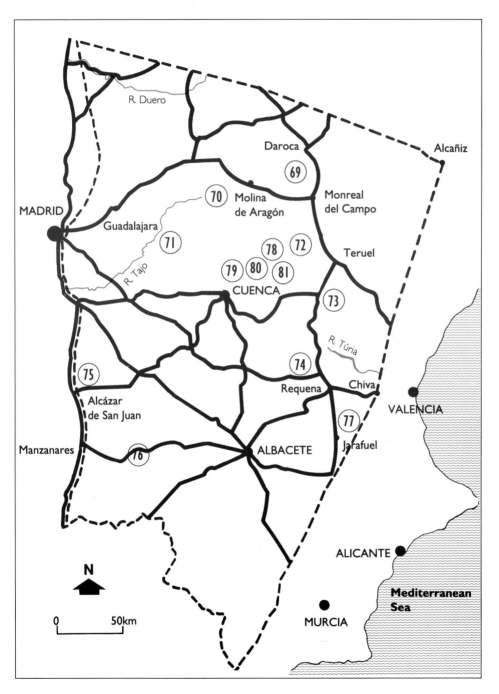

A typical view within the region at Rincón de Ademuz, which clearly shows the rock strata.

FIFTY INTERESTING SPECIES TO LOOK FOR

Short-toed Eagle	Red-necked	Spring Ringlet	Red Pasque Flower
Marsh Harrier	Nightjar	American Painted	*Crocus sativus*
Red Kite	Subalpine Warbler	Lady	*Fritillaria hispanica*
Griffon Vulture	Dupont's Lark	Large Blue	Spanish Juniper
Gull-billed Tern	Woodchat Shrike	Iolas Blue	Bug Orchid
Red-crested	Blue Rock Thrush	Zephyr Blue	Burnt Orchid
Pochard	Rock Thrush	Pine Processionary	Frog Orchid
Shoveler	Rock Bunting	Moth	Pyramidal Orchid
Black-necked	Serin	Angel's Tears	Woodcock Orchid
Grebe	Otter	Narcissus	Broad-leaved
Night Heron	Red Squirrel	*Antirrhinum*	Helleborine
Little Egret	Pardel Lynx	*pulverulentum*	Large White
Pratincole	Wolf	Box	Helleborine
Crane	Spanish Ibex	Brown Bluebell	Red Helleborine
Alpine Swift	Roe Deer	Burnet Rose	

Wintering Cranes (Grus grus) on the Laguna de Gallocanta. There can be as many as 20,000 Cranes in the area during winter, along with many other water-birds. With such vast numbers in the area, the sky can sometimes be alive with birds. The Cranes are nervous and difficult to approach.

69 LAGUNA DE GALLOCANTA

Grid reference:	J 25
Location:	SW of Daroca and NW of Monreál del Campo
Access:	Good
Season:	Spring, autumn and winter
Terrain:	Large lake with extensive marshlands surrounded by flat cereal land
Comments:	For winter visits, warm clothing; bird museum
Specialities:	Crane, Red-crested Pochard, Pochard, Marsh Harrier, Pin-tailed Sandgrouse

Situated about 30km north-west of Monreál del Campo and approximately 25km south-west of Daroca, and reached by the N 234. This is the largest natural lake in Spain, covering some 1500ha within a national game refuge of 7000ha. The surrounding countryside is flat cereal-growing land with sunflower rotation for oil production. The mountains in the distance are covered with evergreen oak.

On the northern side of the lake there is the attractive typical medieval village of Gallocanta, which houses the Museu de Aves (bird museum) situated near the church. This will be opened by request. Several small tracks lead down to the water's edge. The houses in this area are made of stone slabs with very thick walls, making them warmer in winter and cooler in summer when the temperatures are extreme.

The lake is an impressive and important wintering ground for 10–20,000 Cranes, which by day feed in the surrounding lands, doing considerable damage to the emerging crops, and in the evening roost in the large and extensive marsh at the edge of the lake. The lake can dry up almost completely during the hot arid summers, but soon fills again when the autumn rains begin in September or October. Red-crested Pochard, Pochard and Coot are seen in their thousands. Marsh Harriers quarter the ground and with luck the elusive Pin-tailed Sandgrouse may be discovered in the dry areas.

The lake, although in a valley, is at an altitude of 1000m (3280 feet) and therefore can be very cold during the winter. However, this is obviously the best time to visit to see the Cranes. Autumn and spring are also good for other migrating birds.

70 PARQUE NATURAL DEL ALTO TAJO	
Grid reference:	J/K 22/23/24
Location:	SW of Molina de Aragón
Access:	Reasonable
Season:	Spring, summer and autumn
Terrain:	Wooded mountains
Comments:	Can be snow in winter
Specialities:	Egyptian Vulture, Large Blue, Woodcock Orchid, Broad-leaved Helleborine, Box
Subsidiary:	Montes de Picaza, J 24

From Molina de Aragón travel north on the N 211 for about 4km, then turn west onto the GU 914. Several small roads also give access to the park.

Although the Río Tajo begins as a trickle out of the hillside only a few kilometres away in the Montes Universales, by the time it reaches the south-eastern extremity of this park it has gathered enough power to carve a deep gorge 80km long through the limestone bedrock. The area is sparsely populated with one small road running through the park at the bottom of the gorge by the river.

There are some large pine woods, which include Black and Scots Pines, but on the mountainsides, which rise up to well over 1300m (4265 feet) there is extensive grazing land used for sheep. On the more exposed areas maquis scrub occurs with Lavender, Thyme, Box and Juniper. It is a zone noted particularly for a large number of orchids which are at their best in June. Woodcock, Early Spider and Bug Orchids, Broad-leaved Helleborine and many others grow here.

Butterflies are seen in quantity over the whole area. The most notable perhaps is the Large Blue which spends part of its life-cycle within an ants' nest.

The limestone cliffs provide nesting sites for a large colony of Griffon Vultures, fewer Egyptian Vultures and in the woods Eagle Owl.

Wild Boar frequent the region and in the not too distant past Wolves were present.

71 MAR DE CASTILLA	
Grid reference:	K/L 21/22
Location:	E of Guadalajara
Access:	Very easy
Season:	All year round
Terrain:	Reservoirs and maquis scrub
Comments:	Insect repellent may be necessary
Specialities:	Peregrine, Crane, Dartford Warbler, Blackcap, Subalpine Warbler

This is an enormous man-made embalse in the upper reaches of the Río Tajo, which is in reality two large embalses, the Entrepeñas and the Buendía. It is easily accessible from Guadalajara, 60km to the west, via the N 320, then taking one of a number of access roads.

There are large areas of maquis scrub in the hills to the east which hold numbers of small passerines, such as Dartford Warbler, Blackcap, Subalpine Warbler in summer, Stonechat, Chaffinch, Goldfinch and Serin. There are some high limestone cliffs cut by the Tajo which provide nesting sites for a large population of birds of prey, especially Golden Eagle, Peregrine and Bonelli's Eagle.

The lower grain land near the water is a feeding and resting ground for many thousands of Cranes as they pass between their main wintering areas of Laguna de Gallocanta and Extremadura.

Throatwort *Trachelium caeruleum*

A very striking perennial found growing on moist shady banks or on walls in full sun, providing the roots can obtain plenty of moisture. The plant has long branched flowering stems up to 60cm tall which are topped by large flat clusters of individually small tubular flowers of an intense blue. The leaves are oval and toothed along the edges, green but often a deep purple underneath, especially on older plants.

The flowers are very rich in nectar as can be seen by the mass of butterflies which feed on them. In central Spain, on one 10m stretch covered with these beautiful flowers, I have seen Swallowtail, Spanish Marbled White, Escher's Blue, Speckled Wood, Scarce Swallowtail, and that large fritillary, the Cardinal.

It flowers in summer and is common in central, southern and western Spain.

As this is a humid area, there are a large number of amphibians, such as Marsh Frog, Common, Natterjack, Midwife and Western Spadefoot Toads, and with luck you could find the Marbled Newt and Fire Salamander among the stones by the water's edge.

The spectacular Throatwort grows in moist ground by the roadsides and on north-facing cliffs (*see* box).

72 SIERRA DE ALBARRACIN	
Grid reference:	K 24/25
Location:	NW of Teruel
Access:	Very good
Season:	Late spring, summer and early autumn
Terrain:	Fertile valleys, narrow gorges, mountains
Comments:	Snow in winter
Specialities:	Golden Eagle, Zephyr Blue, Spanish Juniper, *Astragalus turolensis*, Red Pasque Flower

This sierra is about 35km north-west of Teruel and is best approached by taking the N 234 from Teruel, turning left after 10km onto the TE 901 to Albarracín and then taking the TE 903. It is on the eastern side of the Montes Universales, the range of hills where the great Río Tajo has its source at El Cubillo, becoming a mighty river emptying into the Atlantic at Lisbon in Portugal.

This is an area which has been inhabited from prehistorical times. Wall paintings can be seen in the local caves which demonstrate this. The town of Albarracín is itself extremely ancient, being heavily fortified with spectacular walls and battlements, which in summer are the haunt of thousands of Swifts and Swallows. As is common in this area, houses have been enlarged right on top of the cliffs and often appear to overhang in a most precarious manner.

The area is full of rare plants and butterflies populating the pine-covered mountain-sides, fertile valleys, and deep narrow gorges where the sun rarely reaches during the winter months but which are baked hard during the summer. The 10m tall Spanish Junipers grow bigger here on the high slopes than elsewhere in Europe. The unusual

Just outside Albarracín on the Río Guadalaviar.

73 RINCON DE ADEMUZ	
Grid reference:	L 25/26
Location:	S of Teruel
Access:	Excellent
Season:	Spring, summer and autumn
Terrain:	Heavily wooded gorge
Comments:	Can be very cold with snow in winter
Specialities:	Dartford Warbler, Crested Lark, Pine Processionary Moth, Woodcock Orchid, Bumble Bee Orchid
Subsidiary:	Javalambre, L 26

Colchicum triphyllum flowers abundantly on the calcareous hillsides. *Astragalus turolensis* grows only in this area in Europe. Near Bronchales on the central north edge of the sierra grows the beautiful dark Red Pasque Flower, while high in the subalpine meadows the spring-flowering prostrate Burnet Rose and Angel's Tears Narcissus are seen.

Butterflies are abundant. The American Painted Lady is surprisingly found on the hillsides as are the uncommon Zephyr Blue and Iolas Blue. Damon, Oberthur's Anomalous and Azure Chalk-hill Blues can also be found.

Birds, especially raptors, are numerous. Golden, Booted, Short-toed and Bonelli's Eagles, vultures and Ravens may all be seen.

This beautiful wild gorge seemingly lost in time is easily reached from Teruel by travelling southwards on the N 420. The Río Turia collects rainfall from the eastern slopes of the Montes Universales and the western slopes of the Sierra de Javalambre before emptying into the Mediterranean Sea at Valencia. At Ademuz it cuts a long deep gorge through ochre-coloured limestone forming the Rincón de Ademuz.

The sides of the gorge are covered with Rosemary and Juniper scrub and pines where they can gain a foothold. Irises and narcissi appear in early spring followed by many orchids, for example Woodcock, Bumble Bee, and Pyramidal Orchids, and Broad-leaved Helleborine. In the valley where there is sufficient soil Poplars are grown and also Osier Willows for basket making. The latter turn deep red in autumn. Some parts of these fertile valleys also provide good deep soil for the production of vegetables and fruit, especially apples, pears and cherries, which thrive in this cooler climate.

Passerines, such as Blackbird, Crested Lark, Meadow Pipit, Sardinian and Dartford

Looking down into the Rincón de Ademuz, a spectacular gorge where the river has carved a deep channel through the limestone rock. The sides of this gorge are covered with vegetation.

Warblers and Grey Wagtail are common amongst the rocks and rushing water in the base of the gorge. Birds of prey are present in small numbers, Kestrel and Peregrine nesting on the cliff sides. Ravens are often seen flying high overhead.

Wild Boar are common in the woods and there are a few Foxes and Rabbits.

Pine Processionary Moth caterpillars are numerous and their silken 'nests' are seen on a very large number of pine trees, some trees being almost denuded of leaves causing death to a great number. This moth is a serious pest in several regions.

74 EMBALSE DE CONTRERAS	
Grid reference:	N 25
Location:	NW of Requena
Access:	Very good
Season:	All year round
Terrain:	Reservoir surrounded by pasture and woodland
Specialities:	Thekla Lark, Dupont's Lark, Green Woodpecker, Brown Bluebell, *Fritillaria hispanica*
Subsidiary:	Carboneras de Guadazaón, M 24

From Requena follow the E 901/N 111 north-west for about 40km to the reservoir. This is a very remote and unpopulated area where the tributaries of the Río Cabriel converge to form the Embalse de Contreras. Open pine woods are a feature with Black and Aleppo Pines the dominant species. In some areas evergreen oak is present with Spanish Juniper, the latter occasionally growing to the exceptional height of 20m.

Crested and Thekla Larks (the Crested with chestnut underwing and the Thekla with grey), and a few Dupont's Larks can be found in the drier areas around the lake. Within the woodland Great Spotted and Green Woodpecker, Jay, Magpie, Woodchat and Great Grey Shrikes are numerous. There are many gorges and cliffs to the north of the dam and it is here that birds of prey nest: Peregrine, Golden, Booted and Bonelli's Eagles, and the large Eagle Owl. Red Kites are frequent and Black Kites may be seen seeking fish in the river.

In the maquis scrub, cistus and Broom are the dominant species with Heather and asphodels, but in spring orchids, *Fritillaria hispanica*, the unusual Brown Bluebell, the Tassel Hyacinth and the Barbary Nut can all be seen.

75 LAGUNAS DE ALCAZAR DE SAN JUAN	
Grid reference:	N 19/20
Location:	N of Alcázar de San Juan
Access:	Easily accessible by small roads
Season:	All year round
Terrain:	A flat plateau with lakes and marshland
Comments:	Insect repellent may be necessary
Specialities:	Black-necked Grebe, Gull-billed Tern, Pratincole, Crane, *Crocus sativus*
Subsidiary:	Laguna de Sánchez Gómez, N 21; Laguna de Manjavacas, N 21; Laguna Grande, N 21

The site is easily reached by taking the C 400 northwards from Alcázar de San Juan and then turning right onto one of several small roads. This is part of the large flat plateau known as La Mancha with vineyards and grain lands as far as the eye can see. South of the town there is a hill crowned with windmills, reputed to be the ones Cervantes saw when he wrote *Don Quixote*.

North of San Juan are the shallow lagoons which form a breeding site for a number of interesting wetland birds: Black-necked Grebe, and a large colony of Gull-billed Terns; Night Heron, Little Egret, Red-crested Pochard and Marsh Harrier in the *Phragmites* at the edge of the lagoons; and Pratincole on the drier land surrounding the pools. Within the adjoining grain lands, Great and Little Bustards, Stone Curlew and Pin-tailed Sandgrouse breed.

Crane, Red-crested Pochard, Pintail, Wigeon, Teal, Mallard and a large number of

Marbled Teal
Marmaronetta angustirostris L 40

A small rare duck related to the Pochard. The basic colour in both sexes is a pale sandy brown, speckled and mottled with darker or lighter spots. Around the eye there is a very dark-brown patch which is discernible at a distance. It is generally gregarious, forming small groups.

Although fairly widespread in distribution once, ranging from the western Mediterranean through the Middle East to India and south Russia, it has been declining in recent years and is now confined to localized pockets. There are signs however, that it could be on the increase in Spain and Morocco due to strict conservation measures.

Most Spanish birds move south to Morocco in winter, returning in spring to breed in lakeside vegetation in either brackish or freshwater.

other ducks winter here.

This part of La Mancha is also noted for being the world's largest producer of saffron. The stigma from the autumn-flowering *Crocus sativus* is collected and dried, requiring 4000 stigmas to produce 28g of dye! This genuine saffron is extremely expensive, but substitutes are now available.

76 PARQUE NATURAL DE LAS LAGUNAS DE RUIDERA

Grid reference:	O/P 21
Location:	E of Manzanares
Access:	Very good
Season:	All year round
Terrain:	Lagoons, wooded hills and maquis scrub
Comments:	Insect repellent may be needed; information centre
Specialities:	Great-crested Grebe, Pochard, Red-crested Pochard, Shoveler, Tufted Duck
Subsidiary:	Montesino's Cave, immortalized by Cervantes in *Don Quixote*, P 21

Situated near Tablas de Daimiel, approximately 52km east of Manzanares on the N 430. An information centre is situated near Laguna Santos Morcillo. These twelve easily accessible lakes run like a necklace through a 20km valley, bounded by hillsides covered with evergreen oaks and maquis scrub, each lake receiving water from the one above either by a surface or underground stream. A thirteenth lake, La Blanca, 5km away, is 128m (420 feet) higher than the lowest, Laguna Cenagosa, which drains into the Río Guadiana and eventually flows into the Tablas de Daimiel.

Most of the lakes have some vegetation giving cover for a large number of water-birds like Mallard, Pochard, Red-crested Pochard, Shoveler, Tufted Duck, Coot and Great-crested Grebe, with the rare Marbled Teal occasionally seen (*see* box). Outside this verdant valley the land is flat and dry, typical La Mancha countryside, with vineyards producing the famous wines of Valdepeñas.

Quite near to La Magdalena is the lowest lake, Cenagosa, surrounded by *Phragmites*. Next comes Coladilla and Cueva Morenilla, both with *Phragmites*, the latter very deep and surrounded by Pines and Poplars. After the village of Ruidera are the two largest lakes, Laguna del Rey and Laguna Colgada; then Laguna Batana, a small lake with a wooded backdrop. Laguna Santos Morcillo has the information centre on its shores and the next lake up-water is Laguna Salvadora, which is very rocky around its edges. Laguna Lengua is tongue shaped as its name suggests and is very deep with rocky sides and no

Laguna Lengua, one of the Ruidera lakes with a heavy snow storm threatening. It is tongue-shaped, and because it is very deep it reflects the sky and the heavily wooded banks to give a deep colour. This and the other lakes at Ruidera are a haven for water-birds, both on the water itself and within the Phragmites which fringes several of the lake shores.

Phragmites. Next comes the small round Redondilla which is shady with little vegetation and San Pedro with much more. Last of the twelve easily accessible lakes is Laguna Conceja surrounded by wooded hills and a marshy shore.

77 RESERVA NACIONAL DE LA MUELA DE CORTES	
Grid reference:	O 27
Location:	SE of Requena
Access:	Comparatively easy
Season:	Spring, summer and autumn
Terrain:	Forest, river and mountain
Comments:	Can be cold in winter
Specialities:	Blue Rock Thrush, Rock Bunting, Alpine Swift, Red Squirrel, Roe Deer

Drive south from Requena on the N 330 and after 50km turn to the east at Jarafuel. This road will take you into the heart of the reserve. The site is partly mountainous, rising to 1017m (3337 feet), and partly river valley with extensive gorges. The Río Júcar passing through the valley rises in the Montes Universales, near the source of the Río Tajo, and empties into the Mediterranean south of Valencia, after flowing through Cuenca and the enormous Embalse de Alarcón.

A large part of the zone is used for forestry, especially in the lower areas near the river, where there are extensive Aleppo Pine plantations. The mountainous part is mainly grassland for sheep grazing. There are areas where maquis scrub is dominant and because it is relatively near the Mediterranean with the influence of its warmer climate, Gum Cistus, Sage-leaved Cistus, Lavender, Rosemary, Heather and Broom are common.

In the gorge, Short-toed Eagle, Golden

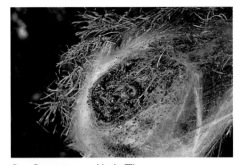

*Pine Processionary Moth (*Thaumetopoea pityocampa*) caterpillars in a communal overwintering nest.*

Eagle and Peregrine are numerous and there is a very large colony of Choughs. Other birds seen here are Blue Rock Thrush, Rock Thrush, Rock Bunting, Alpine and Pallid Swifts, Red-necked and Common Nightjars, Hoopoe, Jay, Magpie and Raven.

Great Banded Grayling and Spanish Gatekeeper are seen and the silky nests of the Pine Processionary Moth can sometimes cause damage in the forested areas.

Within the woods Roe Deer can be found and also the Red Squirrel which here is bright red in colour, unlike the northern Spanish variety which can be almost black.

SERRANÍA DE CUENCA

The Serranía de Cuenca is a sparsely populated range of limestone mountains rising to 1839m (6033 feet), which is traversed by deep spectacular gorges and fast-flowing rivers. Many huge weather-eroded rocks are scattered over the pine-covered mountainsides, and flower-filled meadows cover the lower land. The most exciting place to view one of the gorges is from a point known as Ventano del Diablo (the Devil's Window) where you look out through a large natural

A view from the Devil's Window, looking up the gorge of the Río Júcar.

Griffon and Egyptian Vultures, and Short-toed, Golden and Booted Eagles can often be seen, but the Eagle Owl, although present, is more elusive. Alpine Accentors come down to lower levels during the winter to escape the severe climate in the mountain tops. Within the pine forest there are woodpeckers, and a number of smaller birds such as Goldfinch, Chaffinch, Blackbird, Spotless Starling and Great Grey Shrike.

The best time to visit is either late spring for the flowers, or summer and early autumn for butterflies and vertebrates. There can be heavy snowfall from November to March, when roads become impassable. This is a very diverse area for wildlife and therefore four different sites have been described.

78 PARQUE CINEGÉTICO DEL HOSQUILLO	
Grid reference:	K 24
Location:	NE of Cuenca
Access:	Good
Season:	Spring, summer and autumn
Terrain:	Wooded mountain
Comments:	Permits necessary; snow-bound in winter
Specialities:	Brown Bear, Wolf, Pardel Lynx, Spanish Ibex, Mouflon

hole over a narrow 100m-deep gorge with the Río Júcar flowing fast below. This is in the west of the region, approximately 22km north of Cuenca on the CU 921.

The area is noted for its vast number of orchid species, which include the rare Red Helleborine, the Marsh Helleborine, the amazing Frog Orchid, Burnt, Bug and Pyramidal Orchids, and the Large White Helleborine which rarely opens its flowers.

Butterflies are common with numerous species, including the rare Large Blue, the Spring Ringlet, and the Iolas Blue which has a very scattered distribution. Wild Boar and deer are common in the woods, and Otters can occasionally be seen in the rivers.

Birds are numerous with many raptors.

The Hosquillo Park is under the management of ICONA and is a main breeding station for animals of scientific study. It is approached by heading north from Cuenca on the CU 921 for about 21km and then turning left to Villalba de la Sierra. A long winding minor road goes from here to the park. It is a large enclosed reserve set in some of the most remote and wild country of the Serranía de Cuenca. Within this 1000ha area are Red, Fallow and Roe Deer. Further into the reserve are special pens for breeding Wolves, Pardel Lynx, Spanish Ibex, Mouflon and Brown Bears.

The road up to the reserve is very twisty but offers some spectacular views over the mountains. On the rocks Rock Buntings can be seen and during winter Alpine Accentors come down from the heights. The latter are not timid and are easily seen. Entry is restricted and permission must be obtained from the ICONA Office, 18 de Julio, Cuenca.

79 HOZ DEL JUCAR	
Grid reference:	L 23
Location:	N of Cuenca
Access:	Good
Season:	Throughout the year
Terrain:	River valley
Specialities:	Alpine Accentor, Griffon Vulture, Spring Ringlet, *Antirrhinum pulverulentum*, Large White Helleborine

This is one of the deep ravines characteristic of the area. It is situated along the CU 921 from Cuenca to Villalba de la Sierra. The sierra, which has been cut through limestone by the Río Júcar, has rocky sides coloured with oxides of iron on which Jackdaw, Chough and Griffon Vulture nest. In the valley near the river there are rich pasturelands and maize-growing areas where the Large White Helleborine and *Antirrhinum pulverulentum* can be found. By the river bank large numbers of Poplars are grown to 'feed' the wood-pulp mills which are scattered throughout the region.

In patches where it is excessively wet, Osier Willows are grown for basket making, their stems glowing red in the autumn after the leaves have fallen.

Butterflies are common in the meadows which are alive with fritillaries, ringlets, graylings, blues and skippers. Watch out for the rare Spring Ringlet.

80 LA CIUDAD ENCANTADA	
Grid reference:	L 23
Location:	NE of Cuenca
Access:	Good
Season:	Spring, summer and autumn
Terrain:	Wooded hillsides with fantastic rock formations
Comments:	Spectacular but can be cold in winter
Specialities:	Pine Processionary Moth, *Saxifraga corbariensis*, *Tanacetum pallidum*, Violet Limodore *Tulipa australis*

This site is a geological extravaganza, very easily located 25km north-east of Cuenca on the CU 912, set in the midst of a forest of Black Pine. It is an area where botanical treasures can be found at every turn. At the entrance to La Ciudad Encantada, The Enchanted City, is a large car-park.

Within the area there are a series of well-marked paths winding through a mass of exotically shaped limestone boulders carved by the elements. Most of the formations have imaginative names such as 'The Mushroom' 'The Roman Bridge' and 'The Ships'. Many are as high as three-storey buildings.

From crevices in the rocks the pale-cream flowers of *Antirrhinum pulverulentum* look down. The cushion *Saxifraga corbariensis*, the yellow *Tanacetum pallidum* and *Tulipa australis* can be seen on the top of the flat, cracked limestone area near the part called 'The Toboggan Slope'. On the pine-covered hillsides, the spectacular Violet Limodore exhibits its beautiful flowers.

One of the incredible rock formations at La Ciudad Encantada called 'The Mushroom'.

81 UÑA AND THE EMBALSE DE LA TOBA

Grid reference:	L 24
Location:	NE of Cuenca
Access:	Excellent
Season:	Spring, summer and autumn
Terrain:	River valley
Specialities:	Griffon Vulture, Chough, Little Grebe, Red Helleborine, Marsh Helleborine

Approximately 40km north-east of Cuenca, on the CU 921 or CU 912, past The Enchanted Village and set within the upper reaches of the Río Júcar, is a small freshwater lake at the attractive village of Uña. This is an important centre for the timber industry. The lake is is surrounded by *Phragmites* and there is sufficient cover for a large number of Little Grebes, Mallard and Grey Herons.

Further up the valley there are huge ochre-coloured cliffs, which in places rise almost vertically from the river bank. These crags are the nesting places for a very large colony of Griffon Vultures, and some Choughs. Nearby is the Embalse de la Toba which is devoid of lakeside vegetation, but in the shallower areas Grey Herons and Mallard can be seen feeding. At the edge of the reservoir and on the more gentle slopes of the mountain there is a forest of Black Pine which holds a large number of orchids, most notably the rare Red Helleborine, found only in limestone woodlands. The Marsh Helleborine grows in the wetlands around the lake edge.

The Great Banded Grayling and the Marbled Skipper should be seen.

7. THE MEDITERRANEAN

INTRODUCTION

The Mediterranean region to be described here does not include that part of the coast which falls within Andalucía. It is bounded on the south-east by the Mediterranean Sea, from the French frontier at Portbou to the Andalucían border in the south near Huércal Overa. The north-west border travels north through Lorca, Almansa, Chiva, Alcañiz, Lérida and then to Portbou.

The Scarce Swallowtail (Iphiclides podalirius), one of the more spectacular butterflies found in Spain.

This long coastal strip has many extremes: the stark dramatic cliffs of the Costa Brava with delightful sandy coves so beloved of the tourists, but backed by many high-rise hotels and apartments; the busy city of Barcelona; then the long sandy coast containing the faunistically rich Ebro Delta; and finally Javea where the Costa Blanca begins and continues with cliffs and sandy beaches to the Andalucían border.

Back from the coast magnificent low mountains dominate the horizon. Some are dramatic and awe-inspiring like Montserrat, others are clothed with a mantle of lush forests, and some are high round-topped massifs like Espuña. There are also deep gorges lost to the outside world in Beseit and Date Palm groves like a North African oasis at Elche.

Surprisingly, with such a diversity of magnificent scenery, there is a fairly predictable climate: typically Mediterranean with hot dry summers and warm wet winters. Snow does occur, but only in the mountains back from the coast. Coastal storms are generally short lived.

The southern coastal strip is subtropical and in places near Huércal Overa is semi-desert with cactus and agave plantations. Date Palms are grown commercially and the one at Elche is the largest grove in Europe. Around Valencia, rice, vegetables and fruit, are grown extensively.

The plant life of the region is very varied and in the Costa Brava's more humid zones grazing fields are full of orchids, irises, gladioli, species of *Anchusa*, poppies and other colourful plants. Inland, within the hills, maquis scrub holding Lavender, cistus, Thyme and yellow *Genista* predominates between the large coniferous forests.

With such a wide range of plants the butterfly population is great. The most spectacular amongst a host of beautiful species are the Two-tailed Pasha, with the Swallowtail and Scarce Swallowtail, Painted Lady and the colourful Cleopatra everywhere.

The bird life is impressive. A large proportion of migrating birds to and from Africa pass over this area on their annual migration and with the extensive Ebro Delta in the middle of the zone, ducks and waders are abundant. Mammals, particularly the Egyptian Mongoose, Genet and Wild Boar, are present, and there is a large herd of Mouflon in the Sierra de Espuña.

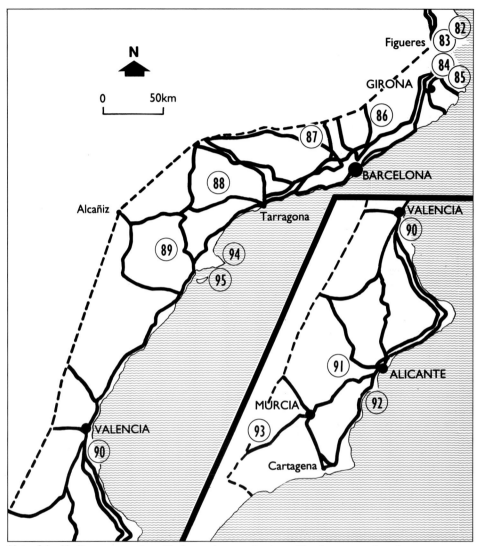

Map of the Mediterranean region with the southern section inset. The sites are numbered as in the text. Only main roads and the major rivers of the region are shown.

Although this is a recognized tourist zone, the high-rise buildings and pleasure areas only occupy a narrow coastal strip. Therefore this remains a wonderful region for the naturalist, with varied habitats of marshes, mountains, woodlands and cliffs.

The grid references used in the following site descriptions relate to Michelin maps numbers 443, 445 and 446.

113

Rugged and undulating countryside just back from the Mediterranean coastline typifies this area.

FIFTY INTERESTING SPECIES TO LOOK FOR

Slender-billed Gull	Crag Martin	Montpellier Snake	Spanish Argus
Little Tern	Alpine Swift	Ladder Snake	*Daphne gnidium*
Cormorant	Pallid Swift	Southern Smooth	Date Palm
Short-toed Eagle	Marmora's	Snake	Limestone
Bonelli's Eagle	Warbler	Savi's Pygmy	Saxifrage
Marbled Teal	Penduline Tit	Shrew	*Saxifraga vayredana*
Squacco Heron	Short-toed	Weasel	*Ramonda myconi*
Night Heron	Treecreeper	Mouflon	Stinking Hellebore
Purple Heron	Blue Rock Thrush	Clouded Yellow	Turk's Cap Lily
Bittern	Stripeless Tree	Cleopatra	Bumble Bee
Little Bittern	Frog	Two-tailed Pasha	Orchid
Baillon's Crake	Natterjack Toad	Great Banded	Common Spotted
Slavonian Grebe	Western	Grayling	Orchid
Lesser Grey Shrike	Spadefoot Toad	Nevada Grayling	Limodore
Pratincole	Iberian Wall Lizard	Spring Ringlet	Man Orchid

82 GOLFO DE ROSES, THE NORTHERN ROCKY CLIFFS	
Grid reference:	F 39
Location:	Northern Costa Brava
Access:	Good
Season:	All year round
Terrain:	Cliffs and valleys
Comments:	Insect repellent could be necessary
Specialities:	Red-breasted Merganser, Cetti's Warbler, Common Scoter, Stripeless Tree Frog, Limodore
Subsidiary:	Cala de Portlligat, F 39

A Stripeless Tree Frog (Hyla meridionalis) *calling.*

From Figueras travel to Castelló d'Empúries on the C 260. Here turn north towards Roses and continue to the cliffs by a small road. This beautiful rocky coastline at the northern end of the Costa Brava is very easily accessible and is a wonderful site for sea-watching. There are also interesting areas in the valleys leading down to the coastline. From vantage points along the cliffs you can see wintering Red-breasted Merganser, Common Scoter and Razorbill. On occasion Velvet Scoter and Eider Duck come in to the protection of this sheltered bay.

Back from the beach there are still vineyards, orchards, areas of Olive groves and occasional patches of maquis scrub with cistus and Heather predominating. It is worth investigating the woods of pine and Cork Oak as you can find groups of *Viburnum tinus*, Lavender, *Daphne gnidium,* a number of *Orchis* species and many Limodores. By the rocky coastline Hottentot Fig has been introduced from South Africa as a sandbinder.

Inland there is a wealth of bird life which includes such interesting species as Blue Rock

Thrush, Alpine and Pallid Swifts, Black-eared Wheatear, Crested Lark, Great Spotted Cuckoo, Melodious, Olivaceous, Sardinian and Dartford Warblers and with luck possibly a rare Marmora's Warbler. In the reeds near streams, Great Reed, Cetti's and Savi's Warblers and Bee-eaters can be seen.

If fortunate a Stripeless Tree Frog can be discovered, blending with the green foliage.

83 AIGUAMOLLS DE L'EMPORDÀ, NORTH	
Grid reference:	F 39
Location:	E of Figueras
Access:	Good
Season:	All year round
Terrain:	Freshwater marshland
Comments:	Insect repellent may be needed
Specialities:	Bittern, Black-winged Stilt, Natterjack Toad, Marsh Frog, Marbled Newt

Access to this site is easy from Figueras by the C 260 to Castelló d'Empúries, where you turn north. This natural park was created in 1983 to preserve one of the last remaining wetlands in the northern part of the Costa Brava.

The northern part (*see also* Site 84) is the

SECTION II: SITE GUIDE

basin of the one-time freshwater lake at Castelló d'Empúries which has been drained to make water-meadows for grazing cattle. It remains basically a freshwater marsh with some open water surrounded by *Phragmites*. Garganey breed here well south of their normal breeding range, Bitterns 'boom' in the marsh and Black-winged Stilts nest in the reeds.

There are many amphibians in the park. In the evenings the Marsh Frogs call loudly; Painted Frogs are here but quite rare; and Natterjack, Common and Western Spade-foot Toads are quite numerous. There are also two newts, the fairly common Palmate Newt and the much larger and beautifully marked Marbled Newt resplendent in bright green and black. Stripe-necked Terrapins can be seen sunning themselves on the banks of the ponds.

84 AIGUAMOLLS DE L'EMPORDÀ, SOUTH	
Grid reference:	F 39
Location:	E of Figueras
Access:	Good
Season:	All year round
Terrain:	Saltwater marsh
Comments:	Information centre; insect repellent advisable
Specialities:	Lesser Grey Shrike, Purple Heron, Slavonian Grebe, Savi's Pygmy Shrew, Montpellier Snake
Subsidiary:	Illa de Caramany (on Río Fluviá), F 39

Like the last site, this one is approached from Figueras on the C 260, but turn south at Castelló d'Empúries. There is an information centre at El Cortalet half-way to Sant Pere Pescador. There are also some hides where birds can be viewed.

It is a saltwater marsh which has been enlarged to encourage migrating birds to rest here on their journeys to and from Africa. It is an excellent place to see large numbers of wintering birds, such as Spoonbill, Crane, Greater Flamingo, Night and Purple Herons, and Black-necked Grebes. Possibly the most interesting species is the Lesser Grey Shrike which in Spain only breeds here.

A large part of the marsh is covered with Golden Samphire, Glasswort and the beautiful Sea Lavender, which is an unforgettable sight when in flower.

Many mammals inhabit the drier part: Savi's Pygmy Shrew is only 3.5cm long and is the smallest mammal known; Water Voles, Field Mice and Hedgehogs are common; and even a family of Wild Boar might come down from the hills to feed. Eleven species of bats have been recorded and also a number of snakes, including Viperine, Grass, Montpellier and Ladder Snakes.

85 ISLAS MEDES	
Grid reference:	F 39
Location:	Islands E of L'Estartit
Access:	By boat from L'Estartit
Season:	Summer when the boats run
Terrain:	Maquis scrub
Comments:	Further information from tourist office
Specialities:	Herring Gull, Cormorant, Shag, British Storm-petrel, Night Heron

The Islas Medes are a small but important group of islands about 1km off the coast at L'Estartit Cape. The islands are covered with maquis scrub and are uninhabited except for lighthouse keepers.

Fishing around the islands is prohibited,

Savi's Pygmy Shrew (Suncus etruscus), reputed to be the world's smallest mammal.

which has a very beneficial effect on the sea-birds which breed here in large numbers, especially the Cormorant, whose only Spanish breeding site is on these islands. A few British Storm-petrels and Shags breed but most notable is one of the largest colonies in the Mediterranean of Herring Gulls, estimated at 8000 pairs. There is now evidence that Little Egret, Cattle Egret and Night Heron have established nesting sites.

Only the largest of the islands, Meda Gran can be visited by boat from L'Estartit, during summer only. Ask at the tourist office in L'Estartit for further details.

about another 10km. You will come to a very heavily wooded area but with bare granite mountain tops rising to 1700m (5577 feet). The lower slopes are covered with a mixture of evergreen oaks, pines, firs and deciduous oak, and some of Spain's finest Beech woods.

Butterflies are numerous and where the Strawberry Tree is plentiful the magnificent Two-tailed Pasha is common in spring and again in late summer. The very rare Spring Ringlet may also be seen on the upper slopes.

Within the woodlands the Violet Limodore is relatively numerous. Other plants which must be mentioned are the endemic *Saxifraga vayredana*, which has resinous aromatic leaves and white flowers, and Mountain Pansy. French Lavender is a common undergrowth shrub with Mountain Cornflower and snapdragons pushing up within. Surprisingly there is an isolated colony of *Sempervivum* on the rocky heights.

Woodland birds are abundant with Jay, woodpeckers, several different tits, Short-toed Treecreeper, Sparrowhawk and other raptors likely to be seen. The park is good to visit all year round but especially in spring and summer for the flowers.

86 PARQUE NATURAL DEL MONTSENY	
Grid reference:	G 36/37
Location:	NE of Barcelona
Access:	Excellent
Season:	All year round
Terrain:	Woodland
Specialities:	Spring Ringlet, Two-tailed Pasha, Limodore, Mountain Pansy, *Saxifraga vayredana*

The park is easily reached from Barcelona by the E 9/N 152. After approximately 65km turn right just before Tona and continue for

87 SIERRA DE MONTSERRAT	
Grid reference:	H 35
Location:	N of Barcelona
Access:	Excellent
Season:	All year round
Terrain:	Mountain with forest and scrubland
Specialities:	Turk's Cap Lily, Limestone Saxifrage, *Ramonda myconi*, Bumble Bee Orchid, Painted Lady
Subsidiary:	Parque natural de Sant Llorenç del Munt, G/H 35/36

The jagged 'teeth' of Montserrat. These are jagged and impressive from whatever angle they are viewed. They can often be seen in the early morning with mist swirling around them. In the monastery on the summit rests the famous Black Madonna.

This site is best approached by the N 11 taking the road to the right at El Bruc, approximately 50km north of Barcelona. The series of giant 'crocodile teeth' towering up to 1238m (4062 feet) is amazing from whichever angle it is viewed. The road eventually winds up and around the high pillars towards the famous monastery situated near the top.

The high slopes are covered with evergreen oak with an undergrowth of cistus and Juniper. In the open grassy areas the Turk's Cap Lily with its lovely red recurved petals can sometimes be found. Remarkable as it may seem, the Alpine *Ramonda myconi* found many kilometres away in the Pyrenees may be seen here clinging to the high rock buttresses, as can the very rare Limestone Saxifrage, which only grows on these high cliffs and near Marseilles in France. There are many species of orchid and in June you should see the Bumble Bee Orchid.

There are many butterflies in the spring and summer. The Painted Lady is particularly numerous and several fritillary species are present. There are many small birds and in the higher areas Buzzards and Ravens wheel around the crags.

The surrounding countryside is fairly heavily wooded with mainly evergreen oaks and pines, although a few Poplars are being grown in the lower land by the rivers. There are also vines and small areas of maize interspersed with vegetable cultivation in the valleys.

88 SIERRA DEL MONTSANT	
Grid reference:	I 32
Location:	NW of Tarragona
Access:	Easy
Season:	All year round
Terrain:	Low mountain and maquis scrub
Specialities:	Peregrine, Great Spotted Cuckoo, Bee-eater, Man Orchid, Dull Orchid
Subsidiary:	Sierra de Roquerole, H 33; Sierra de la Mussara, I 33

The Sierra del Montsant is a relatively unknown area north-west of Tarragona. Take the N 240 from Tarragona through Reus and after about 20km turn north onto the C 242. A winding road through a scenic valley brings you to the sierra after approximately 25km. These are low mountains only rising to 1200m (3937 feet) composed of sandstone and conglomerate rock; deep ravines and cliffs typify this site. Due to a comparatively high rainfall the sierra is fairly heavily wooded with Scots, Black and Aleppo Pines on the upper slopes. In the valley of the Río Montsant there is quite intensive fruit-growing with Olive groves and vineyards. Some scrub areas occur with an abundance of Mastic Trees and Tree Heather. Many orchids can be seen during the spring in the more open regions, especially Pyramidal, Common Spotted, Man and Dull Orchids and in the woods tall spikes of Limodore.

Butterflies are relatively numerous with the Two-tailed Pasha, Scarce Swallowtail, Clouded Yellow and Swallowtail often seen.

The cliffs in the ravines provide nesting ledges for Short-toed, Golden and Bonelli's Eagles while in the woods the Eagle Owl is present.

The orchards hold a large number of Golden Oriole, Great Spotted Cuckoo, Hoopoe, Great Spotted Woodpecker and Jay, as well as Bee-eaters which nest in the softer parts of the sandstone cliffs.

Within the gorge of Beseit.

89 RESERVA NACIONAL DE PUERTOS DE BESEIT	
Grid reference:	J 30
Location:	NW of Morella
Access:	A little difficult to locate
Season:	Spring, summer and autumn
Terrain:	Limestone cliffs and canyons
Comments:	Sensible walking shoes
Specialities:	Rock Bunting, Chough, Great Banded Grayling, Clouded Yellow, Stinking Hellebore
Subsidiary:	The medieval village of Beceite, J 30

Leave Morella (grid reference K 29) northwards on the N 232. Just after Monroyo take the TE 302 to Valderrobres and then the TE 304 to Beceite. Here follow signs to El Parrizal (Parrissal), continuing along this hard core track. Parking is easy.

The reserve is a mountain range inland from the Ebro Delta rising to 1434m (4705 feet). It is deeply dissected by canyons with limestone cliffs reaching up like giant turrets; a wild untamed country with medieval villages and an occasional modern villa on the outskirts. The narrow valleys and gullies, sometimes only a few metres wide, are full of vegetation. Where there is sufficient land Almonds and Olives grow, water for irrigation being drawn from the streams.

Box is the dominant shrub sprouting up between the boulders, with Thyme, Rosemary and sedums clinging to the rocks and

Stinking Hellebore, snapdragons and cistus wherever they can get a foothold.

Birds abound in the vegetation, where Rock Bunting, Grey Wagtail, Crag Martin, Wren, Chaffinch and Spotless Starling may be seen, while the cliffs with their ledges are ideal nesting sites for Griffon Vulture and Chough which can invariably be seen around the cliff tops.

In warmer months butterflies are always in evidence: first the Cleopatra, then a mass of others including the Clouded Yellow (very common), fritillaries, Great Banded Grayling, Painted Lady, Swallowtail and blues.

90 LA ALBUFERA DE VALENCIA	
Grid reference:	N/O 28/29
Location:	S of Valencia
Access:	Good
Season:	All year round
Terrain:	Freshwater lagoon surrounded by *Phragmites*
Comments:	Insect repellent might be necessary
Specialities:	Night Heron, Squacco Heron, Bittern, Penduline Tit, Pratincole

La Albufera is a vast area about 15km south of the large city of Valencia. It is reached by the V 15 which goes to El Salar and continues past the site to Cullera. The shallow freshwater lagoon, 1–2m deep, is separated from the sea by a wide dune area. Its depth is controlled by sluice gates, excess water being channelled to the sea. The dunes are covered with Aleppo Pine and the lagoon itself is surrounded by a large border of *Phragmites*, giving cover for the mass of wintering and breeding birds.

At Mata del Fang bird observatory, 250 bird species have been recorded, including thousands of Cattle and Little Egrets, Red-crested Pochard, Mallard, Shoveler, Wigeon and Teal. Interesting breeding birds within the reeds are Night, Squacco and Purple Herons, the elusive Bittern and the diminutive Little Bittern. Small numbers of Penduline Tits may be seen feeding on the seed heads. On the drier land, Pratincoles looking and behaving like enormous dark-brown Swallows make their nests.

Thousands of hectares of rice to the south hold millions of frogs, the favourite food of the White Stork. Fertilizers and insecticides used to increase rice production are unfortunately polluting the water.

Sunset through the Phragmites *at the Albufera de Valencia. This is so typical of this vast rice-growing area, which unfortunately is now becoming polluted by the chemicals which are used to improve rice production. However, it remains a great wintering ground for many species of duck.*

9 1 ELCHE	
Grid reference:	R 27
Location:	SW of Alicante
Access:	Excellent
Season:	All year round
Terrain:	Palm groves within agricultural land
Specialities:	Date Palm, Golden Oriole
Subsidiary:	L'Hort del Cura Gardens in the western part of Elche, R 27

Elche is approximately 25km south-west of Alicante on the N 340. This is the only place in Europe where the Date Palm is grown commercially, with over 100,000 mature trees. They are thought to have first been planted by the Phoenicians, and it is believed there were about 1,000,000 in the thirteenth century; by the eighteenth century about 500,000 remained. This gives a definite feel of Africa to Spain and reminds you that Morocco is just across the water. In Spain, as soon as the name Elche is mentioned Date Palm trees at once come to mind; they are everywhere! In autumn, great plumes of golden dates hang from the centre crown.

The surrounding countryside is flat and in general highly cultivated with cotton and orange orchards where, especially in spring, the Golden Oriole can be seen.

9 2 SALINAS DE SANTA POLA	
Grid reference:	R 28
Location:	S of Alicante
Access:	Easy
Season:	All year round
Terrain:	Salt- and freshwater lagoons with dense vegetation
Comments:	Parking may be difficult
Specialities:	Marbled Teal, Red-crested Pochard, Greater Flamingo, Black-tailed Godwit, Little Tern
Subsidiary:	Laguna de la Mata, R 27; Laguna Salada de Torrevieja, R/S 27

These salinas form another series of salt- and freshwater lagoons and ponds 20km south of Alicante, on both sides of the main N 332 road. Parking is very limited as you cannot park on the road. The proximity of Santa Pola does not appear to disturb the bird life. These marshes are a birdwatchers' treat.

Commercial Date Palms at Elche. This is a general view of the vast palm groves which have been commercially used for over 2000 years. The surrounding countryside has small groves which must have originated at about the same time as those at Elche.

Greater Flamingos (Phoenicopterus ruber) at Santa Pola. This is one of the special birds to be seen in this area. Flamingos require water of high salinity as it is in this that the crustaceans which form the major part of their diet live. Many of these birds will be resting, passing between southern Andalucía and the Camargue in France, their two major breeding areas in Europe.

They are protected from the coast by a line of sand dunes and are very densely vegetated. They are a very important site for breeding birds, in particular a few pairs of the very rare Marbled Teal. Other breeding species include Great Crested Grebe, Red-crested Pochard, Mallard, Avocet, Black-winged Stilt, Common and Little Terns, Kentish Plover, Moorhen and Coot. To these in winter can be added Greater Flamingo, Teal, Pochard, Shoveler, Black-tailed and Bar-tailed Godwits, Grey Heron, Little Egret, Dunlin, Sanderling, and the ever-present gulls, such as Lesser Black-backed, Herring and maybe Greater Black-backed.

93 RESERVA NACIONAL DE SIERRA ESPUÑA	
Grid reference:	S 25
Location:	SW of Murcia, NW of Totana
Access:	Reasonably good
Season:	All year round
Terrain:	Spectacular cliffs, mountains and forest
Comments:	Maybe snow in winter
Specialities:	Golden Eagle, Mouflon, Wild Boar, Spanish Argus, Nevada Grayling

The Sierra Espuña is a large national park of about 14,000ha situated 40km south-west of Murcia. From Murcia it is reached by taking the N 340/E 15, turning at Alhama de Murcia on to the C 3315 and shortly turning left again. More difficult to find is the turn-off in Totana. This is a small road, sign-posted on a house side to La Santa or Aledo. Once on this road the going is easy.

This park was established in the 1970s to safeguard the untouched Mediterranean pine forest and to introduce a small herd of Mouflon (African Barbary Sheep). They can be seen in the range's higher areas (*see* box).

The park is dominated by two towering peaks: Espuña of 1585m (5200 feet) and Morrón at 1446m (4744 feet). There are forest tracks throughout. On the spectacular cliffs Golden Eagles nest and above Griffon Vultures soar in motionless flight. Lower down in the pine forest, Wild Boar roam. In some of the woodland clearings two rare butterflies can be seen: the Spanish Argus and the Nevada Grayling.

Within the forest of Maritime Pine are several parking areas with built-in barbecues, where you can cook your own food! Lighting fires is otherwise forbidden. This site is good all year round, but in winter there can be up to 10cm of snow making driving difficult.

PARC NATURAL DEL DELTA DEL EBRO

The water which falls on the southern watershed of the Pyrenees finds its way into the mighty Río Ebro. The river brings sediment from the catchment area and deposits it at the Mediterranean exit, forming the great, ecologically important delta, which is the wintering ground for countless ducks, Coot and waders (grid reference J/K 31/32).

The delta is mainly devoted to rice cultivation, but there are large areas of *Phragmites* which make ideal habitat for a wide variety of bird life, especially Bittern, Little Bittern, Night, Squacco and Purple Herons, Water Rail, Black-winged Stilt, Avocet, Little Tern and the rare Baillon's Crake. In the saltwater bay the majestic Greater Flamingo wades and Slender-billed and Mediterranean Gulls feed.

As might be expected, there are many reptiles and amphibians. The Marsh Frog is present in large numbers but the Painted Frog is more local. Water snakes include Montpellier, Southern Smooth, Grass, Viperine, Ladder and Horseshoe Whip Snakes.

Mouflon *Ovis aries* var. *musimon*
L 120 (head and body)

In 1970 the nature conservation organization ICONA decided to import some wild sheep, to see if a flock could be established in the Sierra Espuña natural park. The Mouflon or Barbary Sheep found in North Africa is native from the High Atlas to the Red Sea and has the ability to go without water for very long periods. More importantly, it will not eat young trees, preferring the grass and vegetation which grows between them. It looks like a cross between a sheep and a goat, short hair replacing wool. The ram has magnificent curved horns.

The initial few animals have now proliferated and there is an estimated flock of over 700 well established in the sierra. Some new flocks are now being created in other similar areas.

Adult Night Heron (Nycticorax nycticorax), one of the many species of wetland birds found in the Ebro delta.

Argiope lobata

This is a beautiful spider of dry sand regions and scrubland. The body is fawn coloured and looks as though it has been sculptured in alabaster. It weaves a large circular web where the female can often be seen, legs outstretched, head downwards in the centre, waiting for a grasshopper or other unsuspecting prey to be ensnared.

Many of the genus *Argiope* are highly colourful, in particular the Garden Spider which has a large fat abdomen striped in yellow and black.

Many people have an innate fear of spiders, which can be well understood when confronted with a huge hairy bird-eating spider from the tropics; a truly fearsome creature. Here in Europe, we have none of these! There is only one which is slightly poisonous, the European Black Widow, which is uncommon.

The Iberian Wall Lizard is fairly common.

Large mammals are not present, but Rabbits and Red Foxes breed commonly, and Otters, Hedgehogs and Weasels less so.

Mention must be made of the large and beautifully marked spider *Argiope lobata* which makes its web amongst the scrub on the sand dunes (*see* box).

There are mussel beds to the north and south and fishing and crustacean culture is of great economic importance in the vicinity. Rice growing within the area is of major importance and accounts for 98% of the total Catalan output. The urbanization at Riumar and Deltebre does not seem to have affected the wildlife in the area. To do full justice to the area it has been divided into two. The river makes a natural division.

94 PARC NATURAL DEL DELTA DEL EBRO, NORTHERN SIDE	
Grid reference:	J 31/32
Location:	SE of Tortosa
Access:	Good
Season:	All year round
Terrain:	Marshland
Comments:	Insect repellent might be necessary; information centre
Specialities:	Bittern, Night Heron, Baillon's Crake, Painted Frog, Montpellier Snake

The northern delta is approached from Amposta on the N 340. To the north after crossing the river turn east towards the town of Deltebre. This attractive small town contains the main information centre of the area at its western end; it is well signposted. Here there is usually an English-speaking attendant who is very helpful, showing the best routes to follow and giving out leaflets. Many books are available for purchase, some in

English, with many in the Catalan dialect.

The areas Bassa de les Olles, Punta del Fangar, Canal Vell, El Gerxal and the Illa de Buda are all protected and a permit must be obtained for access. There are many road-ways however, from which the vast number of waders which are usually in this area can be viewed, and it is worth asking at the reception what is around at the time of your visit.

Although Night Heron, Baillon's Crake and Bittern are all present, they are rarely seen, keeping hidden in the reed beds. Pain-ted Frog and Montpellier Snake are fairly common on the edges of the rice paddies.

*Montpellier Snake (*Malpolon monspessulanus*) feeding. This is one of many snakes to be found in the Ebro delta.*

95 PARC NATURAL DEL DELTA DEL EBRO, SOUTHERN SIDE	
Grid reference:	J/K 31/32
Location:	SE of Tortosa
Access:	Good
Season:	All year round
Terrain:	Marshland
Comments:	Insect repellent may be necessary; information centre
Specialities:	Slender-billed Gull, Greater Flamingo, Southern Smooth Snake, Horseshoe Whip Snake

The southern delta is approached from Am-posta on the N 340. At St Carles de la Ràpita take the coastal road to the delta. There is a well signposted information centre and museum at La Casa de Fusta to the north of El Poblenou del Delta. This museum con-tains a large collection of stuffed birds, other land vertebrates and fish which either breed or pass through on passage. Various leaflets showing the different roadways can be obtained here.

There are a large number of protected areas. The Lagunas de l'Encanyissada and de la Tancada are *Phragmites* edged; Punta de la Banya is almost an island with access along a narrow sandbank. This has pine woods and some interesting salt-pans with Greater Flamingo and several gulls, Mediterranean and Slender-billed in particular.

The Southern Smooth and Horseshoe Whip Snakes, and the Iberian Wall Lizard can often be seen, all of which sun themselves on the sand dunes.

A pass is necessary to visit these three sites, but there are many accessible paths from which they can be viewed without entering.

8. WEST ANDALUCÍA

INTRODUCTION

This area is bounded on the west by Portugal, the north by Extremadura province, the south by the Atlantic as far as Algeciras and with its eastern line running due north from that town, slightly east of Sevilla, continuing to the Extremadura border.

It is a low-lying area with four main rivers: the Río Guadiana, which forms the natural boundary between Spain and Portugal; the mighty Río Guadalquivir, which is navigable as far as Sevilla; and the two lesser rivers, Tinto and Odiel, which rise near Aracena in the Sierra Morena quite near to the great copper and manganese mines. The highest point in the region is 959m (3150 feet) and lies in the Sierra Morena, covered with evergreen oak and pine forest.

The lowlands along the south from Ayamonte to Sevilla have been transformed into an area for orange and early strawberry growing for export to northern Europe. South of Sevilla towards Cádiz, sunflower, cotton and sugar beet are grown on irrigated land. Near Jerez de la Frontera and towards Sanlúcar de Barrameda the land is covered with vineyards for the sherry industry.

The climate is mild during the winter, when most of the rain falls, Sevilla for example having an annual average of 50cm (20 inches). The summers can be hot, especially inland where the temperature reaches 35°C, but nearer the coast there is usually a breeze to temper the heat. Within the region the natural history emphasis is on wet and marshland sites, because this is one of the main spring and autumn migratory routes between Europe and Africa. Also ducks and geese come down from northern

Opposite: Chameleon (Chamaeleo chamaeleon).

FIFTY INTERESTING SPECIES TO LOOK FOR

Audouin's Gull	Black Stork	Dartford Warbler	Swallowtail
Slender-billed Gull	Greater Flamingo	Ocellated Lizard	Painted Lady
Little Tern	Spoonbill	Chameleon	Marsh Fritillary
Osprey	Purple Heron	√ Marsh Frog	Common Blue
Spanish Imperial Eagle	Black-necked Grebe	Stripe-necked Terrapin	Lorquin's Blue
Montagu's Harrier	Crested Coot	Pardel or Spanish Lynx	Silver-studded Blue
Marsh Harrier	Avocet	Wild Cat	Fritillaria hispanica
Black Vulture	Whimbrel	Wolf	Iris filifolia
√ Black Kite	Green Sandpiper	Egyptian Mongoose	Mandrake
Marbled Teal	Crane	Wild Boar	Sea Daffodil
White-headed Duck	Great Bustard	Red Deer	Shrubby Blue Pimpernell
Red-crested Pochard	White-rumped Swift	Fallow Deer	Three-leaved Snowflake
	Rufous Bush Robin		Yellow Broomrape

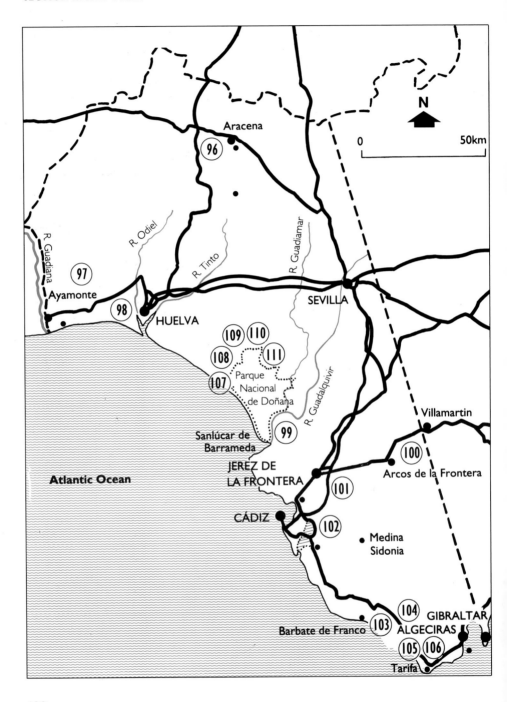

Europe to winter here as can be seen from the huge Coto Doñana Reserve, where birds come in their thousands onto the marshes in the evening. Not only ducks and geese, but also thousands of Chiffchaffs and Robins, which are absent in the summer, overwinter throughout the region.

The range of habitats is large. In the Sierra Morena there are coniferous forests interspersed with maquis scrub, especially in the foothills. There are lowland mixed forest in the Coto del Rey with Cork and Ilex Oak and pines predominating. Salt- and freshwater marshes are found in the Coto Doñana, Cádiz, Bonanza and Marismas de Barbate, with freshwater marshes at Embalse de Bornos and beside the village of El Rocio. Coto Doñana also has the most extensive dunes in Iberia. The sea-cliff habitat between Tarifa and Algeciras is superb for migrant watching, raptors in particular.

The grid references used in the following site descriptions relate to Michelin map number 446.

96 PEÑA DE ARIAS MONTANO	
Grid reference:	S 10
Location:	W of Aracena
Access:	Very good
Season:	All year round, especially spring and early summer
Terrain:	Mountainous with wooded slopes
Specialities:	Wolf, Pardel Lynx, Black Vulture, Lorquin's Blue, Brown Bluebell
Subsidiary:	Aracena, Gruta de las Maravillas: Spain's largest cave, S 10; Río Tinto opencast mine, S 10

Opposite: map of West Andalucía. The sites are numbered as in the text. Only main roads and the major rivers of the region are shown.

Situated 12km west of Aracena. Turn north from the H 521 near Alajar and the road rises rapidly. The site is a heavily wooded mountainside with evergreen oak and Gum Cistus predominating. From Nossa Señora de los Angeles you overlook the typical village of Alajar and can see the majority of the Sierra de Aracena and beyond.

Specialities which still exist in the woodlands are the Wolf and Pardel Lynx (*see* box).

Pardel or Spanish Lynx
Lynx pardina L 85–110

The Pardel Lynx is very much an endangered species and is found in the wild woodlands of southern and western Spain. Due to its mainly nocturnal habits and its retiring nature it is not often seen.

A stronghold with forty pairs is the Coto Doñana Reserve and it is here that investigations are being carried out to find out more about these beautiful animals. They are smaller than the Lynx from northern Europe, being up to 30kg in weight compared to about 38kg in their northern cousin. Their ground colour is buff but it is handsomely spotted with dark brown. They have long cheek whiskers and tufted ears. The tail is short with a black tip. Their main food consists of rabbits and ducks.

The Black Vulture may be seen soaring on broad wings and with luck a Spanish Imperial Eagle with white shoulder patches may also be seen. Great Grey and Woodchat Shrikes, Azure-winged Magpies, Bee-eaters, Hoopoes and a large number of woodland birds are common.

The rare Lorquin's Blue butterfly which is confined in Europe to southern Iberia is still found locally in this area. The Swallowtail, Scarce Swallowtail and Cleopatra are relatively common with several of the blues and skippers.

Late spring and early summer are the best times, when the flowers will be at their peak. Gum Cistus, Rosemary, French Lavender, peonies, Spanish Iris and Gladiolus adorn the hillsides. Look out for the rare Brown Bluebell and many of the orchids, especially the Bug Orchid.

Guadiana. Embalse del Piedras is a man-made freshwater reservoir situated in the middle of undulating open farmland, with a large coniferous forest nearby.

Within the reservoir there are a number of small islands where migrating birds rest, notably Black Storks, which pass through on their autumn migration from Extremaduran breeding sites to African wintering quarters. On occasions Ospreys will winter in the area, feeding on the fish which abound.

The edge of the lake is relatively shallow, allowing tamarisk to establish and give cover for smaller birds. The coniferous woods nearby hold a large number of Azure-winged Magpies, Short-toed Treecreepers, woodpeckers and Little Owls, with Bee-eaters nesting in the sandy banks.

97 EMBALSE DEL PIEDRAS	
Grid reference:	T 8
Location:	NE Ayamonte, NW Huelva
Access:	Reasonable
Season:	Spring and autumn migrations
Terrain:	Rolling agricultural land
Comments:	Strong footwear
Specialities:	Black Stork, White Stork, Grey Heron, Osprey, Montagu's Harrier
Subsidiary:	Coastal marshes at Isla Cristina, U 7

98 LAS MARISMAS DEL ODIEL	
Grid reference:	U 9
Location:	W bank Río Odiel, Huelva
Access:	Good; metalled road and car-parks
Season:	All year round
Terrain:	Confluence of Ríos Odiel and Tinto, about 7000ha, including large working salt-pan area
Comments:	Insect repellent advised
Specialities:	Greater Flamingo, Spoonbill, Little Tern, Marsh Harrier, Purple Heron
Subsidiary:	Laguna de Aljaraque, U 8; Laguna El Portil, U 8; Marismas Gibraleón, U 9

Situated 22km north-east of Ayamonte and 32km north-west of Huelva. Turn north from the N 431 at Cartaya towards Tariquejo. After approximately 8km turn left onto Carretera Forestal road, signposted Ch Guadiana Presa del Piedras. At the end turn left, heading away from Vivendas Ch

Leave Huelva heading west on the H 414 towards Punta Umbria. After the long river bridge, take the Ayamonte turning, and

A Little Egret (Egretta garzetta) contemplating its next meal on the salt-marshes at Bonanza. This elegant bird almost became extinct at the end of the nineteenth century due to the millinery trade using the white breeding head plumes to adorn ladies' hats. It was this that lead to the formation of the Royal Society for the Protection of Birds (RSPB) to protect endangered species and their habitats.

almost immediately turn left over the road, as though returning to Huelva. Shortly turn right onto Dique Juan Carlos I Rey de España road.

This area is a tidal salt-marsh on the western banks of the rivers Odiel and Tinto, with a large area of marshland scrub, extensive mudflats and salt-pans. Effluent from the oil refineries and industrial sites on the eastern banks causes considerable pollution.

It is a major resting area for migrating birds, especially Black and Whiskered Terns, Avocets and Black-winged Stilts, Whimbrel and Curlew. In summer, there are Greater Flamingo in their hundreds, and large numbers of breeding Little Terns.

Through the reserve there is a 20km public road, with good vantage points. 15km from the entrance a large car-park gives access to the beach area, ideal for watching seabirds. A small woodland, viewed from the road, may produce Great Spotted Cuckoo, woodpeckers and Azure-winged Magpies.

The dry mudflats are carpeted with *Spergularia purpurea* in spring. The larger lagoons are tidal, with Kentish and Ringed Plover, Redshank and Greenshank, godwits, herons and Marsh Harrier common.

99 SALINAS DE BONANZA AND NEARBY CONIFEROUS FOREST	
Grid reference:	V 10/11
Location:	NW of Jerez de la Frontera
Access:	Good
Season:	All year round
Terrain:	Salt-pans and forest surrounded by vineyards
Comments:	Insect repellent advised
Specialities:	Slender-billed Gull, Audouin's Gull, Whiskered Tern, Greater Flamingo, Spoonbill

These salinas are 27km north-west of Jerez de la Frontera and are reached from Jerez by the C 440 to Sanlúcar de Barrameda. In Sanlúcar turn right at Petronor and drive straight into town. At the second set of traffic lights (just after Adega Manzani) turn right into Avenida de San Francisco, continue straight, and 200m beyond Apromasa Sales Lavadas bear left onto a track. Park on reaching the large gates on the right. Walk through the left-hand gates, which are the service gates for the

*A male Lesser Kestrel (*Falco naumanni)*, much smaller than the common Kestrel and gregarious.*

100 EMBALSE DE BORNOS	
Grid reference:	V 12
Location:	NE of Arcos de la Frontera, W of Villamartin
Access:	Good
Season:	All year round
Terrain:	Reservoir with tamarisk at the end
Comments:	Insect repellent may be necessary
Specialities:	Purple Heron, Night Heron, Little Egret, Cormorant, Great Crested Grebe
Subsidiary:	Arcos de la Frontera, V 12, for Lesser Kestrel

salt-pans. For the forest continue on to La Algaida.

This is a vast area of salt-pans on the eastern bank of the Río Guadalquivir, opposite the Coto Doñana Reserve. It therefore has a very similar avifauna. The salt-pans are private property, but if your car is parked outside the main gates, you may walk through, keeping to the main paths.

Greater Flamingo, Spoonbill and Avocet are usually seen in quantity and with luck Slender-billed Gull, and in winter Audouin's Gull may be seen on the river banks.

Next to the salt-pans is a large coniferous forest which holds Azure-winged Magpie, Hoopoe, and Dartford and Sardinian Warblers. Overhead, Red and Black Kites circle looking for carrion or fish. Between Bonanza and Jerez the countryside is gently undulating, dry and calcarious, planted almost entirely with vines, producing grapes for the world-famous sherry industry.

This large man-made reservoir lies to the south of the N 342 which runs north-east from Arcos de la Frontera to Villamartin. There is good access on the northern side via the N 342. On the south-eastern side a track passes between the C 444 and the CA 523.

The reservoir covers 4000ha on the Río Guadalete. At the northern end is a large tangled mass of tamarisk and aquatic vegetation which produce ideal nesting sites for various species of the heron family, the most numerous of which are the Cattle Egrets. It is also important for small numbers of Night Heron, Little Egret and Purple Heron. In winter large numbers of Coot will be seen with smaller numbers of Cormorant and Great Crested Grebe.

The surrounding area is dry cereal-growing land rotated with sugar-beet and sunflower production. Vines and Olive plantations predominate on the hillsides. This site can be productive bird-wise at any time of the year, especially if combined with a visit to the geologically interesting Arcos de la

Frontera escarpment, which holds the world's largest population of Lesser Kestrel during their breeding season.

101 LAGUNA DE MEDINA	
Grid reference:	W 11
Location:	SE of Jerez de la Frontera, NW of Medina Sidonia
Access:	Very good
Season:	Autumn, winter and spring
Terrain:	Shallow lagoon with *Phragmites* and tamarisk
Comments:	Insect repellent may be necessary
Specialities:	Crested Coot, Black-necked Grebe, Marbled Teal, White-headed Duck, Ocellated Lizard

An ICONA reserve situated 11km south-east of Jerez de la Frontera and 25km north-west of Medina Sidonia, marked as a lake on the map but not named. It is well signposted from the C 440 immediately opposite the cement factory, and has a small car-park. There is a picnic site and shelter just inside the reserve to the right.

This freshwater lake, within dry, rolling, arable land can dry out in summer. Surrounded by *Phragmites* and tamarisk, it attracts large numbers of waders, ducks, Coot and Greater Flamingo. Most notable are White-headed Duck, Marbled Teal, Red-crested Pochard, Black-necked Grebe and the fabulous Purple Gallinule. Do watch for the rare Crested Coot which breeds here. During the breeding season the two red knobs on top of their heads are very obvious, looking like headlamps!

Sardinian and Great Reed Warblers nest, while in the autumn migration clouds of martins and Swallows roost in the reed beds.

Colourful dragonflies and some butterflies are in evidence in early summer. Marsh Frogs and Stripeless Tree Frogs, Viperine Snakes and Ocellated Lizards may all be seen.

The quarry on the north side does not seem to be an ecological problem. The southern path is best for morning viewing with the western one for evening.

102 SALINAS DE CADIZ	
Grid reference:	W 11
Location:	SE of Cádiz
Access:	Excellent
Season:	All year round
Terrain:	Typical salt-land scrub amongst the salt-pans
Comments:	Off-road parking may be a little difficult
Specialities:	Avocet, Whimbrel, Little Tern, Green Sandpiper, Yellow Broomrape
Subsidiary:	Lagunas de Terry, N of El Puerto de Santa Maria, W 11 (marked but not named on map)

Situated 17km south-east of Cádiz on the N IV/E 25. A huge expanse of shallow water on the main road between El Puerto de Santa Maria and Chiclana, with the important naval base of Cádiz on the north-west side.

There are vast areas of salt-pans, some abandoned, where large flocks of waders pause during migration. Many Black-tailed and Bar-tailed Godwits, Redshank, Spotted Redshank, Greenshank, Avocet, Ruff, Green Sandpiper, Whimbrel and some Curlew winter within the area. During spring, Black and Whiskered Terns hawk for insects over the water, with the largest concentration of breeding Little Terns in Spain looking for nesting sites. White Storks are frequent and

Mandrake *Mandragora autumnalis*

Few plants have more mythology and folklore attached to them than the Mandrake. It is said to shriek when pulled out of the ground, no doubt due to its thick fleshy root fancifully thought to represent a human! It has a rosette of dark-green crinkly leaves radiating from a stout rootstock and a mass of large lilac flowers are produced from the centre of the plant followed by a round fleshy yellow fruit 2.5cm in diameter.

The sap is slightly poisonous containing a number of narcotic substances. It has long been used as a 'love potion' and is said to have aphrodisiac properties.

It is a lovely plant despite all the myth attached to it, and sometimes grows by the roadside in such profusion that it imparts a lilac tinge to the whole area.

103 MARISMAS DE BARBATE

Grid reference:	X 12
Location:	Immediately E of Barbate de Franco, NW of Tarifa
Access:	Very good
Season:	All year round
Terrain:	Freshwater river and salt-marshes
Comments:	Insect repellent may be necessary
Specialities:	Black Kite, Red-crested Pochard, Marsh Frog, Stripe-necked Terrapin, Mandrake
Subsidiary:	Tajo de la Barbate, coastal cliffs; Pinar de la Barbate, pinewoods; both between Cabo de Trafalgar and Barbate de Franco, X 11/12

Little Egrets feed in the shallow waters.

This area with its typical salt-land and scrub provides cover for a large number of smaller birds: Crested and Short-toed Larks, Sardinian and Dartford Warblers, and Bluethroats in the autumn.

A spectacular plant in the spring is the extraordinary large Yellow Broomrape, parasitic on Saltwort and goosefoot.

Unfortunately there is a lot of disturbance for breeding birds due to the large port and naval base of Cádiz, and further construction is projected.

Situated just outside Barbate de Franco on a small road to the east. Also 50km north-west of Tarifa approached by the N 340, then the small road from Casas de los Hierros. It is an area of salt-marshes and disused salt-pans by the estuary of the Río Barbate. North and west is a low range of hills covered in Stone Pine, while eastwards a craggy range rises to 316m (1037 feet). This is within a military zone.

Large numbers of Pochard, Red-crested Pochard, Mallard and Wigeon overwinter. Greater Flamingo and Spoonbill are common, especially in the salt-pans near the road. During migration Black-tailed and Bar-tailed Godwits, Ringed Plover, Ruff, Little Stint and Grey Heron appear as well as good numbers of raptors, such as Black Kite and Booted Eagle with an occasional Osprey.

Salicornia and other salt-marsh plants

surround the pans. During winter Mandrake (*see* box) and Friar's Cowl are by the roadside with quantities of Paper-white Narcissi in the freshwater meadows. In spring, irises and Summer Snowflake can be found and there is an abundance of dragonflies.

Marsh Frogs and Stripe-necked Terrapin are common in the river and freshwater wetlands.

104 LA JANDA	
Grid reference:	X 12
Location:	NW of Tarifa, SE of Cádiz
Access:	Can be difficult due to fencing
Season:	Autumn, winter and spring
Terrain:	Cultivated grain lands which can flood
Comments:	Summer can be very hot
Specialities:	Crane, Great Bustard, Marsh Fritillary, Painted Lady, *Iris filifolia*

This important area, not named on the map, is situated north of the N 340 between Tarifa and Cádiz. Access is by roads near Tahivilla to either Las Hebas or El Aciscar. It was formerly a large shallow inland lake which was drained in the 1950s for agricultural purposes. It is now a flat plain covered with grain fields and cattle ranches.

Surrounded by ranges of high wooded hills, it can become an 'oven' in summer but during autumn, winter and spring it still tends to flood if the drainage channels overflow. As in former days a multitude of wintering birds still congregate here. Cranes in small numbers and with luck Great and Little Bustards may be seen, especially in the early morning. During the summer Griffon Vultures and Bonelli's Eagles glide on the warm thermals looking for food. During migration in late summer many White Storks congregate with the occasional rare Black Stork.

Pine woods at the base of the hills hold some interesting plants including the long fine-leaved *Iris filifolia*, *I. xiphium* variety *taitii* and Three-leaved Snowflake. On the roadsides and grasslands where it is wet the Paper-white Narcissus is abundant.

During early summer butterflies are numerous: fritillaries (in particular the variable Marsh Fritillary), Silver-studded and Common Blue, Swallowtail, and especially in late summer the Painted Lady. This is a site to visit all the year round, but summer can be very hot.

105 TARIFA BEACH	
Grid reference:	X 12/13
Location:	NW of Tarifa
Access:	Reasonably good
Season:	All year round, but especially during migratory periods
Terrain:	Long sandy beach backed by coniferous forest and grassland
Comments:	Normal clothing
Specialities:	Audouin's Gull, Sandwich Tern, Kentish Plover, Sea Daffodil, Shrubby Blue Pimpernel
Subsidiary:	Puerto del Cabrito Mirador, X 13; Punta del Carnero, X 13

Situated just north-west of Tarifa, several small tracks from the main Algeciras to Vejar de la Frontera road (E 5 N 340) give access to this huge sandy beach, which is washed by the Atlantic Ocean and backed by pine woods and pasture-lands.

Except for the summer season, when the

Inland from Tarifa Beach on the migratory route.

nearby campsites are busy, this beautiful beach is almost deserted. It is a noted site for Audouin's Gull, especially during the winter. Nesting birds include Kentish Plover, and Crested and Short-toed Larks further inland. During the spring and autumn migration, many thousands of birds pass over this area, some resting until favourable conditions enable them to continue their journey. Slightly inland is the only European breeding area for the White-rumped Swift, although its range is now extending.

In late summer, Sea Daffodil makes a wonderful show with pure white trumpet-shaped flowers, while earlier in the season the large-flowered Blue Pimpernel carpets the ground back from the beach.

Car-parking is comparatively easy. All times of the year are good to visit, but preference must be given to the main migration times in spring and autumn.

106 SANTUARIO DE NOSSA SEÑORA DE LA LUZ VALLEY	
Grid reference:	X 13
Location:	N of Tarifa and W of Algeciras
Access:	Good
Season:	All year round, but especially during the migratory periods
Terrain:	pasture-land, tree-clad stream courses and rolling countryside
Comments:	Beware of straying animals as much of area is unfenced
Specialities:	Rufous Bush Robin, White-rumped Swift, Dartford Warbler, Ocellated Lizard, *Fritillaria hispanica*
Subsidiary:	Sierra de Fates, X 12/13; Sierra del Niño, X 13

Situated almost due north of Tarifa and approached from the main E 5/N 340 road. Travelling westwards from Tarifa turn between two large gates (signposted) to the north onto the CA P2214. This turning can easily be missed as it looks like a private entrance.

It is a wide, mainly pastoral valley with scattered evergreen oaks. The surrounding wood-covered hills hold Golden and Bonelli's Eagles and Egyptian and Griffon Vultures, while in the Gum Cistus scrub lower down Dartford Warblers and Rufous Bush Robins can be found. During the autumn migration, hundreds of White Storks rest and feed in the grasslands.

During springtime many orchids, irises and fritillaries can be seen. Several varieties of lizards can be found, amongst them the enormous Eyed Lizard.

During late spring and early summer there are many butterflies including the Spanish Gatekeeper, the Spanish Marbled White and on occasion the Two-tailed Pasha.

This site can be visited at any time of the year and should always produce something of interest.

COTO DOÑANA

The Coto Doñana on the delta of the Río Guadalquivir is one of the most important wetland sites in Europe. It comprises a pre-park area and the enclosed Doñana National Reserve, in all totalling 165,000ha. It is situated in the south-west (grid reference U/V 10/11), 50km south-east of Huelva and about 60km south-west of Sevilla. It is approached via the A 49 which runs between Sevilla and Huelva, turning south at Bollullos where it is signposted. Alternatively from Huelva you can take the C 442 as far as Torre de la Higuera, turning north onto the H 612.

Doñana's importance lies in the fact that it is on a major migratory route and is also a wintering ground for thousands of northern European waterfowl. However, maybe its most important feature is that it combines seven different ecosystems. A 30km beach, which is within the protected area, has a few licensed shell-fishermen. Here can be seen Oystercatcher, Sanderling and Kentish Plover in large numbers, Lesser Black-backed, Herring and Black-headed Gulls in abundance, Sandwich and Little Terns, and the occasional Audouin's Gull. The saltwater marshes adjacent to the river, and protected on the west bank, hold Greater Flamingo and many duck species. Freshwater marshes and the non-tidal river are located in the pre-park and reserved area nearer El Rocio making ideal habitat for Black-winged Stilt, Black-tailed and Bar-tailed Godwit, and heron species.

The coniferous forest, which is within the protected area, is the nesting area for the Spanish Imperial Eagle (see box overleaf) and gives cover for Red and Fallow Deer, Wild Boar and the rare Pardel Lynx. The lowland mixed forest is in the protected area at El Acebrón and in the pre-park area of Coto del Rey, areas perfect for Hawfinch, Greenfinch, Serin, Great Spotted Cuckoo and Azure-winged Magpie.

The desert and sand-dune area, with moving dunes, are within the protected zone. Spur-thighed Tortoise, Lataste's Viper and Montpellier Snake can be seen here, with thousands of wintering Greylag Geese.

Finally, the areas of maquis scrub, between the dunes and the marsh, also within the protected zone, hold Mongoose, Stonechat, Woodchat and Great Grey Shrikes, Wall Lizards, Sun Rose, French Lavender, Thyme and cistus species.

Due to its international significance,

Spanish Imperial Eagle *Aquila heliaca adalberti*
L 70–80, W 175–210

A large magnificent eagle that truly deserves the name 'Imperial'. The bird found in Spain is a subspecies, distinguished from the subspecies *heliaca* found in Asia by the white shoulders which are quite visible from a distance; the rest of the adult plumage is rich brown. The immatures are pale brown with a dark-streaked breast and characteristically pale, creamy-white lower back.

There are only 100 pairs left in Spain. Their main stronghold is in the Parque Nacional de Coto Doñana where twenty pairs breed in most years. They build their large nests on the upper branches of the Umbrella Pine and the male can often be seen perched on the topmost branches keeping guard. Another major breeding area is within the Monfragüe Natural Park. Both these areas have integral reserves with restricted entry.

Their main food is Rabbit and other small mammals, but they will also take duck.

access to a large area has been completely restricted and a scientific research centre has been built next to the Palacio de Doñana. There are two established information centres, closed on Mondays and also for ten days over Whitsun. The smaller one, near El Rocio bridge, has a large car-park, and is the stepping-off point for the hides, with a drive to the Acebrón Palace Museum. The larger one is near Matalascañas. This also has a large car-park. The centre is built in the form of an old 'cortijo' (manor house). One wing is a museum explaining the importance of the Spanish wetlands and in particular Doñana. The second wing is a snack bar and sales area, while in the centre section is an auditorium where film shows are held several times daily highlighting Doñana's importance. This centre is the meeting place for the 'safari trips' and for viewing the various hides.

This extremely important area has been threatened by tourist developments which would have lowered the water table. Such development now seems to have been halted.

As this is such a large and important ecological area, five separate sites are described.

107 SAFARI TOUR AND THE ACEBUCHE HIDES	
Grid reference:	U/V 10
Location:	SE of Huelva and SW of Sevilla
Access:	Excellent
Season:	All year round
Terrain:	Marshland, dunes, woodland and beach
Comments:	Information centre; closed for 10 days over Whitsun; no safaris on Mondays
Specialities:	Purple Gallinule, Marbled Teal, Spanish Imperial Eagle, Pardel Lynx, Wild Boar

The El Acebuche main centre is 4km from Matalascañas on the El Rocio road and is well signposted. Here there are some well-marked pathways leading to a series of hides which overlook the 33ha Laguna de los Pájaros. Directions are given on a leaflet obtained from the centre. From the well-appointed

Sand dunes in the Coto Doñana Reserve which can be seen on the safari tour. Fallow Deer (Dama dama) are resting in the shade of an Umbrella Pine (Pinus pinea). There are large numbers of Fallow and Red Deer (Cervus elaphas) within the reserve and although they are shy, they are very easily seen, especially in the morning when they move to the watering holes.

hides you can observe a large variety of duck, including with luck the rare Marbled Teal, as well as Purple Gallinule, Great Crested and Little Grebes, Kingfisher and, within the trees, Azure-winged Magpies. Little and Cattle Egrets nest on the far side of the lake and part of one hide may be 'out of bounds' to protect the nesting Swallow! On returning to the centre, take note of the White Stork's nest on the reception tower.

From the reception, the safari tours can be joined. These must be booked in advance, as part of Andalucía's education programme is to introduce the young to the importance of wildlife conservation and several coach-loads arrive daily, bringing children to join the tours. There are two tours each day, but none on Mondays.

A typical 80km tour leaves the centre, travelling in overland vehicles, passes Matalascañas and enters the park through a series of sand dunes. You then enjoy an exciting 30km beach drive, seeing the Sanderlings, Oystercatchers, Sandwich Terns and Kentish Plovers take to the wing as the vehicles pass. You may also see the Peregrine on the ruined

Carbonero tower. The tour then heads inland through a wooded area and past the reed-built charcoal burners' homes. A stop at a glade, followed by a short walk produces fine views of deer and Wild Boar, and with extreme luck the Pardel Lynx. From here you continue on past the river and salt marshland, travelling by the newly renovated Palacio de las Marismillas to a marshland stop, seeing waders and Greater Flamingo, and possibly a distant glimpse of the Spanish Imperial Eagle.

After an area of garigue countryside you reach the moving sand-dune area with another stop. These dunes move at a rate of 5m per year. As they move the slack (depression) left behind becomes moist and soon rejuvenates with young pines and scrub, only to be overtaken again by another wave of sand a few years later. Mature trees become submerged as the dunes can attain a height of 30m. This is an important roosting place for Greylag Geese in winter. This sand area is interesting as many fascinating tracks can be seen in the rippled sands. Finally after about four hours the trip returns to the centre.

Although, as it is an organized party, you cannot stop when and where you want, the guides are excellent and pause if anything of interest appears. They are all well trained and conversant with Latin and Spanish names, and an occasional English one.

The tour described here may be changed slightly, due to the time of day, nesting birds (the Spanish Imperial Eagle in particular must not be disturbed), track conditions or maybe the whim of the leader!

108 ROCINA HIDES AND THE PALACIO DEL ACEBRON	
Grid reference:	U 10
Location:	SE of Huelva and SW of Sevilla
Access:	Very good
Season:	All year round
Terrain:	Woodland and river
Comments:	Information centre; closed on Mondays and over Whitsun El Rocio Festival
Specialities:	Crested Tit, Hawfinch, Red-crested Pochard, Fallow Deer, Swallowtail

The Rocina information centre is situated just inside the wrought-iron gates south of the El Rocio bridge (see Site 109). There is a good car-park. This centre has leaflets giving directions to the hides and also about the Palacio del Acebrón exhibition entitled 'Man and Doñana'.

The hides are situated along a well-marked route and pass through three types of habitat: a *Phragmites* marshland, where there are numerous Cetti's, Great Reed and Dartford Warblers and in summer multitudes of Nightingales singing; a mature pine wood with Crested, Great and Blue Tits, Short-toed Treecreeper, Chaffinch and Hoopoe;

and finally along the river bank where there are three hides from which Red-crested Pochard, Shoveler, Coot and with luck Marbled Teal can usually be seen.

Drive to the Palacio del Acebrón where there is another good car-park. This is now an exhibition centre depicting the marismas and the life of man past and present within them. In the grounds there is another well-marked walk through mature woodland of pines, evergreens and some deciduous trees. Here can be seen a large number of woodland birds, in particular the rare Hawfinch.

A multitude of butterflies in the area include Swallowtail, Painted Lady, Two-tailed Pasha and Great Banded Grayling.

109 'THE BRIDGE', EL ROCIO	
Grid reference:	U 10
Location:	SE of Huelva and SW of Sevilla
Access:	Excellent
Season:	All year round
Terrain:	Freshwater marshes
Comments:	For birdwatching, avoid Whitsun weekend
Specialities:	Spoonbill, Greylag Goose, Ruff, Black Kite, Whiskered Tern

This insignificant bridge over the small river outside the town of El Rocio is world famous as one of the finest places in Europe for watching marshland birds, and is a great meeting place for ornithologists. During the evening many thousands of birds fly over to feed on the marshes. During summer, the marshes are usually dry and grazed by horses, but Coot, Black-winged Stilts and Avocets breed by the river.

As soon as the first rains come, usually in late September, the marsh becomes shallowly flooded and is soon covered with ducks

A famous view of El Rocio from 'The Bridge'.

which winter there. Groups of Spoonbills will be feeding with a sweeping motion and later in the autumn they will be joined by thousands of Greylag Geese which have come down from northern Europe. Immature Greater Flamingo still in their drab brown plumage stand around in small groups. Waders in their hundreds will stop to feed on the annual migration: Redshank, Spotted Redshank, Greenshank, Ringed Plover, Kentish Plover, Common Sandpiper and Ruff all occur. Many White Storks feed on the frogs which abound, and Black and Whiskered Terns pick insects off the water's surface. Red and Black Kites play acrobatically looking for food, while during summer, Bee-eaters, those beautiful kaleidoscopic birds, catch insects which fly near their perch. This is an enthralling spot.

110 COTO DEL REY	
Grid reference:	U 10
Location:	SE of Huelva and SW of Sevilla
Access:	Fair, either by sand tracks or better on foot
Season:	All year round
Terrain:	Woodland
Comments:	Can be extremely wet in the rainy season
Specialities:	Red Kite, Azure-winged Magpie, Great Spotted Cuckoo, Hoopoe, Egyptian Mongoose

Situated almost due east of the town of El Rocio, which is famous for the Whitsun pilgrimage. It is within easy walking distance of the town. Walking is advised as the sandy tracks at times make it almost impassible for non four-wheeled drive vehicles.

The Azure-winged Magpie (Cyanopica cyana) is one of the more spectacular birds found in Spain. Originally introduced from the Far East, it can now be found throughout much of Iberia.

III THE MARISMAS OF THE NORTH PRE-PARK	
Grid reference:	U 10
Location:	SE of Huelva and SW of Sevilla
Access:	On foot from Coto del Rey
Season:	All year round
Terrain:	Marshland and cereal-growing land
Specialities:	Calandra Lark, Marsh Harrier, Pin-tailed Sandgrouse, Purple Heron, Squacco Heron

This is a magnificent woodland area, adjacent to the enclosed Coto Doñana Reserve and known as the pre-park. The sandy track goes through a wooded area, where Umbrella Pines, Cork Oak and Ilex Oak provide excellent feeding grounds for Azure-winged Magpie, Woodpigeon, Hoopoe, Black and Red Kites, Great Spotted Woodpecker, Great Spotted Cuckoo and a host of small woodland birds.

Mongooses may be seen hunting in the area, but are very shy. Rabbits in vast numbers dig their burrows in the soft sandy land. From this pre-park area Wild Boar and Fallow Deer roam within the Coto perimeter and can easily be seen. The Spanish Imperial Eagle may be seen hunting overhead.

Situated beyond the Coto del Rey, the marismas can, ground permitting, be approached by continuing along from the woods at Coto del Rey, bearing to the right and thus reaching the causeway. Failing this, a long detour is necessary, for which the Parque

Nacional de Doñana 1/50,000 map is necessary if the ground is waterlogged (available at Acebuche information centre), with the aim to reach Estacion de bombeo de los Caracoles (37° 01" N 6° 17" W) on the border of the enclosed National Park. This area is private marshlands and borders the Doñana Park which is enclosed on the southern side. It is used for grazing or has been reclaimed for cereal growing. Fallow Deer can often be seen in the park. Rabbits abound in the sandy burrows on the edge of the woodland.

An astounding variety of birds can be seen from the roads which criss-cross this vast area: Pin-tailed Sandgrouse, Marsh and Montagu's Harriers, Calandra Lark, Yellow Wagtail, many waders in the shallow pools, Night, Purple and Squacco Herons, Black and White Storks, Greater Flamingo and Pratincole. Breeding birds include Avocet, Black-winged Stilt, Mallard, all the species of heron, Black and Whiskered Terns, Bee-eater and a host of other birds.

During migration Green, Marsh and Wood Sandpipers, Redshank, Spotted Redshank and Greenshank can be found and during the winter Pintail, Wigeon, Shoveler and Pochard abound. Red-crested Pochard, White-headed Duck, Marbled Teal and Mallard can be seen throughout the year.

Do not forget to look overhead, as there are many high-flying birds to be seen. Griffon and Egyptian Vultures soar on the thermals, clouds of migrating waders and ducks race past, or a lone Spanish Imperial Eagle might glide into view. Dead trees and fence posts nearer the Coto del Rey are used as lookout posts for raptors, such as vultures and kites, and many smaller birds including shrikes and wheatears. Beside the roadways in the reedbeds, the Purple Heron hides with his neck held motionless like a walking stick.

Cattle Egrets (Bubulcus ibis) at a watering hole bordering the north pre-park marismas. Herons of many species abound in the Coto Doñana.

9. CENTRAL ANDALUCÍA

INTRODUCTION

The border of Central Andalucía, moving clockwise, begins in the west at Algeciras, moves north through Sevilla to Extremadura Province, follows the province border as far east as Desfiladero de Despeñaperros, then moves south through Jaén and Granada to Motril on the Mediterranean. Its southern border is formed by the sea.

This region is very mountainous with the smooth-topped, rolling, wooded range of the Sierra Morena in

The Marsh Frog (Rana Ridibunda) *is found throughout Spain. It grows to 12cm in length.*

the north. The wide valley of the famous Río Guadalquivir is an enormous dry, treeless, cereal-growing area. In the vast plains of lighter soil are extensive plantations of Olive trees cultivated mainly for oil. This is economically a very important crop and Andalucía is Spain's major olive oil centre. The southern half of the region consists of high craggy limestone mountains rising to 2065m (6775 feet) in the sierras just north of Malaga. These mountains are heavily wooded but have some grasslands for grazing goats and sheep. Near villages in the flatter land, fields of vegetables and Olive groves predominate.

The narrow coastal strip, just a couple of kilometres wide, is devoted to mass tourism: golf courses, villa developments, some high-rise apartments and hotels, as well as

beautiful subtropical gardens abound.

The climate is very variable, with the mountains near Grazalema having 210cm (83 inches) of rain annually, while the coastline receives less than half that amount, mostly during the winter months. Storms can occur during the summer in the mountainous regions. Summer can be very hot, especially in the Guadalquivir basin where temperatures often reach 40°C. Near the coast the temperature is cooler due to sea breezes. In winter, it can be cold in the mountains with frequent snow. Frost and even a little snow can occur on the lower ground in the interior, but in the coastal strip with an almost subtropical climate the daytime temperature rarely drops below 10°C.

There is a vast range of habitats within this region. The mountain tops of the Sierras of Grazalema and Ronda are subalpine in nature and are rich in plants. The peaks are a stronghold of the Spanish Ibex. Coniferous forest covers large areas, especially on the southern slopes of Sierra Bermeja in the south and Sierra Morena in the north. Near Ronda there are broad-leaved evergreen woodlands containing extensive areas of Cork Oak. Salt and freshwater marshes are almost non-existent due to the lack of river exits and the abrupt fall of the mountains towards the sea. However, freshwater is provided by the Río Guadalquivir from which large areas of land are irrigated between Andujar and west through Cordoba and Sevilla. Maquis scrub occurs in the foothills

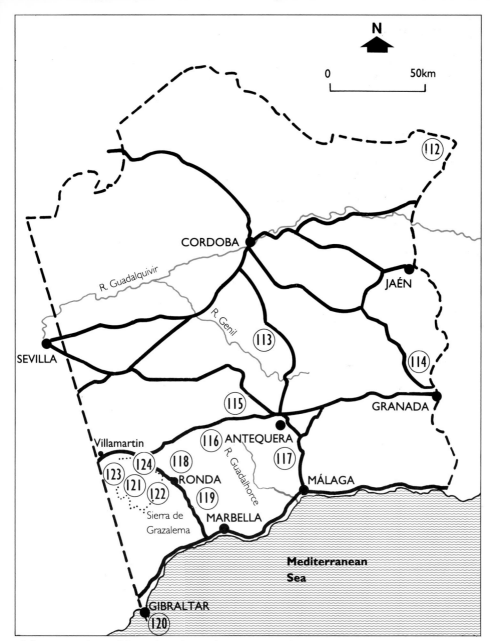

Map of central Andalucía. The sites are numbered as in the text. Only main roads and the major rivers of the region are shown.

of the mountains and in spring gives colour to this fascinating area.

The grid references used in the following site descriptions relate to Michelin map number 446.

A common scene with colourful Oleanders, which typifies the inland moist valleys of central Andalucía.

FIFTY INTERESTING SPECIES TO LOOK FOR

Slender-billed Gull	Black Wheatear	Wild Boar	*Linaria platycalyx*
Short-toed Eagle ✓	Rock Bunting	Spanish Ibex	*Narcissus rupicola*
Spanish Imperial	Woodchat Shrike ✓	Swallowtail	*Ornithogalum*
Eagle	Chough ✓	Scarce Swallowtail	*reverchonii*
Honey Buzzard ✓	Parsley Frog	Cleopatra	*Paeonia broteroi*
Marsh Harrier	Marsh Frog	Cardinal	*Papaver rupifragum*
Black Kite ✓	Western	Clouded Yellow ✓	*Tulipa australis*
Griffon Vulture ✓	Spadefoot Toad	Escher's Blue	*Viola demetria*
Purple Gallinule	Psammodromus	*Biscutella frutescens*	Hoop Petticoat
Black Stork	Lizard	*Centaurea clementei*	Narcissus
Eagle Owl	Egyptian	*Digitalis purpurea*	Bee Orchid
Scops Owl	Mongoose	*ssp. mariana*	Giant Orchid
Red-crested	Badger	Gibraltar	Lizard Orchid
Pochard	Genet	Candytuft	Pink Butterfly
Barbary Partridge	Otter	*Iris planifolia*	Orchid

112 DESFILADERO DE DESPEÑAPERROS	
Grid reference:	Q 19
Location:	N of Bailén
Access:	Excellent
Season:	All year round
Terrain:	Rugged cliffs
Comments:	Parking is difficult and may have to be on local minor roads
Specialities:	Golden Eagle, Egyptian Mongoose, *Paeonia broteroi, Digitalis purpurea ssp. mariana, Jasione crispa ssp. mariana*
Subsidiary:	Coto Nacional de Cortadero, Q/R 18; Santuario Virgen de la Cabeza, R 17

Paeonia broteroi, a common gem within the hilly areas around Desfiladero de Despeñaperros.

This gorge is about 40km north of Bailén on the N IV/E 25. The long mountain range of Sierra Morena forms a 500km barrier between the Río Guadalquivir basin and the dry La Mancha plain of central Spain. At Desfiladero de Despeñaperros is a deep natural gorge giving access from Madrid to southern Spain. Through it runs a train link, and a dual carriageway with one track on each side of the ravine, up to 1km apart.

During May the hillsides, which are covered with the sticky-leaved Gum Cistus, become smothered with large white flowers up to 12cm across, each with a purple spot at the base of each petal, looking like handkerchieves put out to dry! In the rocky areas are two endemic plants, *Jasione crispa ssp. mariana*, and the foxglove *Digitalis purpurea ssp. mariana*.

In the valley there are mixed woods containing broad-leaved evergreen oak and here may be seen the beautiful *Paeonia broteroi* with large rose-coloured flowers, the yellow Palmate Anenome and *Tulipa australis*. Also look out for the Bug Orchid.

Foxes and Rabbits are plentiful but are hunted during the open season. A few Wolves are still in the high mountain and are rigorously protected. Wild Boar, Mongoose, Badger and Genet are present but are mainly nocturnal and therefore not often seen.

Imperial and Golden Eagle, Eagle Owl, Black Stork, Rock Bunting, Rock Thrush, Black-eared and Black Wheatears, and Great Grey and Woodchat Shrikes may all be seen.

113 LAGUNAS DE CORDOBA	
Grid reference:	T/U 15/16
Location:	S of Cordoba
Access:	Good
Season:	All year
Terrain:	Saltwater lakes, reservoirs, within undulating farm land
Comments:	Can be hot in summer
Specialities:	White-headed Duck, Purple Heron, Purple Gallinule, Avocet, Black-winged Stilt
Subsidiary:	Natural Park, Sierras Subbéticas Cordobesas, T/U 16/17

White-headed Duck
Oxyura leucocephala L 46

The White-headed Duck is a member of the 'stiff-tail' group, where the tail is held almost vertically, giving it an unmistakable appearance. The bill of the drake is very distinctive, very large and in spring-time during the breeding season a beautiful pale blue.

At the beginning of this century there were estimated to be at least 500 breeding pairs in southern Spain. With the drainage of the wetlands and the general destruction of the habitat, the population decreased to only fifty breeding pairs by 1979. A group of ornithologists and enthusiasts, lead by Francisco Palma Flores, realized that if immediate remedial action was not taken this species would be extinct in Spain. 'The Friends of the White-headed Duck' was formed in the Andalucían area and the results of their labours have paid off, with 500 pairs again recorded each year after ten years of conservation.

The world-wide population at the end of the 1980s was 12,000 birds, existing mainly in Asia and eastern Europe. Spain is proud of her achievement in having a good proportion of the overall number.

An area with ten lakes and two reservoirs situated south of Cordoba. The first six lakes were designated Integral Reserves in October 1984. One of the more important, Laguna de Zóñar, is situated on the C 329 between Aguilar and Puente-Genil. At the lake there is a reception and information centre.

Lagunas de Zóñar, del Rincon and Amarga are permanent, with Lagunas del Salobral, de Tiscar and de los Jarales seasonal. Dulce, Santiago, Vedohondo and Taraje are semi-permanent lakes and Malpasillo and Cordobilla are reservoirs.

The first six lakes are all important breeding or wintering areas for birds. Laguna del Rincon is the most important for the breeding White-headed Duck (*see* box), with Zóñar and Amarga important for some breeding pairs and for wintering birds of this species.

During migration many waders stop to feed and often Greater Flamingo can be seen. In the *Phragmites* reeds and other growth at the sides of the lakes, Purple Heron, Purple Gallinule, Avocet, Black-winged Stilt, Red-crested Pochard, Mallard and Coot all breed. During winter Tufted Duck, Shoveler and Lapwings will be seen. Great-crested and Little Grebes are present all year round, as is the Marsh Harrier.

114 MOCLIN	
Grid reference:	T 18
Location:	NW of Granada
Access:	Good
Season:	Spring and autumn
Terrain:	Coniferous woodland
Comments:	Can be hot in summer and cold in winter
Specialities:	Peregrine, Egyptian Vulture, Griffon Vulture, Chough, Sardinian Warbler
Subsidiary:	Sierra de Cabra, Luque, Priego y Rute, T 17

Moclin is approximately 25km from Granada, approached from the south by the N 432. Just north of Pinos Puente turn right towards Tiena and on to Moclin. The road winds across an undulating plain through Olive groves almost as far as the eye can see. Each large village has its own cooperative for processing and refining Olive oil which gives an unmistakable aroma. The oil is of major economic importance.

Moclin, a fortified village reached by a steep road, is clustered around the high promontory which rises dramatically from the eastern plain to 1307m (4300 feet) giving a panoramic view towards the Sierra Nevada 50km to the south. The local coniferous woods with a thick undergrowth of Gum Cistus, Sage-leaved Cistus and *Genista*, hold irises and orchids, especially the Green-winged Orchid in spring.

Near the village are small cultivated plots with vegetables and cherry trees predominating. Small birds such as Chaffinch, Great Tits and Sardinian Warbler are evident in the woodlands, while within the craggy outcrops are a large number of breeding birds, notably Peregrine, Chough, and Egyptian and Griffon Vultures.

115 LAGUNA DE LA FUENTE DE PIEDRA	
Grid reference:	U 15
Location:	NW of Antequera
Access:	Good
Season:	All year round
Terrain:	Large shallow lake, surrounded by agricultural land
Comments:	Insect repellent may be needed; information centre
Specialities:	Greater Flamingo, Gull-billed Tern, Stone Curlew, Parsley Frog, Psammodromus Lizard
Subsidiary:	Laguna Dulce, U 15

This lake is situated about 22km north-west of Antequera. Take the N 334 as far as the village of Fuente de Piedra, cross the railway line onto the MA 454 and turn left after 150m on to the signposted track. Parking is available at the information centre.

This is the largest natural lake in Andalucía. It is highly saline and surrounded by dry cereal farmland, Olive groves and vines. The

View from Moclin overlooking the village of Tiena, with the Sierra Nevada in the far distance. After a drive through an arid plain and cool woods, this magnificent panorama appears, revealing a landscape far below dotted with Olive trees.

Greater Flamingo
Phoenicopterus ruber L 135, W 155

There is no more beautiful sight than a large flock of Greater Flamingo rising as a pink cloud when the sun is setting on a still summer evening, necks outstretched, legs trailing and their black-tipped vivid pink wings flapping slowly, the colour enhanced by the sinking sun.

Flamingos are very particular in their feeding habits, requiring high salinity which sustains the crustaceans and vegetable matter on which they feed. They filter this particular matter using their strongly modified bills.

The Greater Flamingo can be found in most highly saline areas on the Mediterranean and south Atlantic coasts of Spain. It is also often seen at a variety of sites while on migration from the Camargue in France or Fuente de Piedra. The latter is now the foremost breeding site in Europe; in 1990 14,000 pairs reared 12,000 young here.

This has become the foremost area in Europe for breeding Greater Flamingos (*see* box). Slender-billed Gulls and Gull-billed Terns breed by the lake, with Marsh Harrier and Stone Curlew breeding in the surrounding fields. It is a wintering area for small numbers of Crane. Many waders are also seen.

The surrounding marshy area has many amphibians and reptiles: Marsh and Parsley Frogs, Western Spadefoot Toad and Psammodromus Lizard to mention just a few.

116 TEBA GORGE	
Grid reference:	V 15
Location:	W of Antequera, NE of Ronda
Access:	Excellent
Season:	All year round, but best in spring and early summer
Terrain:	Limestone hills covered with Olive trees
Comments:	Heavy footwear is advised
Specialities:	Bonelli's Eagle, Egyptian Vulture, Blue Rock Thrush, Cardinal, Oleander

Situated 28km west of Antequera and 36km north-east of Ronda on the C 341. From Antequera join the N 342 and at Campillos take the C 341 towards Ronda. At kilometre post 14, at the bridge over the Río de la Venta, is a small, deep and rugged gorge cut into the hard limestone hills, the river emptying into the nearby reservoir Embalse del Guadalteba-Guadalhorce, near the picturesque hill-top village of Teba.

Opposite: Teba Gorge is a small but beautiful gorge cut into the limestone hills.

edge of the lake is fairly open, but where there is vegetation it is of the typical salt-marsh variety with abundant Glasswort (*Salicornia*). The lake, 2000ha in extent, is very shallow. In the past, it tended to dry up during the hot, dry, summer months, but recent work has prevented this from happening again in the future.

This small gorge is very well worth a visit, as the smallest of the European vultures, the Egyptian, nests here in association with Bonelli's Eagle. Black Kites and Choughs can usually be seen patrolling the skies. Black-eared Wheatear, Black Redstart and Blue Rock Thrush can commonly be seen hopping from rock to rock, whilst in the valley by the river, Oleanders have secured a foothold amongst the boulders.

Look out for butterflies: the Swallowtail and Scarce Swallowtail, numerous blues and the Cardinal, one of the largest of the fritillaries.

From the road-side bridge, a steep rugged path winds downwards. This is well worth taking as it meanders through the gorge where most of the birds can be seen.

117 EL TORCAL DE ANTEQUERA	
Grid reference:	V 16
Location:	S of Antequera
Access:	Good
Season:	Spring, summer and autumn
Terrain:	Spectacularly sculptured limestone rocks
Comments:	Normal clothing with good walking shoes; information centre
Specialities:	Griffon Vulture, Black Wheatear, Iris subbiflora, Clouded Yellow, Woodcock Orchid
Subsidiary:	Menga and Viera Dolmen Caves on the N 342 to Archidona immediately outside Antequera, U 16

Situated approximately 14km by road to the south of Antequera. Leave on the well-signed

C 3310. Shortly after passing the panoramic view over the Sierra de las Cabras, turn right towards Torcal de Antequera. The road continues until it reaches the official car-park with the AMA information centre which is open during the morning and late afternoon.

This is one of the most spectacular geological karstic formations in Europe. It is an amazing collection of sculptured limestone rocks covering 1200ha, that wind and rain have weathered into bizarre forms, many of which have been given fanciful names!

There are two arrowed walks, red and yellow, easily followed. The 1.5hr yellow walk is considerably easier than the 6hr red one. The time allowed is generous. Griffon Vulture, Black Redstart and Black Wheatear should be seen. Thirty species of orchids occur at this site, including the rare Lizard, Pink Butterfly, Woodcock and Dense-flowered Orchids. *Iris subbiflora*, the yellow annual *Viola demetria*, the violet Spring Rock Cress and the endemic *Saxifraga biternata* should be seen. Various species of lizard are common. Butterflies include many blues, skippers and the Swallowtail.

118 RONDA GORGE	
Grid reference:	V 14
Location:	Within the town of Ronda
Access:	Excellent
Season:	All year round
Terrain:	High limestone mountains with intensive cultivation in the valley
Comments:	Normal walking shoes
Specialities:	Chough, Rock Dove, Alpine Swift, Blue Rock Thrush, Black Redstart
Subsidiary:	Sierra Bermeja, W 14

The deep gorge at Ronda taken from the bridge looking towards the Serranía de Ronda. The gorge is a haven for birds and species such as Alpine Swift, Blue Rock Thrush, Black Redstart and Chough should all be seen.

Swallows and Alpine Swifts can be seen screaming, diving and turning, capturing insects in flight, whilst overhead, Choughs, with their broad wings and red bills perform their acrobatic flight. Blue Rock Thrush and Black Redstart can be seen foraging amongst the rocks on the cliff face.

The surrounding countryside is mountainous, but the valleys are well cultivated with maize and vegetables, and the hillsides are wooded with Olive and Cork Oak trees.

In spring some areas are blue with *Iris planifolia*, which is very local in limestone areas.

119 RESERVA NACIONAL DE SERRANIA DE RONDA	
Grid reference:	V/W 14/15
Location:	S of Ronda, NW of Marbella
Access:	Basically good, but tracks must be found for walking
Season:	All year round
Terrain:	Forest and mountain
Comments:	Sensible walking shoes
Specialities:	Golden Eagle, Spanish Ibex, *Erinacae anthyllis, Genista triacanthos, Narcissus cantabricus*
Subsidiary:	Cueva de la Pileta, V 14; interesting for plants in the area, but the cave itself has paintings dating back to 25,000BC

Situated within the town of Ronda, this amazing limestone gorge, 100m in depth, cuts the town in two. A short road bridge built in 1793 (for its time a great feat of engineering) joins the old town with the new. The new town is built on a 100m precipice with fantastic views over the surrounding countryside.

Ronda, whether one approves or not, is still noted for its classical bullfighting school, with strict observance of the rules. Its bullring, built in 1785, is one of the oldest in the country.

From the bridge, looking down, Swifts,

This site is north-west of Marbella and southeast of Ronda, and is reached by the C 339. Several interesting tracks can be explored. The highest peak is Torrecilla at 1919m (6296 feet). The large reserve is noted not only for its flora and butterflies, but also for the Spanish Ibex which is well established but

Orobanche foetida

The broomrape family Orobanchacea is parasitic. The sticky seeds have to actually touch the roots of host plants before they germinate.

This particular plant feeds from the roots of Leguminosae species, especially of the gorse group. They cannot manufacture chlorophyll and therefore have no green colouring.

O. foetida has a very strong flower stem up to 60cm high. The flowering spike is conical in shape and has a large number of striking deep blood-red flowers. Unfortunately it has a rather disagreeable odour, hence its name. It is not uncommon, but because of its habit it is botanically interesting, being found in most places where its host plants grow, especially in southern, sandy, scrubland areas where Gorse and *Coronilla* predominate.

elusive, keeping to higher rocky slopes.

A few groups of the highly protected Spanish Fir are present. The occasional *Biarum carratracenae* is found, its pink spadix appearing after the leaves have died, followed later by the red seed heads. Cork Oaks can be found on the lower ground with Maritime Pine higher up, where *Narcissus cantabricus* pushes through the pine needles and peonies flower in the more open areas. Many orchids can be found throughout the reserve.

Above the treeline the land is rocky and bare with little pockets of soil in which the prostrate *Prunus prostrata* grows flat against the rocks, and two interesting 'hedgehog' plants, *Erinacae anthyllis* and *Genista triacanthos* dot the landscape. Throughout this region butterflies are plentiful in number and variety. Look out for the Scarce Swallowtail, which is more striped and less colourful than the Swallowtail which is also found here.

The rocky mountainsides provide ideal nesting sites for a large variety of birds, mainly Golden, Bonelli's and Booted Eagles higher up, while in the lower wooded areas many smaller birds, such as Short-toed Treecreeper, woodpeckers, Magpie and Little Owl nest. As well as the Ibex, Wild Cat and Genet can be seen in the higher zones, with Roe Deer common in the woods.

120 GIBRALTAR	✓
Grid reference:	X 13
Location:	Peninsula SW of Marbella and E of Algeciras
Access:	Excellent
Season:	All year round, but particularly migration periods
Terrain:	Huge limestone outcrop
Comments:	Normal clothing
Specialities:	Barbary Ape, Barbary Partridge, Honey Buzzard, Gibraltar Candytuft, *Antirrhinum majus*

This site is situated 58km south-west of Marbella and 10km east of Algeciras. It is a huge limestone bastion linked with Spain by a narrow isthmus from la Linea de la Concepción. Gibraltar covers an area of 5.8km², rising to 398m (1300 feet). It is only 14km from Africa and therefore forms the most important 'bridge' for migrating birds in western Europe. For example, during the southward passage of migration between July and October, as many as 20,000 Honey Buzzards have been recorded in a single season.

'The Rock', as it is called, is the only place in Europe where the Barbary Ape is wild, although very heavily protected (*see* box). The Barbary Partridge is found only here in Iberia, in areas where there is sufficient scrub for cover.

A plant which should not be missed is the Gibraltar Candytuft with pink flowers, blooming in May. In Europe, its only location is on the limestone scree on the eastern side of the Rock.

This site is good all the year round, with emphasis on the spring and autumn migratory periods, and spring for the flowers. A flourishing ornithological and natural history society has its headquarters at the Gibraltar Museum.

SIERRA DE GRAZALEMA NATURAL PARK

The Sierra de Grazalema is an area virtually bounded by the towns of Grazalema, Ubrique, El Bosque and Zahara, situated to the west of Ronda and approached by the C 344. It is a vast botanical treasure house within high craggy limestone mountains. A restricted reserve has been designated on the north side of the Sierra del Pinar to protect the rare Spanish Fir (*Abies pinsapo*), which is only

Barbary Ape *Macaca sylvanus* L 60–71

This is not in fact an ape, but one of the twelve species of macaque normally found in Asia. This is the only species found outside Asia, in North Africa and Gibraltar, and is the only wild monkey in Europe. How they came to the Rock is unknown. They either could have been brought over from North Africa or are a remnant of a species once common throughout Europe before the last ice age.

There are about fifty within the two packs which roam their own territories in the middle and upper regions of the Rock. At the beginning of the century they became a nuisance within the town and were consequently allotted a keeper from the British Army, whose job it still is to feed and be responsible for their welfare. They are wild animals and must be treated with respect as they can be vicious if touched.

found here and in one or two adjacent sites and is easily destroyed when young by goats.

It is one of the wettest areas in Spain, with an annual rainfall of 210cm (83 inches). There is usually luxuriant vegetation in the valleys which hold *Iris planifolia*, Hoop Petticoat Narcissus, Jonquil and many orchids, such as Bee, Mirror, Woodcock, Lizard, Man, Pale-flowered, Green-winged and Sawfly Orchid to mention but a few. On the

A general view of the Sierra de Grazalema.

mountainsides and in crevices the rare endemic *Papaver rupifragum*, a brick-red poppy, *Biscutella frutescens, Saxifraga globulifera, S. boissieri* and *S. haenseleri*, may all be found with the small *Narcissus rupicola*.

The mountains are rich in bird life: Griffon Vulture, Bonelli's, Booted and Short-toed Eagles, Buzzard, Chough and Raven all nest. Scops Owl will be heard in the woods, and Great Spotted Woodpecker, Short-toed Treecreeper, Woodlark, Wren and Stonechat feeding amongst the foliage should be seen. Dippers and Otters can with luck be found along the river banks, on high lives the Spanish Ibex and in the meadow lands deer graze. In Grazalema there is a small information centre, with a large one in El Bosque. One- and two-day riding tours (on horseback) can be arranged with details from the Ronda Tourist Office.

121 GRAZALEMA	
Grid reference:	V 13
Location:	W of Ronda
Access:	Good
Season:	All year round
Terrain:	High limestone mountains
Comments:	Good walking shoes essential; information centre
Specialities:	Scops Owl, Bonelli's Eagle, Spanish Ibex, *Iris planifolia*, Sawfly Orchid

This is a delightful and typical 'white village' of Andalucía, with narrow flower-bedecked streets nestled in a valley and huge rocky limestone cliffs towering above. It is reached by taking the C 339 west from Ronda for approximately 17km and then turning left

156

Grazalema village in the early morning, nestling within the mountain valley.

onto the C 344. A small but useful information centre is situated just off the main square.

Walking is the best way to explore the area which is wonderfully rich in plant life. In crevices in the rocks *Centaurea clementei*, a knapweed with large woolly leaves and yellow flowers, the rare *Linaria platycalyx*, a toadflax with small yellow snapdragon-like flowers and a purple-lipped spur, and the endemic *Ornithogalum reverchonii*, a star-of-Bethlehem with white bluebell-type flowers, all make a spectacular show. The earliest flower to appear in spring is the delightful *Iris planifolia*, which can turn areas blue-violet with its flowers. This is almost immediately followed by the yellow Hoop Petticoat Narcissus and a mass of orchid species, especially the Sawfly Orchid.

You will almost always see Griffon Vultures gliding on thermals and Choughs playing around the craggy peaks, and if lucky a Bonelli's Eagle may be seen hunting. The Spanish Ibex is here in small numbers on the higher ground.

122 GRAZALEMA TO UBRIQUE	
Grid reference:	V 13
Location:	W of Ronda
Access:	Easy on the C 3331
Season:	All year round
Terrain:	Scrub-covered valley and occasional farmland
Specialities:	Chough, Cleopatra, Escher's Blue, Lizard Orchid, *Papaver rupifragum*

The C 3331 from Grazalema to Ubrique is a fascinating road. It first follows a very well-cultivated valley with grazing cattle and sheep, but soon becomes wild, with high rocky sides which are well worth exploring. There is Verbascum by the roadside and a very fine Salvia near the little village of Villaluenga del Rosario. Orchids are common in the meadows, especially the spectacular Lizard Orchid. The rare *Papaver rupifragum* can also be found here. Just after this point it is worth taking a diversion to the right to the village of Benaocaz and exploring the adjoining area. Here there is a typical glacial valley, with high walls and a gently rounded valley bottom. The mountain crags are inhabited by breeding Bonelli's and Booted Eagles, with Griffon Vultures and Choughs usually seen.

Butterflies abound on the flowering hillsides. The yellow and orange Cleopatra is one of the earliest to appear. The Cardinal is striking and common, whilst there is always a mass of skippers and blues, notably Escher's Blue.

Pinsapo, the rare Spanish Fir (Abies pinsapo) *in the environs of El Bosque.*

123 EL BOSQUE

Grid reference:	V 13
Location:	W of Ronda
Access:	Excellent
Season:	All year round
Terrain:	Woodland and river valley
Comments:	Information centre
Specialities:	Short-toed Treecreeper, Great Spotted Woodpecker, Spanish Ibex, Spanish Fir, *Ornithogalum reverchonii*

El Bosque is another 'white village' situated on the western edge of Sierra del Pinar amongst fine woods of evergreen oaks and pines. It is 18km west of Grazalema (*see* Site 121) on the C 344.

There is a reception centre situated within

the outskirts of the village on the road to Arcos de la Frontera, on the southern side. Here there is a small museum of some interest. Leaflets and information about the various walks are available within the Grazalema Natural Park, all graded according to ability from a gentle one-way only walk to more exerting ten-hour treks for experienced walkers.

One gentler walk is from Benamahoma to El Bosque, suggested this way round because one follows the river on its downward course. It is approximately 5km long and drops from 420m to 240m (1380–790 feet) in altitude. To appreciate it to the full, the woodlands, the river, the various ways in which the river has been used to benefit the surrounding countryside, takes approximately two and a half hours.

During this downward walk a number of the river inhabitants can be seen as well as a number of the woodland ones There may be a ripple as a Water Vole crosses the stream or an Otter may slide silently into the water. The latter are not over-popular as there are a number of fish farms in the area! Look for the Spanish Ibex which has been introduced onto the high craggy mountains, and the rare Spanish Fir.

Within the woods Great Spotted Wood-pecker, Short-toed Treecreeper, and tits, finches and warblers, including the Sardinian, may be seen

124 GRAZALEMA TO ZAHARA	
Grid reference:	V 13
Location:	W of Ronda
Access:	Easy
Season:	All year round
Terrain:	Rugged mountains
Specialities:	Griffon Vulture, Crested Lark, Giant Orchid, French Lavender, *Linaria platycalyx*

This road, the CA 531, is tortuous, with high cliffs rising straight up from the road and spectacular views. These rocks yield a wealth of interesting sedums, saxifrages, and campanulas with many other botanical gems such as *Linaria platycalyx* . In small pockets of soil French Lavender is both colourful and fragrant.

Lower down towards the village of Zahara the land levels out and large plantations of Olive appear. It is here that you should find one of the largest and finest of the European orchids, the Giant Orchid (*Barlia robertiana*). This early flowering orchid (January to May) can reach up to 80cm high and has a long dense flower spike; the large flowers are reddish-violet in colour.

Griffon Vultures are common on the mountain crests, while the orchards hold an interesting warbler population, including Sardinian, Spectacled, Olivaceous, Orphean and Melodious. On sandy pathways Crested Larks are common. Swallowtail and Scarce Swallowtail are frequently seen.

On the mountainsides, herds of sheep and goats browse. Economically there is little else for which this land is suitable.

The road from Grazalema to Zahara is a spectacular mountain route. It is a botanist's paradise with the rocky cliffs producing many gems including sedums, saxifrages and campanulas. For the ornithologist, a host of raptors soar on the air currents.

10. EAST ANDALUCÍA

INTRODUCTION

This is an amazing region full of surprises and contrasts. The western edge runs from Motril through Granada to Desfiladero de Despeñaperros, then follows the Andalucían border east to Sierra de Alcaraz then south-east along this provincial border eventually reaching the sea near Huércal Overa. The southern Mediterranean boundary takes in part of the Costa del Sol.

This mountainous region has the highest peak in mainland Spain. The 3482m (11,424 feet) Mulhacén summit in the Sierra Nevada is covered with snow for nine months of the year. The Río Guadalquivir rises in the Sierra de Cazorla and in this great river's plain the largest plantations of Olives are grown, sometimes extending as far as the eye can see.

South of Sierra de los Filabres is the only true desert on mainland Spain. The harsh dry habitat of limestone and sandstone with deep canyons, has sometimes been used for 'Western' film locations, the so-called 'Spaghetti Westerns'. Cave dwellings are common here. The southern coastal strip is subtropical with plantations of bananas, avocados, custard apples and of course citrus.

Perhaps the most unbelievable area is between Almería and Adra where literally thousands of hectares are devoted to early

Kilometre upon kilometre of Olive groves cover the inland plains in east Andalucía.

vegetables for export to northern Europe. Peppers, cucumbers, tomatoes, dwarf and runner beans, melons and some strawberries are all packed in co-operatives, then cooled and loaded into enormous refrigerated transporters which speed their way day and night to northern Europe, where out of season the produce commands very high prices. The fruit and vegetables are all grown in plastic houses, which from a distance look like vast lakes.

Climatically the contrasts are great. The rainfall is substantial in the Sierra de Cazorla y Segura, often falling as snow during the winter. Heavy snow, lasting from October until June, makes the high areas of the Sierra Nevada a favourite zone for winter sports based at the Solynieve ski resort, complete with ski lifts to the highest slopes. The Cabo de Gata area is the driest in Spain with an average annual rainfall of 10cm (4 inches).

Temperatures can be hot in summer throughout the region, but the highest peaks of the Sierras, even in the height of summer are usually cool. Winter along the coastline is mild with extremely low temperatures unknown.

Alpine and subalpine habitats are common on all the mountains from 2000m (6500 feet) upwards, with many small plants clinging in crevices, while in the wet meadows exposed by the retreating snow, crocuses and gentians flower in early July. Coniferous forest covers many parts, especially in Sierra de Cazorla. Maquis scrub is

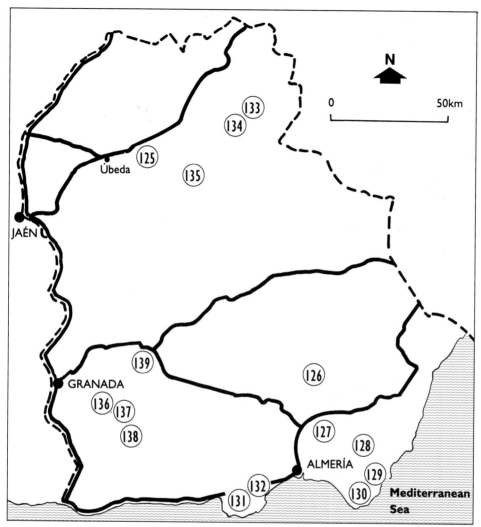

thick on a number of dry hillsides right down to sea level, while the desert-like area near Cabo de Gata represents steppe land inhabited by Stone Curlew, sandgrouse and Little Bustards which typify this kind of habitat.

Freshwater sites are located around the Guadalquivir with the Embalse del Tranco and Embalse del Negratín the largest areas. Salt-marsh is found at Roquetas de Mar and

Map of east Andalucía. The sites are numbered as in the text. Only main roads and the major rivers of the region are shown.

Cabo de Gata with the wild cliffs at Cabo de Gata lighthouse dramatically spectacular.

The grid references used in the following site descriptions relate to Michelin map number 446.

FIFTY INTERESTING SPECIES TO LOOK FOR

Audouin's Gull	Short-toed	Red Deer	*Campanula herminii*
Golden Eagle	Treecreeper	*Graëllsia isabellae*	*Cistus clusii*
Booted Eagle ✓	Trumpeter Finch	moth	*Convolvulus boissieri*
Bearded Vulture	Azure-winged	Clouded Yellow ✓	*Crocus nevadensis*
Greater Flamingo	Magpie	Spanish Argus	*Erinacea anthyllis*
Black-tailed Godwit	Chough	Spanish Brassy	Marsh Gentian
Avocet	Great Spotted	Ringlet	*Narcissus*
Black-winged Stilt	Woodpecker	Glandon Blue	*cantabricus*
Purple Gallinule	Iberian Wall Lizard	Nevada Blue	*monophyllus*
Stone Curlew	Italian Wall Lizard	Escher's Blue	*Narcissus*
Black-bellied	Lataste's Viper	Long-tailed Blue	*hedraecanthus*
Sandgrouse	Egyptian Mongoose	*Aconitum nevadense*	*Narcissus nevadensis*
Dartford Warbler	Pine Marten	*Aquilegia cazorlensis*	*Paeonia cariacea*
Black Wheatear	Red Squirrel	*Arenaria nevadensis*	*Pinguicula*
Alpine Accentor	Spanish Ibex	*Arenaria tetraquetra*	*vatisneriifolia*

125 EMBALSE DEL PUENTE DE LA CERRADA

Grid reference:	S 20
Location:	SE of Ubeda, NW of Cazorla
Access:	Very good
Season:	All year round
Terrain:	Freshwater reservoir with plenty of cover
Specialities:	Bar-tailed Godwit, Black-tailed Godwit, Greenshank, Purple Gallinule, Shoveler
Subsidiary:	Embalse de Doña Aldonaza, S 20; Embalse de Pedro Marin, S 19

Access to this interesting site is easy. It is situated approximately 20km south-east of Úbeda and is reached by first taking the N 322 and then the J 314. Alternatively leave Cazorla west on the C 328 and join the J 314 north at Peal de Becerro. The Guadalquivir is born in the mountains of Cazorla. After it has burst through the gorge of Tranco it levels out in the gently undulating lowlands in the province of Jaén. Here there are a series of freshwater lakes, many of which have been adapted for hydro-electric power and to provide irrigation.

Puente de la Cerrada is a shallow reservoir with its dam by the roadside. It is surrounded by a thick edge of *Phragmites* and has at its centre two islands with willow growing in abundance. These conditions are ideal for breeding and wintering ducks and waders.

Birds which may be seen are Purple Gallinule, Black-tailed and Bar-tailed Godwits, Greenshank, Redshank, Spotted Redshank, Mallard, Teal, Shoveler and many others.

The surrounding land is dry and almost entirely planted with extensive Olive groves with the occasional area of cereal. The soil is almost white due to it being very calcareous.

An interesting plant here is the Squirting Cucumber which can take you unawares!

126 SIERRA DE LOS FILABRES	
Grid reference:	U 22/23
Location:	N of Almería
Access:	Very good
Season:	Spring, summer and autumn
Terrain:	Mountain and desert-type canyons
Comments:	Summer can be very hot, winter with snow
Specialities:	Hoopoe, Long-tailed Blue, Clouded Yellow, Stinking Hellebore, *Narcissus cantabricus monophyllus*

This range is in reality a continuation of the Sierra Nevada, rising to 2168m (7113 feet) at the Observatorio del Calar Alto. To the south lies the Desierto de Tabernas and north the Sierras de Cazorla and Segura. It is easily reached from Almería. Leave on the N 340 northwards. At Los Yesos turn onto the C 3325 for approximately 40km.

Rivers have cut deep canyons giving a formidable aspect to the area which is honey-combed with many cave dwellings for human habitation and livestock. The valley of the Río Almenzora has many high-quality marble quarries.

The vegetation is mainly scrub with cistus, Rosemary, Lavender, Curry Plant, Broom and Gorse. Look for foxglove species. In the valleys and gorges there are pines and evergreen oak, and Poplars where there is sufficient water. One of the specialities of the area is *Narcissus cantabricus monophyllus,* a beautiful white-flowered form of the Hoop-petticoat Narcissus, which is also found in the Moroccan Atlas Mountains. Stinking Hellebore is also found.

The Prickly Pear cactus is grown in the area for its fruit. Xerophytic plants grow on very dry land with tamarisk and False Esparto grass in the ravine bottoms, and thyme species which are visited by masses of butter-flies, including Clouded Yellow, Painted Lady, Red Admiral and Long-tailed Blue.

Crested Lark, Stonechat, Spotless Star-ling, Black Wheatear, Redstart, Hoopoe, Magpie, Great Grey Shrike, Peregrine, Kestrel and Little Owl can all be seen.

127 TABERNAS/MINI HOLLYWOOD	
Grid reference:	U 22
Location:	N of Almería
Access:	Very good
Season:	All year round
Terrain:	Desert with deep canyons
Comments:	Very hot in summer
Specialities:	Stone Curlew, Black-bellied Sandgrouse, Trumpeter Finch, Black Wheatear, Long-tailed Blue

Tabernas is easily located 24km north of Almería on the N 340. It is true 'badland' country, with desert and deep canyons, sand and rocky wasteland. The area was the film set for a large number of Westerns. (These sets are now tourist attractions.)

Due to the very low rainfall (10 cm or 4 inches per year), the river-formed canyons now rarely contain water. This dry arid land is sparsely vegetated with xerophytic scrub, with Oleander and tamarisk in the dried-up depressions. A few cactus and agaves scattered amongst the rocks give slight shelter to many goats which roam the area.

Various species of thyme grow on the sides of these canyons and when in flower are attractive to butterflies, such as Escher's Blue

The typical 'badland' country of mini Hollywood. A group of riders are leaving the corral to ride the trails once used by Clint Eastwood in some of his films. The sets including saloon bar, sheriff's office, jail and stage-coach post are still here. The American Indian camps are also still in place.

various skippers and the migratory Painted Lady and Long-tailed Blue. Birds which inhabit semi-desert terrain can be found, such as Stone Curlew, Black-bellied Sandgrouse, Trumpeter Finch, Black Wheatear and the occasional Little Bustard and Eagle Owl.

Caves have been hewn out of the sandstone cliff sides for human habitation and animal shelter. Autumn, winter and spring are the best times to visit as the summer months can be very hot.

128 CAMPO DE NIJAR	
Grid reference:	U/V 23
Location:	NE of Almería
Access:	Good
Season:	All year round
Terrain:	Soft rounded limestone, semi-desert landscape
Comments:	Can be very hot in summer months
Specialities:	Trumpeter Finch, Hoopoe, Black-bellied Sandgrouse, *Launaea spinosa, Androcymbium gramineum*
Subsidiary:	Sierra de Alhamilla, V 22/23

This area is situated to the north-east of Almería a distance of about 25km and is easily reached by the N 344. It is a wild desert-like area with soft rounded limestone hills and a backdrop of the Sierra Filabres and Sierra de Alhamilla. This desert-like area of xerophytic grasslands is virtually uncultivated. False Esparto grass is collected and used in the making of baskets and mats. Previously *Agave sisalana* was cultivated for rope making and the rows are still clearly visible. It has an interesting natural flora, such as *Launaea spinosa,* with its 'barbed wire' stems dominating part of the landscape, while occasionally

A little piece of Africa in southern Europe at Campo de Níjar.

Cabo de Gata, the wild promontory in the evening sunlight.

the rare endemic *Androcymbium gramineum* can be found, with its white starry flowers poking between the stones. Other rarities include *Senecio auricula var. major*. Occasional groups of Date Palms give this entire area an African appearance.

Black-bellied Sandgrouse, Stone Curlew, Little Bustard, and Calandra and Lesser Short-toed Larks can be seen in the area. This is the most important area in Europe for the Trumpeter Finch, normally an African species. During the migration season, thousands of Pallid and Alpine Swifts, Swallows and martins can be seen.

The best visiting times are spring and autumn as the summer months can be extremely hot, and this is one of the driest areas in Europe.

129 SIERRA DEL CABO DE GATA

Grid reference:	V 23
Location:	SE of Almería
Access:	Good if approached by the inland route to San José, otherwise needs to be negotiated with care
Season:	All year round, but summer can be extremely hot
Terrain:	Spectacular rugged cliffs
Comments:	Strong walking shoes
Specialities:	Bonelli's Eagle, Black Wheatear, *Antirrhinum charidemi*, *Limonium thouinii*, *Tamarix boveana*
Subsidiary:	Carboneras, V 24

Salinas with Sierra del Cabo de Gata in the background. This photograph was taken from the northern end of the salinas, overlooking the denser vegetation where thousands of waders congregate during the migration period. Greater Flamingo (Phoenicopterus ruber) can also be seen here.

Situated about 30km south-east of Almería, with good access from Almería to Cabo de Gata point, but from there to San José the road is hardcore and should be negotiated with care. Access to San José by the inland route is good. Continuation along the coastal route of the Cabo de Gata range also needs care, but is well worth the drive.

This wild and rugged area is the driest in Europe with an annual rainfall of 10cm (4 inches). The cliffs are spectacular and precipitous with few beaches. The arid semi-desert produces some interesting plants, usually clinging to the rock face wherever they can get a roothold. An endemic, *Antirrhinum charidemi* with pale lilac flowers is only found in this sierra, as is *Limonium thouinii*, an annual sea lavender, found in sandy soil near the sea. *Tamarix boveana*, another rarity, is found on the beach of San José and is truly a North African species. Also near this village there are fields of the Prickly Pear cactus being grown for its fruit.

On the crags Bonelli's Eagles nest and Eagle Owls can be found. Black Redstart, Blue Rock Thrush and Black Wheatear are commonly seen among the rocks.

130 SALINAS DEL CABO DE GATA AND ACOSTA	
Grid reference:	V 23
Location:	SE of Almería
Access:	From Almería very good
Season:	All year round
Terrain:	Marshy with mountainous backdrop
Comments:	Insect repellent may be necessary; in summer can be very hot
Specialities:	Audouin's Gull, Trumpeter Finch, Thekla Lark, Iberian Wall Lizard, Italian Wall Lizard

These salt-pans are situated approximately 30km south-east of Almería. Leaving Almería on the AL 100 the road is good.

This is one of the major wetland areas in Iberia. It is important both for breeding birds and migrants as it is on a well-known flight path, especially for waders. The salinas at the south end of the area are a commercial enterprise, but the owners do not object to visitors. Please do not abuse their hospitality

An Italian Wall Lizard (Podarcis sicula), one of the rarest lizards in Spain, which can be found at the Salinas del Cabo de Gata.

131 PUNTA ENTINAS-SABINAR	
Grid reference:	V 21/22
Location:	E of Almerimar, SW of Roquetas de Mar
Access:	Very good
Season:	All year round
Terrain:	Sand dune and salt-marsh
Comments:	Insect repellent may be necessary
Specialities:	Greater Flamingo, Black-winged Stilt, Avocet, Garden Dormouse, Lataste's Viper
Subsidiary:	Albufera de Adra, V 21

in letting you walk around. The salinas are in a depression surrounded by desert-like scrub, with a backdrop of the rugged Sierra de Gata.

Between the road and the long shallow salt-pans there is an area of steppe vegetation which shelters many of the smaller birds, including Lesser Short-toed, Thekla and Crested Larks, Dartford and Sardinian Warblers, and the occasional rare Trumpeter Finch. The pans themselves have up to 2000 Greater Flamingo, Black Winged-Stilt and Avocet. At the northern end there is a lot more vegetation which gives cover for large numbers of ducks and waders. With luck Audouin's Gull may be seen.

Within the area are a number of interesting lizards: the Iberian Wall Lizard can be found, but more interesting is the Italian Wall Lizard, which in mainland Spain is only found in this southern strip of Almería.

Within the salt marsh a spectacular parasitic plant, feeding on legumes and species of goosefoot, is the yellow-flowered *Cistanche phelypaea*. It is large and very striking.

The sandy coastal strip leading to the Cabo de Gata promontory is relatively isolated and is visited by numerous gulls, including the rare Audouin's Gull.

Situated on the coast about 12km east of Almerimar and 6km south-west of the tourist centre of Roquetas de Mar. It is easily located from the road joining the two.

This small important area, which has been designated a natural park by AMA, comprises a beach, sand dunes and salt-marsh. The long narrow salt-marsh, between the main road and the sand dunes is well vegetated with *Salicornia* and other salt-loving plants. In the shallow open pools Greater Flamingo, Black-winged Stilt, Redshank, Greenshank, Mallard and Shoveler are found.

The sand-dune area between the beach and the marsh is stabilized with thickets of tamarisk, Mastic Tree and Phoenician Juniper, which give cover for Black Redstart, Stonechat, Crested Lark, Woodchat and Great Grey Shrikes, and Dartford and Fantailed Warblers.

The Garden Dormouse, Mediterranean Pine Vole and Lataste's Viper may be seen in the dune area.

The surrounding area is a vast 'sea' of plastic houses for the cultivation of early vegetables for the north European market.

132 LAS MARINAS DE ROQUETAS DE MAR	
Grid reference:	V 22
Location:	S of Roquetas de Mar
Access:	Good
Season:	All year round, especially during migration
Terrain:	Well-vegetated saline marshes
Comments:	Insect repellent may be necessary
Specialities:	Greater Flamingo, Little Egret, Pintail, Avocet, White Wagtail
Subsidiary:	Salt pans N of Roquetas de Mar, V 22

This salina area is approximately 5km south of Roquetas de Mar and is reached by passing the Urbanización Roquetas de Mar and continuing to Las Marinas. There are one or two subsidiary tracks which can also prove interesting when explored on foot.

This is virtually an extension of the Punta Etinas-Sabinar AMA Natural Park, but this area has substantially greater width and more vegetation at the lake-side. It has a fairly high tamarisk growth, especially near the side of the road, giving more cover for birds.

Although plastic-house cultivation and tourism are expanding, taking valuable water for irrigation and domestic use respectively, there is still a lot of wildlife to be seen.

Greater Flamingos are usually seen here in quantity as are Little Egrets wading through the shallow waters on the edge of the lake. Ducks, especially Pintail, Mallard and Shoveler, are usually present during the winter, while Avocets are resident. The White Wagtail, a common winter visitor, is very similar to the northern European Pied Wagtail, but much paler.

The best times to visit are spring, winter and autumn, as in summer there are usually large numbers of tourists who tend to disturb the birds.

LAS SIERRAS DE CAZORLA Y SEGURA

This is a 214,000ha reserve with check points on entering and leaving. It is approached from Úbeda travelling northwards on the N 322. At Torrepenogil turn towards Cazorla on the J 314 then the C 328. Within these mountains the great Río Guadalquivir is born. It has been dammed near its source producing the vast Embalse del Tranco, which floods an entire valley 24km long and 2km across at its widest point. The high mountains rise to 2107m (6913 feet) and are composed of Jurassic and Cretaceous limestone with a band of red clay and sand which can be seen by the red muddy banks of the embalse. This incredibly beautiful location has deep ravines, towering cliffs and wooded valleys, where, in the rutting season the air vibrates with the roar of the Red Deer stag.

There are high Alpine peaks and scree where a large number of endemic plants have survived since the last ice age, and tranquil flowering meadows, alive with butterflies, with tree-lined streams running through them.

Spanish Ibex have now re-established themselves and can be seen climbing seemingly impossible cliffs, while Wild Boar remain hidden during the daytime within the undergrowth, coming out at night to drink and to forage for roots in the scrubland.

Woodland birds are numerous, in particular noisy groups of Azure-winged Magpies, woodpeckers (Green, and Great and Lesser

The mountain village of Hornos, which due to its fortifications must have been almost impregnable. Today its narrow streets overlook the magnificent Embalse del Tranco; pine woods clothe the mountains to the east. It is a good area for the naturalist to visit.

Spotted varieties), Short-toed Treecreeper, Hoopoe, and Dartford and Sardinian Warblers. On the mountain tops Golden and Booted Eagles, many Griffon Vultures and Chough, Peregrine and with great luck the Bearded Vulture (Lammergeier) may be seen in this its only Spanish location outside the Pyrenees.

The best times to visit are late spring, summer and early autumn. Winter can be very wet and cold and sometimes closed by snow. Summers are very hot and dry.

133 HORNOS AND THE EASTERN BANKS OF EMBALSE DEL TRANCO	
Grid reference:	R 21
Location:	NE of Cazorla
Access:	Good
Season:	Spring, summer and autumn
Terrain:	Mountain and wooded river valley
Comments:	Can be snow-bound
Specialities:	Dartford Warbler, Azure-winged Magpie, Pine Marten, *Graëllsia isabellae*, *Narcissus longispathus*

At the northern extremity of the Embalse del Tranco stands a pinnacle with the village of Hornos built on its top. It must have been impregnable to invaders and has the most magnificent view up the widened river. Hornos is reached by turning east from the N 322 onto the C 3210, 28km north of Villacarrillo.

An interesting walk can be taken along the eastern banks of the reservoir. Here the mountainsides are covered with Aleppo Pine. It is the home of the rare and beautiful moth *Graëllsia isabellae*, the caterpillar of which prefers leaves of Scots Pine which is scattered throughout this area. Also to be found are the Woodland Grayling, Large Grizzled Skipper and the Spanish Marbled White.

Further up the mountain above the treeline there are two endemic narcissi, *Narcissus longispathus* and *N. hedraeanthus*. Both of these will grow below the treeline but their most usual habitat is well-watered scree. Other interesting plants include the Yellow-flowered Flax and Throatwort growing in crevices on the moist rock faces. Interesting mammals in the area include Red Squirrel, Fox, Egyptian Mongoose, Pine Marten, Genet, Badger, Red Deer and Wild Cat, with Otter down by the river.

134 INFORMATION CENTRE AT TORRE DEL VINAGRE	
Grid reference:	R 21
Location:	NE of Cazorla at km post 17
Access:	Excellent
Season:	Spring, summer and autumn
Terrain:	Woodland
Comments:	Museum and Botanical garden
Specialities:	The botanical rarities of the area

The centre is situated at kilometre post 17 (AMA marking post). It is a beautifully built building sited within woodland halfway along the western side of Embalse del Tranco. It is closed on Mondays but is otherwise open from 11am to 2pm and then again from 4pm to 7pm. It has a very informative ecological museum which explains each area within the region with diagrams, photographs and examples. From the centre various excursions are available or can be arranged by horse, Landrover, or minibus, with walks or eighteen-gear mountain-bike rides. All are lead by a competent guide.

The information centre at Torre del Vinagre, which houses a very informative ecological museum and has a botanical garden in its grounds containing many of the local plants.

Attached to the centre is a hunting museum which traces the weapons used and the animals and birds hunted within the region, from the very earliest times to the present day.

In front of the centre is a very comprehensive botanical garden containing many of the local plants, all arranged in 'height zones' and well labelled with the Latin name and corresponding Spanish one.

In the woods around the centre, Golden Oriole, Great Spotted Woodpecker and Sardinian Warbler can be found. Some of the open spaces can become blue with *Linum narbonense* or pink with *Silene colorata*.

At AMA kilometre post 28 is a large car-park, from which the Parque Cinegético del Collado del Almendral can be visited. Here the majority of the animals of this sierra are kept and bred in large enclosures.

135 PARADOR EL ADELANTADO ROUTE	
Grid reference:	S 21
Location:	E of Cazorla
Access:	Very good
Season:	Spring, summer and autumn
Terrain:	Woodland and mountain
Specialities:	Red Squirrel, Red Deer, *Narcissus hedraeanthus*, *Viola cazorlensis*, *Aquilegia cazorlensis*

The parador is reached by travelling east from Cazorla. It is well signposted. The road is spectacular with deep valleys to the south and east and high mountains to the north and west. Parking is easy for walking in the woods or generally enjoying the views.

On the cliffs the beautiful *Trachelium caeruleum* grows with its large cluster flower heads often covered with a variety of

Just before entering the parador route near the source of the Río Guadalquivir. This is a quiet tranquil spot, which makes it difficult to appreciate that this trickle widens into the enormous Embalse del Tranco. Beyond the embalse, the river has carved a narrow gorge, through which the water rushes before emerging onto the flat plains and eventually exiting at the sea at the Coto Doñana.

butterflies, especially the Painted Lady, Cardinal and Long-tailed Blue.

The woods at this height are mainly of Black Pine, a few Aleppo Pine and evergreen oak, with the Strawberry Tree and Mastic Tree forming the undergrowth. Towards the parador *Viola cazorlensis* is found amongst the rocks and also the beautiful, rare, purple-flowered *Pinguicula vallisneriifolia* with its strap-shaped sticky leaves for catching flies. *V. cazorlensis* is one of the rarest violets found only in the Sierras Cazorla y Segura. A more common colourful plant is *Centaurium erythraea ssp. grandiflorum* with its lovely head of almost shocking-pink flowers. The endemic *Aquilegia cazorlensis* grows much higher up beyond the parador near Pico de Cabañas, as does *Narcissus hedraeanthus*.

SIERRA NEVADA

The Sierra Nevada contains Spain's highest mountain, Mulhacén, rising to 3478m (11,411 feet) which is higher than any peak in the Pyrenees. Pico Veleta, the second highest peak at 3398m (11,148 feet), is easily accessible by car during the summer months and boasts a car-park and mobile hamburger bar! The road across the Sierra Nevada at this point is the highest in Europe. Only 48km to the south is the Mediterranean with its sub-tropical climate, sugar cane, custard apple and orange groves.

The rocks of the Sierra Nevada are composed of mica-schist and tend to flake giving a more gentle outline without the majestic splendour of the Alpine peaks in the Pyrenees. Rising up from the south-east of Granada there is a good but winding road passing through all stages of vegetation from tobacco fields and orange orchards to bare Alpine scree, which is snow covered for nine to ten months of the year.

After almost reaching Pico Veleta, the tarmac road becomes a hard-core track which continues over the top of the sierra and down the southern slopes towards the Alpujarras. This needs to be driven with care and only in summer, but is well worth the effort.

The wealth of plant life is incredible, with about forty endemic species, mainly in the Alpine zone above 2000m (6560 feet). In spring, as soon as the snow recedes, crocuses, colchicums, narcissi and gentians appear in the short brown turf, while lower down is the 'hedgehog' zone with neatly rounded shrubs, which are often very spiny, with yellow, blue

A view from the Balcón de Canales on the northern lower slopes of the Sierra Nevada at 1300m (4265 feet), overlooking the Embalse de Canales. This embalse produces some of the water and electricity for the large city of Granada. It is fed by the melting snow from the higher northern slopes of the Sierra Nevada.

or violet flowers predominating.

The butterflies in this area are also noteworthy, with many blues, such as the Glandon Blue (often more brown than blue) and the Nevada Blue. The Spanish Brassy Ringlet is yet another rarity in the area.

Raptors play on the air currents and up at the very summit of Pico Veleta the Alpine Accentor wanders amongst the tourists picking up crumbs, migrating to lower altitudes during the harsh winter months (altitude migration). Because this area is covered with snow for a large proportion of the year, there is no great mammal population.

136 NORTHERN LOWER SLOPES OF THE SIERRA NEVADA	
Grid reference:	U 19
Location:	E of Granada
Access:	Good
Season:	All year round
Terrain:	Mountain slopes
Specialities:	*Paeonia coriacea, Salvia lavandulifolia,* Spanish Rusty Foxglove, Stinking Hellebore, Curry Plant

Leaving Granada on the GR 420, the road initially follows a small river, lined with Poplars and other deciduous trees. The road then climbs steeply, passing terraced agricultural land, Olives and cereals. From this point onwards, it is worth parking periodically and exploring the roadsides and areas at different levels, and also appreciating the view overlooking Granada.

In the early stages, within the trees and orchards, Magpie, Stonechat, Bee-eater and woodpeckers may be seen. Above 1200m (3940 feet) an area of conifers is reached with *Daphne,* Thrift, *Genista,* Broom, Hawthorn, Gorse, *Rosa micrantha* and *Berberis hispanica.* Up to about this height, look out for many of the orchid species, in particular members of the *Ophrys* genus (insect orchids). In the region to 1700m (5580 feet) Lavender, *Salvia lavandulifolia,* hawthorn, Gorse, *Genista* and the Curry Plant can be found. It is well worth looking for the Stinking Hellebore, *Paeonia coriacea, Geum heterocarpum* and the Spanish Rusty Foxglove.

Magpie, Redstart, Crested Lark, Wheatear, Blackbird, Swallow and House Martin are all common with many more species.

The peak of Mulhacén in the Sierra Nevada, the highest point in mainland Spain at 3478m (11,411 feet). This peak is covered with snow for ten months of the year, with patches showing even in August. From the roadside on the southern slopes, it is a comparatively easy walk to reach the summit.

137 NORTHERN HIGHER SLOPES OF THE SIERRA NEVADA	
Grid reference:	U 19
Location:	E of Granada
Access:	Good
Season:	Summer
Terrain:	High mountain
Comments:	Warm clothing advisable as it is snow-covered for nine months of the year
Specialities:	Alpine Accentor, *Narcissus nevadensis*, *Erinacae anthyllis*, *Crocus nevadensis*, *Arenaria nevadensis*

Above 1700m (5580 feet) the mountain is snow covered during the late autumn, winter and early spring, but as the snow recedes a wealth of plants spring into life. The endemic *Narcissus nevadensis* is one of the first to push up its yellow trumpets followed by thousands of *Crocus nevadensis* covering the land with shades of blue.

The 'hedgehog' zone is reached by 2000m

(6560 feet) and is mainly composed of *Erinacea anthyllis* with mauve flowers and *Echiospartum boissieri* with yellow flowers. Higher up near the top of the mountain, where there is snow for nine months of the year, plants have to grow fast and be hardy to withstand the harsh Alpine climate. Rock-clinging plants dominate, taking advantage of every crack where there is moisture and a little soil. Species to been seen include *Arenaria nevadensis* and *A. tetraquetra*, both with white flowers, *Saxifraga globulifera*, *S. oppositifolia*, *Chaenorhinum origanifolium*, *Campanula herminii*, *Chrysanthemum radicans*, *Convolvulus boissieri*, *Eryngium glaciale*, *Gentiana alpina*, *Sempervivum nevadense (see box)* and *Potentilla caulescens*.

In the Alpine meadows there is usually an abundance of butterflies. The rare Nevada Blue, Spanish Chalk-hill Blue, Glandon Blue (Nevada form), Spanish Argus, Spanish Fritillary, False Grayling and many others are present.

As noted in the introduction, the Alpine Accentor, rare in most localities, is possibly the most common bird near the top! Chough and Kestrel are also often seen.

173

Typical of the Alpine flora on the southern side of the Sierra Nevada is Campanula hirminii.

138 SOUTHERN SLOPES OF THE SIERRA NEVADA	
Grid reference:	U/V 19/20
Location:	NE of Lanjarón
Access:	Hardcore road
Season:	Summer
Terrain:	High mountain
Comments:	Only for the intrepid driver
Specialities:	Golden Eagle, Nevada Blue, Marsh Gentian, *Aconitum nevadense*, *Linaria glacialis*

The road on the south side of the Sierra Nevada from Pico Veleta descends fairly slowly through bare Alpine scenery before it finally reaches a well-vegetated lush valley. In the Alpine reaches, where car parking is possible with care, there are some interesting steep climbs with many fascinating plants to be found, and several lagunas, producing Marsh Gentian, *Aconitum nevadense* and *Leontodon microcephalus* with its tiny pink flowers. On the central slopes *Daphne* and Rosemary are common. The Buff-coloured Foxglove is unusual as is the pink-flowered *Helianthemum*, while higher up the cliffs tufts of *Dianthus* show their pink flowers.

Sempervivum nevadense

This is one of the endemic plants found in the rock cervices of the Alpine zone near the summits of the Sierra Nevada. It is considered by some to be a variety of *Sempervivum cantabricum* found in the Picos de Europa many kilometres away, but over several thousand years it has developed into a separate species.

For nine months of the year these plants remain dormant under the snow, but as soon as this recedes the tight rosettes unfold and rapidly send out more offshoots and the occasional reddish flower. This species is monocarpic, so the rosette dies after the flowers have set seed. The rosettes are fairly small, only 3cm in diameter. When actively growing, the hairless leaves are green, each tipped with dull red.

Linaria glacialis is found on the rocky screes.

The lower valley is wide and terraced, and planted where possible with a large variety of crops: apples, cherries, Spanish Chestnut, walnuts, potatoes and a variety of vegetables. Butterflies other than those mentioned in the area introduction which might be seen are Spanish Argus and Escher's Blue.

Birds on the rocky higher parts which can be included on the list of species to be seen are Black Redstart, Wheatear, Black-eared Wheatear, Black Wheatear, Alpine Accentor,

Golden Eagle, Kestrel and Chough, while in the valleys many of the smaller passerines can be seen. There are a number of very attractive villages in the foothills from which mineral water springs emerge, and where people visit to 'take the waters'.

Peppers drying on the balconies in Guadix; a common and colourful sight in this area.

139 GUADIX	
Grid reference:	U 20
Location:	NE of Granada
Access:	Excellent
Season:	All year round
Terrain:	Dry steppe
Specialities:	Hoopoe, Bee-eater, Spanish Argus, *Cistus clusii, Opuntia Ficus-indica*

This amazing town lies on the northern slopes of the Sierra Nevada 68km east of Granada on the N 342. It lies in dry desert-like country with canyons cut deep into the limestone/sandstone rock. It is within these cliffs that many hundreds of families have excavated their cave dwellings. These caves are warm in winter and cool in summer. They usually have electric power and adequate plumbing. They are spotlessly clean inside with four or five good-sized rooms and an open fireplace in the sitting-room.

The surrounding countryside is inhospitable and has a lunar aspect, but where water is obtainable vegetables are grown, especially a very excellent sweet red pepper. After harvesting, this is threaded onto strings up to 1m long and dried in the sun, suspended from the eaves or balconies of houses.

Natural plants are generally scarce on the desert landscape although *Cistus clusii, Opuntia Ficus-indica* and *Lithospermum* can be seen. Many species of thyme, and Rosemary are good nectar plants for Spanish Argus, and Common and Escher's Blues.

Bee-eaters nest in the sandy cliffs where they can dig into the softer sand, while Hoopoes are often seen in the scrub.

11. THE BALEARIC ISLANDS

INTRODUCTION

The Balearics are a series of islands in the Mediterranean nearer to the Spanish mainland than to Africa. The main island is Mallorca, then Menorca and Ibiza, and finally the much smaller islands of Formentera and Cabrera.

Geologically Mallorca, Ibiza, Formentera and Cabrera are Triassic and Jurassic limestone, a continuation of the great Baetic Cordillera (the ranges of mountains in southern Spain). Menorca is slightly different, being composed of much older rocks similar to those found in Sardinia.

The Two-tailed Pasha (Charaxes jasius) is one of the largest European butterflies.

The mountain ridge in north Mallorca is dramatic and high, rising to 1436m (4711 feet) at the summit of Puig Major. The cliffs of the northern coastline are some of the highest and wildest in Iberia; in some areas there is an almost precipitous drop for 300m (985 feet). In contrast the southern half of the island is relatively flat, the limestone overlaid with gravel and pockets of the rich terra-rossa. Here orchards of almonds, figs and citrus are grown.

Ibiza is also mountainous, secondary limestone rising to 475m (1558 feet), but not as dramatic as Mallorca. Formentera and Cabrera are very much smaller, but similar geologically to their near neighbours, Ibiza and Mallorca respectively. Menorca, on the other hand is basically old siliceous rock rising to 357m (1171 feet) and is much flatter than the other islands.

The rainfall on the islands differs greatly. On the mountains in Mallorca, which act as a barrier protecting the southern plain, the annual average rainfall is up to 150cm (59 inches) while on the plain it is as low as 60cm (24 inches). On all the other islands the average is about 80cm (31 inches) but on Menorca the climate is generally windy. The rain normally begins in late autumn, but by April is infrequent. Warm, sunny days are enjoyed throughout the year and from May through to September the sun usually shines from cloudless skies.

Botanically the islands are exciting most of the year, the large variation in height producing a great diversity of plants, from almost Alpine habitat on the tops of the mountains to lush woods in the valleys. Because the islands have been separated from mainland Spain for thousands of years, many endemic plants have evolved, good examples being *Cyclamen balearicum* and *Paeonia cambessedesii*.

This effect of isolation is also evident in the reptile population and each island seems to have its own particular species of lizard, either Lilford's Wall, Ibiza Wall, Italian Wall or the Moroccan Rock Lizard.

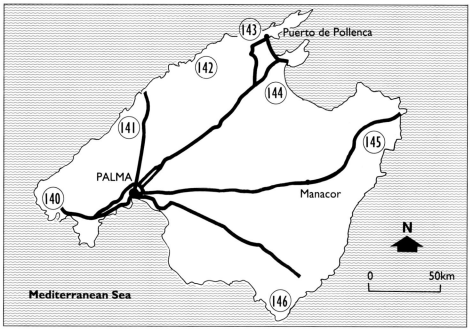

Map of Mallorca. The sites are numbered as in the text. Only main roads are shown.

FIFTY INTERESTING SPECIES TO LOOK FOR

Cory's Shearwater	Black-necked Grebe	Italian Wall Lizard	*Helleborus lividus*
Balearic Shearwater	Black-winged Stilt	Lilford's Wall Lizard	*Hypericum*
Audouin's Gull	Red-rumped	Ibiza Wall Lizard	*balearicum*
Black Tern	Swallow	Turkish Gecko	Large Yellow
Peregrine	Crag Martin	Moorish Gecko	Restharrow
Osprey	Moustached	False Smooth Snake	*Paeonii cambessedesii*
Eleonora's Falcon	Warbler	Two-tailed Pasha	*Primula vulgaris ssp.*
Booted Eagle	Marmora's Warbler	Common Blue	*balearica*
Bonelli's Eagle	Blue Rock Thrush	*Aristolochia bianorii*	*Teucrium lancifolium*
Black Vulture	Rock Sparrow	*Astragalus balearicus*	*Teucrium*
Marsh Harrier	Pied Flycatcher	*Cistus clusii*	*subspinosum*
Little Bittern	Cirl Bunting	*Crocus cambessedesii*	Bertoloni's Bee
Purple Heron	Hoopoe	*Cyclamen balearicum*	Orchid
Little Egret	Moroccan Rock	*Daphne rodriguezii*	
Spoonbill	Lizard	*Erica multiflora*	

A typical Mallorcan scene showing high rugged cliffs, beautiful bays and lush green vegetation. The pathways down to the beaches are very steep and difficult for walking. Great care must be exercised when venturing down from the recognized tracks.

Ornithologically, the islands are fascinating with a large number of species to thrill any birdwatcher, such as Eleonora's Falcon, which is a late breeder enabling it to feed its young on small migrating birds, the majestic Black Vulture gliding on the thermals, and Marmora's Warbler hiding in the scrub.

The grid references used in the following site descriptions, beginning with Mallorca, relate to Michelin map number 443.

140 PUERTO DE ANDRATX AND ENVIRONS, MALLORCA	
Grid reference:	N 37
Location:	W point of Mallorca
Access:	Very good
Season:	All year round
Terrain:	Limestone cliffs, maquis scrub, woodland
Specialities:	Audouin's Gull, Cory's Shearwater, Eleonora's Falcon, Black Vulture,
Subsidiary:	Isla Dragonera, N 36/37

An area easily located on the westernmost point of Mallorca. Access is by smaller roads from the C 719. The mountains drop straight down to the sea at this point. The high limestone cliffs are covered with maquis scrub underneath the woodlands of Aleppo Pine and Ilex Oak. The scrubland consists of Mastic Trees with Grey and Narrow-leaved Cistus, Rosemary and *Erica multiflora*, which is very similar to the maquis scrub on the adjacent Spanish mainland. It is used mainly for sheep and goat grazing.

Audouin's Gull is relatively common at this point and Ospreys can often be seen fishing from the cliffs, but the most spectacular are the large numbers of Eleonora's Falcons, which can be seen when they return to breed at the end of April, and the rare Black Vulture with its huge 3m wingspan.

141 NORTH-WEST COAST, MALLORCA	
Grid reference:	M/N 37/38
Location:	From Andratx to Sa Calobra
Access:	Good
Season:	All year round
Terrain:	Rugged coastline
Comments:	Walking shoes
Specialities:	False Smooth Snake, Two-tailed Pasha, *Ranunculus weyleri*, *Cyclamen balearicum*, *Crocus cambessedesii*
Subsidiary:	Valldemossa wood, M 37

Cyclamen balearicum

This beautiful plant was at one time distributed and common in all the wooded and shady parts of the island of Mallorca. Now, due to indiscriminate collecting, it has become more localized but can still be found in quantity within the woods and shaded areas on the northern half of the island. It is always found on moist but well-drained soil with plenty of humus.

This is one of the smaller species of cyclamen, the corm being only about 2cm in diameter. It flowers in spring with dainty white flowers tinged with pale pink in the throat. The leaves are dull green with whitish spots and purple underneath.

Situated along the C 710 from Andratx to Sa Calobra. This is a wild and rugged coastline with towering limestone cliffs backed by the high mountain ridge of Sierra de Alfabia. The Puig Major mountain on the eastern edge at 1436m (4711 feet) is the highest on Mallorca, with the peak of the Galatzó mountain to the west of this area rising to 1026m (3366 feet).

The lower slopes are mainly covered by Aleppo Pine and Ilex Oak, while the high land is covered with heath or devoid of vegetation. There are also scattered terraces of aged gnarled Olive trees clinging to the hillsides. It is here that many of the endemic plants are found. *Cyclamen balearicum* (*see* box) is a particularly beautiful plant often seen nestling around the roots of Olives and frequently growing in association with the autumn-flowering *Crocus cambessedesii* which has lilac flowers. *Erica multiflora* is prolific in lower areas.

Puig Major's summit is inaccessible to the public as it is a military zone, but in the hollows on the northern slopes there is a rich flora including *Ligusticum lucidum ssp. huteri*, the rare *Ranunculus weyleri* and *Primula vulgaris ssp. balearica*.

There is a good variety of butterflies including the Balearic form of the Common Blue and the Two-tailed Pasha which are both common. Wall Lizards may be seen in normal or melanistic forms. The lizard-eating False Smooth Snake, and Moorish and Turkish Geckos are all in evidence.

Throughout this area Peregrine, Kestrel, Booted and Bonelli's Eagles, Black Vulture and Eleonora's Falcon can all be seen. It is truly a naturalist's paradise all the year round.

142 NORTH-EAST COAST, MALLORCA

Grid reference:	M 38/39
Location:	Sa Calobra to Sant Vicenç
Access:	Good
Season:	All year round
Terrain:	High, wild limestone cliffs
Comments:	Good walking shoes
Specialities:	Eleonora's Falcon, Marmora's Warbler, *Helleborus lividus*, *Hypericum balearicum*, *Paeonia cambessedesii*
Subsidiary:	Ternellés Valley. Permit necessary from the bank in Pollença; Mondays only, M 39; Cabo Formentor Peninsula, M 39

179

The craggy north-eastern point of Mallorca. This sticks out into the sea like a bare finger. It is a wonderful place for watching birds of prey hunting for food.

This takes in the route from Sa Calobra to Puerto de Pollença along the C 710. It is a continuation of the high limestone cliffs ending at Sant Vicenç, and has as its backbone wild, rugged mountains of between 650m and 1000m (2130–3280 feet), with Puig de Massanella (1348m; 4423 feet) on the outer western part of this region, the highest accessible mountain in Mallorca. The lower slopes are heavily wooded with Aleppo Pine.

This area has the highest rainfall in Mallorca and is therefore probably the best region on the island for plants, which include the endemic *Paeonia cambessedesii* with its large deep rose-coloured flowers, *Hypericum balearicum*, a distinctive evergreen shrubby St John's wort with large yellow flowers and *Helleborus lividus*. *Aristolochia bianorii* grows at sea level near Puerto Pollença, while in the hills *Teucrium subspinosum and Astragalus balearicus*, two 'hedgehog' plants, are common.

The bird life of this area is equally fascinating, especially near the sea cliffs where you can catch glimpses of many Eleonora's Falcons gliding in the thermals, and also the huge Black Vulture. Within the scrubland look out for Marmora's Warbler which is a Mallorcan speciality.

143 BOQUER VALLEY, MALLORCA

Grid reference:	M 39
Location:	S of Formentor Peninsula
Access:	Easy from Puerto de Pollença
Season:	All year round
Terrain:	Rocky with maquis scrub
Comments:	Sensible shoes
Specialities:	Rock Sparrow, Blue Rock Thrush, Subalpine Warbler, Marmora's Warbler, Black Redstart

This is a delightful small valley, easily reached by foot from Puerto de Pollença. No permit is needed. This important rock-strewn valley is covered with Dwarf Fan Palms, an exceptionally blue form of Rosemary, *Erica multiflora* in profusion, and some aged Olive trees.

It contains a number of very interesting and rare birds, with possibly the best known being the elusive Marmora's Warbler. Other notable warblers are Sardinian, Subalpine and Melodious. Marmora's is very similar to the Dartford Warbler, having a pale grey breast unlike the latter species' ruddy breast.

The entrance to the fabulous Boquer Valley. Many birds are concealed in the undergrowth, such as Marmora's Warbler, Sardinian Warbler, Blue Rock Thrush and Rock Sparrow. This lovely valley is full of rocks with interesting plants forming the undergrowth. In particular, there is the Dwarf Fan Palm which gives an African feel to the surroundings.

Crossbill, Rock Sparrow (particularly in the bottom of the valley), Blue Rock Thrush, Black Redstart and Stonechat can be seen as well as Hoopoe and maybe the Wryneck if you are lucky, amongst the higher-growing cover. Pied Flycatchers and Swallows pass in numbers during migration, and Crag Martins winter in the region. Serin, Linnet, Chaffinch, Greenfinch, Firecrest, Cirl Bunting and the ubiquitous House Sparrow are all in evidence. Hopefully construction around this area will not disrupt this interesting site.

144 ALBUFERA DE ALCUDIA, MALLORCA	
Grid reference:	M 39
Location:	S of Puerto de Alcudia
Access:	Easy from the C 712
Season:	All year round; mainly spring and summer
Terrain:	Mainly freshwater marsh and lagoons
Comments:	Permits obtained from the reception area
Specialities:	Little Bittern, Purple Heron, Osprey, Red-rumped Swallow, Moustached Warbler
Subsidiary:	Cabo de Pinar, M 39

This marsh is situated south of Puerto de Alcudia, between the C 712 and PM 343. There are several connecting roads with the entrance to this marsh on the C 712 at English Bridge just south of Lago Esperanza. There is a large car park and reception area from which permits can be obtained. The 1700ha mainly freshwater reserve is formed by the Ríos Miquel and Muro, and has extensive areas of *Phragmites* and sedge plus large areas of open water. At one end is an area of abandoned salt-pans and there is a sand bank between the reserve and the sea.

The combination of fresh and saltwater makes this a great site for birds. Little Bittern and Purple Heron hide within the undergrowth. There are hundreds of pairs of Great Reed Warblers with their unmistakable 'croak', many Fan-tailed Warblers 'zip-zip-zipping', Cetti's Warblers with their strident call and Moustached Warblers in quantity. Black-winged Stilts and Little Egrets stride slowly through the water with Cattle Egrets feeding on the dry land. Marsh Harriers quarter the reed beds and Osprey can be seen diving for fish. Red-rumped Swallow, House Martin and Swallow search for insects above the water while Black Terns delicately pick insects from the surface. Spoonbill and Greater Flamingo may be seen on passage.

145 PORTO CRISTO TO CABO DEL FREU, MALLORCA	
Grid reference:	M/N 40
Location:	East coast
Access:	Small roads from PM 404
Season:	All year round
Terrain:	Sandy coves, limestone hills, fertile valleys
Comments:	Sensible shoes
Specialities:	Bee-eater, Golden Oriole, Woodchat Shrike, Grey-leaved Cistus, Narrow-leaved Cistus
Subsidiary:	Cuevas del Drac, N 40; Cuevas de Artá, N 40; spectacular caves; not to be missed

In this area there are many small sandy coves with high limestone hills inland rising to 315m (1033 feet). The Aleppo and occasional Umbrella Pines in places come right down to the beach; the valleys are cultivated with fruit orchards.

The inland maquis scrub consists of Mastic Trees, Grey-leaved and Narrow-leaved Cistus, with Rosemary and several thyme species making this a very aromatic area. Shags, shearwaters and gulls should all be seen while inland in the valleys you can find many warblers, swarms of Serins, Woodchat Shrike, Golden Oriole amongst the fruit orchards and Bee-eaters nesting in the sandy areas.

146 SALINAS DE LEVANTE TO CABO SALINAS, MALLORCA	
Grid reference:	N/O 38/39
Location:	Southern-most area
Access:	From Campos del Puerto or Santanyí by various small roads
Season:	All year round
Terrain:	Salt-marsh, salt-pans, limestone cliffs and agricultural land
Specialities:	Night Heron, Mediterranean Gull, Scops Owl, Hoopoe, Stone Curlew

This is the most southern area in Mallorca. The salinas are low-lying coastal marshes and lagoons with commercial salt-pans. Although closed to the public, permits may be available. There is, however, good viewing from the public road. Migrating wading

Friars Cowl (Arisarum vulgare), a typical plant seen very early in the year.

Two wader chicks showing the camouflage of the juvenile plumage soon after hatching.

birds in April and May might include Spotted Redshank, Greater Flamingo, Ruff and Little Stint, with Black-winged Stilt, Kentish Plover, Night Heron, Little Egret and Avocet amongst the breeding birds.

The undulating land behind is intensively cultivated. Here you can hope to see Crested and Short-toed Larks, many warblers including Sardinian, Dartford, Marmora's and Fan-tailed, Woodchat and Great-grey Shrikes and Hoopoe, with Stone Curlew and Quail in the drier areas. Scops Owl, strictly nocturnal, may be heard during the night.

Cabo Salinas, the most southern point, has limestone cliffs from which there are fabulous sea views towards Isla de Cabrera. It is good for sea birds, such as Shag, Cory's and Balearic Shearwaters, and Mediterranean, Herring, Lesser Black-backed and with luck Audouin's Gulls.

147 MENORCA	
Grid reference:	L/M 41/42
Location:	NE of Mallorca
Access:	By air or ferry from Spanish mainland
Season:	All year round
Terrain:	High limestone cliffs, coastal lagoons, scrub and agricultural land
Comments:	Can be very windy
Specialities:	Egyptian Vulture, Moroccan Rock Lizard, Italian Wall Lizard, *Daphne rodriguezii*, *Teucrium lancifolium*

Menorca is the most northern of the Balearic Islands, situated north-east of Mallorca. It is a big tourist resort with access by air from many European countries, by ferry from the Spanish mainland (Barcelona and Valencia), or by ferry from Mallorca's capital Palma.

Paeonia cambessedesii

This species is a true endemic and one which can only be described as local, but where it is found, it is usually in profusion. It is a beautiful plant, whether in flower or not. It is small, not more than 25cm high, with fairly large dark-green leaves, the undersides of which are a deep shining purple.

The flower is solitary, up to 9cm in diameter and deep rose in colour with a mass of bright-yellow stamens. It flowers during March and April and this is followed by the appearance of 5cm-long seed pods, which ripen in the autumn. When the pod splits open, both red and black seeds are revealed. The red ones are infertile, but the black ones should germinate.

It is usually found growing in scrubland, often in association with *Helleborus lividus*, on hillsides from sea level to 1000m (3280 feet) and mainly on the eastern side of Mallorca.

The terrain is varied with limestone cliffs, rocky beaches, maquis scrublands, and rich grasslands for dairy farming. There is an important protected marshland at El Grau and more marshes on the southern side at Son Bou. There are also small areas of Aleppo Pine and Ilex Oak woodlands.

Floristically it is less interesting than the other islands, but it has the endemic Menorcan Loosestrife, and also *Daphne rodriguezii*, *Teucrium lancifolium*, *Paeonia cambessedesii*, *Digitalis dubia* and the Caper Plant.

Cory's Shearwater, Peregrine, Osprey and

Shag can all be seen. Egyptian Vultures prefer Menorca to other Balearic Islands. Some white-backed escapee vultures are here, so do not be surprised by the unexpected!

Lilford's Wall Lizard, green, brown or melanistic forms, the Moroccan Rock Lizard and the Italian Wall Lizard may all be seen.

148 IBIZA	
Grid reference:	O/P 33/34
Location:	SW of Mallorca
Access:	By ferry from Valencia; seasonal service from Alicante and Denia; or by air
Season:	All year round
Terrain:	Limestone cliffs, coniferous woodland, maquis scrub
Specialities:	British Storm-petrel, Audouin's Gull, Ibizan Hound, Ibiza Wall Lizard, Bertoloni's Bee Orchid
Subsidiary:	Outlying islands

This island is situated south-west of Mallorca and is usually reached by air. It has high limestone cliffs, and is wooded with Aleppo Pine on the higher ground, with orchards of almond, carob bean, citrus and fig trees lower down. Within the dryer areas there is cistus scrub, Phoenician Juniper, Everlasting Curry Plant, with its curry smell when the plant is bruised, myrtle and Large Yellow Restharrow. Oleander is a feature of the dried-up river beds. Around Aubarca Cove on the north side of the island there are several interesting species. Amongst the bulbous plants look out for Bertoloni's Bee Orchid (sometimes called Mirror of Venus and not to be confused with the Mirror Orchid), Sea Squill and Barbary Nut. The Ibiza Wall Lizard has a vivid green back.

Ibiza also lends its name to the Ibizan Hound, accepted as a breed within the dog-showing world. In Spain it is known as the Podonco Ibicenco (with several varieties) but on Ibiza it is called Ca Eivissenc. It is an old breed, sculptured in stone before the reign of King Tutankhamun (1350BC) and depicted in cave paintings. It is probably of Egyptian origin and is a coursing and hunting dog.

149 ISLA DE FORMENTERA	
Grid reference:	P/Q 34
Location:	S of Ibiza
Access:	By ferry from Ibiza or Spanish mainland
Season:	Spring, summer and autumn
Terrain:	High limestone cliffs and salinas
Comments:	Sea-sickness pills advised
Specialities:	Balearic Shearwater, Shag, Black-necked Grebe, *Chaenorhinum origanifolium*, Toothed Lavender

This is the most southern of the Balearic Islands, reached by ferry from neighbouring Ibiza some 20km to the north, or from Denia on the mainland of Spain during the tourist season. It is a small island which has an area of saline salt-pans and ponds with *Salicornia* scrub, high limestone cliffs with maquis scrub and a coastal sand-dune area. The salt-pans are interesting and are situated at the northern end of the island. The largest ponds are at the south of this area and hold in particular quantities of Black-necked Grebes during the winter. Near La Mola on the eastern-most point, the high limestone cliffs make ideal nesting sites for Balearic Shearwaters and the Mediterranean race of the Shag (*Phalacrocorax aristotelis desmarestii*), the Brown-legged Shag, with its yellow webbed feet.

These cliffs are covered with maquis scrub which includes *Cistus clusii, Helianthemum origanifolium,* Toothed Lavender, Dwarf Fan Palms and the Barbary Nut, an afternoon-flowering iris. The dune area west of La Mola grows *Tamarix africana,* the violet-flowered *Chaenorhinum origanifolium* and Sea Squill which flowers in autumn with the leaves appearing during early spring.

The race of Ibiza Wall Lizard here is larger and more brightly coloured than the one on Ibiza.

150 ISLA DE CABRERA	
Grid reference:	O 38
Location:	S of Mallorca
Access:	By boat from Mallorca
Season:	Late spring, summer and early autumn
Terrain:	Mediterranean scrub and high cliffs
Comments:	Permit needed to visit interior; sea-sickness pills advisable
Specialities:	Cory's Shearwater, Balearic Shearwater, British Storm-petrel, Audouin's Gull, Lilford's Wall Lizard

Isla de Cabrera is situated south of Mallorca and is reached by an approximately 20km boat trip. The normal trip goes from Colonia Sant Jordi on Mallorca to the harbour and ruined castle only. Should you wish to venture further inland permission must be obtained from the tourist office in Palma. There is a move afoot to try to make this a National Park rather than a military post which it is at present. It is a small island consisting of high rocky limestone cliffs, Mediterranean scrub

The magnificent Bertoloni's Bee Orchid (Ophrys bertolonii) which can be found growing in the Balearics.

with some small pine woods.

On the boat trip there is a good chance that dolphins will be seen. As this island has numerous breeding birds for which it is noted you should see Cory's Shearwater, Balearic Shearwater, British Storm-petrel, Shag, Eleonora's Falcon, Osprey and the rare Audouin's Gull. Here Lilford's Wall Lizard is darker and larger then those found elsewhere. Because of the lack of habitation it is also much less wary. It is very hardy and will eat vegetable food.

Day trips only are possible as there is no accommodation. Trips run during the late spring, summer and early autumn depending on the weather.

SECTION III:
FIELD GUIDE TO COMMONER
ANIMALS AND PLANTS

This field guide section is intended to assist in the identification of a number of the more common birds, mammals, reptiles, amphibians, butterflies and plants which you may see. The choice of plants was difficult, as Spain has some 5500 species of which 2500 are found in Andalucía alone.

The mammal plates do, however, have some of the more uncommon, or very localized species, which may occasionally be seen, but they are extremely wary and in a number of cases are almost entirely nocturnal. Only within the national reserves where they are strictly protected can they be seen frequently, often in the daytime.

This book is about Spanish wildlife as a whole, but it has only been possible to illustrate vertebrates, butterflies and plants. Many of the more beautiful and common insects have had to be omitted because of lack of space. Moths are not included because the vast majority are nocturnal, although hawk moths are relatively common and can be seen visiting flowers. Dragonflies which can be seen throughout the region, mainly near water, are extremely colourful and numerous. The Praying Mantis, beetles and wasps can all be fascinating. However, one could go and on forever with insects. Let us also not forget the interesting Arachnids (spiders), of which the 'tiger-striped' garden spider and the trap-door spider with its ingenious home are two examples.

The colour identification plates are largely

self-explanatory but to help you with the text a few of the descriptive points should be clarified:

Birds: the measurements are in centimetres, from the tip of the beak to the tail tip. If the size is variable, the average is given.

Mammals: again the measurements are in centimetres with weights given in kilograms, except for the Noctule Bat and the Weasel's which are in grams. For the Spanish Ibex and Chamois, the males are illustrated with their large horns; the females have only small ones. The Roe Deer male is illustrated with the palmate antlers but the female has none.

Amphibians and Reptiles: with the exception of the Ladder Snake all are depicted as adults. Juveniles can vary in colour and markings.

Butterflies: the width measurements are from forewing tip to forewing tip across the body. To add interest, a description of the caterpillars of the butterflies depicted has been included and their food plants described. The flight periods given are those for when the adults are most actively egg laying.

Plants: these are measured in metres or centimetres.

For vertebrates and butterflies the Spanish names which are recognized throughout the country have been included. Regional names do differ but with the limited space available they have not been included. Only the English and Latin names have been given for the plants as many do not have a specific Spanish equivalent.

Opposite: Cattle Egret (Bubulcus ibis).

Little Grebe *Tachybaptus ruficollis*
Sp. Zampullín Chico **L 25**
Common resident. Freshwater pools, lakes, rivers with plenty of vegetation. Smallest grebe. Dark crown, reddish neck, grey-brown back. Winter, paler. Frequently diving for several minutes. Food, small fish and aquatic insects. Call, loud *whit whit.* Moorhen similar, larger, red bill, white tail coverts.

Cattle Egret *Bubulcus ibis*
Sp. Garcilla Bueyera **L 50**
Common resident. Amongst livestock or following plough. White plumage. In breeding season, back, crown and breast, buff. Bill and legs yellow or reddish (juvenile black). Gregarious. Food, grassland insects. Call, soft grunt or croak. Little Egret similar, larger, black bill, yellow feet.

Little Egret *Egretta garzetta*
Sp. Garceta Común **L 60**
Common resident. Ponds, marshes, rivers, preferably saline. Elegant with white plumage, long sharp black beak, long black legs, yellow feet. Gregarious in nesting sites only. Food, small fish, aquatic insects. Call, harsh *kark* usually heard when rising from the water. Cattle Egret similar, smaller, yellow beak, black feet.

White Stork *Ciconia ciconia*
Sp. Cigüeña Blanca **L 110**
Partial migrant. Marshes and meadows. Very large, black and white. Long bright-red beak and legs. Rides the thermals, gliding vast distances. Nests on chimneys, belltowers, battlements, trees, occasionally communal. Food, fish and amphibians. Communicates by bill clapping. Black Stork similar, rare, smaller, much darker.

Mallard *Anas platyrhynchos*
Sp. Anade Real **L 56**
Most common duck, resident. Marshes, rivers, lakes, occasionally inshore. In breeding plumage, drake extremely colourful, in eclipse very like duck. 'Upends' for aquatic seeds, plants and invertebrates. Call, a loud *quack.* Likely to be confused in eclipse with other surface feeders.

Shoveler *Anas clypeata*
Sp. Pato Cuchara **L 51**
Common winter visitor. Freshwater marshes and occasionally estuaries. Male very colourful with unmistakable spatulate bill. Sweeps bill in shallow water, feeding on aquatic vegetation and insects. Call a two-syllable *tuck* by the drake, a loud *quack* by the duck.

Red-legged Partridge *Alectoris rufa*
Sp. Perdiz Roja **L 35**
Common resident game bird. Agricultural land, open woodland, low mountain. Colourful with red legs and bill, heavily barred sides, black flecked bib. More likely to run than fly. Eats seeds and insects, with occasional vegetation. Call *chur cuch.* Grey Partridge similar but only found in northern Spain. Quail considerably smaller.

Quail *Coturnix coturnix*
Sp. Codorniz Común **L 18**
Fairly common partial migrant. Agricultural land and open woodland. Heavily streaked brown; male has a dark throat. Hides in undergrowth, difficult to flush. Food, seeds and insects. Call distinctive far-reaching *kwick me kwick.* Grey Partridge similar, larger and only in north Spain.

Moorhen *Gallinula chloropus*
Sp. Polla de Agua **L 33**
Common resident. Freshwater marshes, ponds, lakes and rivers with sufficient vegetation to hide and nest. Red bill and frontal shield unmistakable, white under tail. Swims well and often seen 'bobbing' on waterside banks. Food, insects, aquatic plants, small shellfish. Call, loud *kik-kik.* Coot similar, larger with white frontal shield.

Coot *Fulica atra*
Sp. Focha Común **L 37**
Common resident. Freshwater ponds and lakes with well-vegetated margins. Large, black, with white frontal shield. Frequently dives, makes quarrelsome chases, gregarious in winter. Food, vegetable matter and small aquatic insects. Call a loud *kowk.* Crested Coot similar but with two red knobs on forehead.

summer

winter

Little Grebe

female

male

Mallard

female

male

Shoveler

summer

summer

Cattle Egret

Little Egret

Red-legged Partridge

female

male

Quail

White Stork

Moorhen

Coot

Honey Buzzard *Pernis apivorus*
Sp. Abejero **L 55**
Summer visitor. Mainly confined to deciduous forests. Plumage variable. Notable for migration over Gibraltar. Feeds mainly on wasps, their larvae, frogs, small mammals and birds. Call, high *whee-oo*. Other buzzards similar, lack broad black band at tail end and two finer bars nearer body.

Black Kite *Milvus migrans*
Sp. Milano Negro **L 56**
Locally common summer visitor. Open ground near marshes, rivers, seashore and rubbish dumps. Dark plumage, pale head and square 'cut off' tail used as a rudder. Often gregarious and noisy. Food, fish and other carrion. Call, a loud trill. Red Kite similar, but has forked tail and is more chestnut coloured.

Red Kite *Milvus milvus*
Sp. Milano Real **L 60**
Widespread resident. Open and wooded areas. Plumage rich chestnut, two distinct pale 'windows' on underside of wings; deeply forked tail. Very buoyant flight using tail as rudder. Food, carrion and small animals. Call a mewing. Black Kite similar, slightly smaller, darker, 'cut off' tail.

Griffon Vulture *Gyps fulvus*
Sp. Buitre Leonado **L 101**
Locally common. Partial migrant. Mountainous craggy areas. Huge bird of prey, extremely broad wings. Usually gregarious. Circles on thermals. Food, carrion. Call a series of grunts and hisses when feeding. Black Vulture similar, rare, black. Egyptian Vulture, smaller, black and 'dirty' white.

Marsh Harrier *Circus aeruginosus*
Sp. Aguilucho Lagunero **L 52**
Resident, locally common. Marshes, lakes with extensive reed beds, rice fields. Female uni-coloured dark, pale head. Male, chestnut, with grey and black wings. Glides with V-shaped wings, low over reed beds. Hunts birds and small mammals, also carrion. Call, shrill *chinka*. All other harriers similar, smaller, males grey with black wing tips, females have pale ring at tail base.

Buzzard *Buteo buteo*
Sp. Ratonero Común **L 54**
Comparatively common resident. Frequents scattered woodland areas. Extremely variable plumage, ranging from almost black to pale buff with black wing tips. Often seen in pairs circling on thermals. Food, small mammals and birds. Call a high-pitched mewing. Similar species all other buzzards and Black Kite.

Booted Eagle *Hieraaetus pennatus*
Sp. Aguila Calzada **L 50**
Widespread summer visitor. Open woodland. Pale phase the most common: pale body, and wings with broad black trailing edge. Migrates in large numbers over Gibraltar. Food mainly small birds. Call, short whistles. Egyptian Vulture similar but much larger with wedge-shaped tail.

Kestrel *Falco tinnunculus*
Sp. Cernícalo Real **L 34**
Very common resident. Open country. Brightly coloured. Male grey head and tail. Both sexes reddish brown wings, black tips, light mottled underparts, yellow legs. Hovers. Food, small animals and large insects. Call, loud *kee-kee-kee*. Lesser Kestrel, smaller, gregarious, migratory.

Little Owl *Athene noctua*
Sp. Mochuelo Común **L 23**
Common resident. Open fields, woodland, scrubland, villages. Small, dumpy, speckled with brown; yellow eyes. The only partly diurnal owl in region. Perches on posts and wires, bobs when alarmed, head can turn through 180°. Food, small mammals, birds and insects. Call, loud kiew-kiew. Scops Owl similar, slimmer with broad ear tufts.

Tawny Owl *Strix aluco*
Sp. Cárabo Común **L 38**
Common nocturnal resident. Prefers woodland. Large, brown, streaked, with dark eyes. Concealed in trees during daytime and often mobbed by birds. Mainly dawn and dusk hunting. Food, small birds and mammals. Call, quavering hoot. Little Owl similar, smaller, yellow eyes. Barn Owl, smaller, paler with very obvious facial disc.

Honey Buzzard

Buzzard

dark
phase

light
phase

Booted Eagle

Black Kite

Red Kite

female

male

hovering

Kestrel

Griffon Vulture

Little Owl

male

female

Marsh Harrier

Tawny Owl

Black-winged Stilt *Himantopus himantopus*
Sp. Cigüeñuela **L 38**
Common partial migrant. Salt and freshwater marshes, shallow lakes, ponds. Black and white, exceptionally long, pink legs. Juveniles brown and white. Gregarious, noisy, mobs intruders during breeding season. Food, aquatic insects. Call sharp *kik-kik*. Avocet similar, black-and-white wings, upturned bill, shorter grey legs.

Ringed Plover *Charadrius hiaticula*
Sp. Chorlitejo Grande **L 18**
Common winter visitor. Fresh and brackish marshes, shoreline. Small dumpy wader, distinctive black breast band, orange legs. Juvenile paler. Typical plover movement, runs then stops. Gregarious, often large flocks. Food, aquatic invertebrates. Call, *too-li*. Little Ringed Plover similar, smaller, frequents inland rivers.

Kentish Plover *Charadrius alexandrinus*
Sp. Chorlitejo Patinegro **L 16**
Common resident. Salt-pans, estuaries, seashores, freshwater mudflats. Small dumpy bird, black legs. Typical plover movement; gregarious in small numbers. Food, aquatic insects. Call, quiet *whit-whit-whit*. Little Ringed Plover, yellowish legs, inland waterways.

Redshank *Tringa totanus*
Sp. Archibebe Común **L 27**
Common resident. Marshes, estuaries, wet grasslands. In flight, distinctive white trailing edge to wings; orange-red legs. Often solitary, sometimes flocks during winter. Food, aquatic insects, crustaceans. Call unmistakable *twek-twek*. Spotted Redshank similar, larger, no white trailing wing edge. Greenshank, larger, paler, greenish legs.

Mediterranean Gull *Larus melanocephalus*
Sp. Gaviota Cabecinegra **L 37**
Relatively common winter visitor. Some immatures during summer. Marshlands, coastal waters, rarely inland. Summer plumage, distinctive black head, winter white head. Adults, white wing-tips. Food, fish. Call *kee-ow*. Black-headed Gull similar, head markings less, black wing marks.

Lesser Black-backed Gull *Larus fuscus*
Sp. Gaviota Sombría **L 53**
Very common resident.. Sea, shore, marshes, rivers, lakes, rubbish dumps. Juvenile heavily mottled with brown. Adult very dark grey and white, yellow legs. Follows fishing boats, adorns lamp-posts and sea walls. Aggressive and noisy when feeding. Food, carrion, fish and refuse. Call, *keou-keou*. Herring Gull similar, pale grey back. Greater Black-backed much larger, pinkish legs.

Little Tern *Sterna albifrons*
Sp. Charrancito **L 23**
Local summer visitor. Sea and estuaries. Black cap, white forehead, yellow bill with black tip, yellow legs. Smallest sea tern, graceful, frequently dives for small fish. A chattering call. Sandwich Tern similar, much larger, all black bill and black legs.

Black Tern *Chlidonias niger*
Sp. Fumarel Común **L 24**
Mainly passage migrant, spring and autumn. Occasional breeder, Inland lakes, marshes. Very dark black-grey. Small elegant tern. Winter plumage paler grey and white. Acrobatic flight, frequently taking insects from water, without ripples. Call, occasional *kik*. Whiskered Tern similar, red-bill and legs, paler plumage, frequently dives, very noisy.

Rock Dove *Columba livia*
Sp. Paloma Bravía **L 33**
Localized resident, sea cliffs. Distinctive white rump. Fast flight. Usually small groups. Food, mainly seeds. Call a soft *coo*. Stock Dove similar, lacks white rump. Feral Pigeon (domesticated pigeon) bred from the Rock Dove developing many forms.

Turtle Dove *Streptopelia turtur*
Sp. Tórtola Común **L 27**
Common summer visitor. Scattered woodlands. Smallish, highly coloured, a mixture of browns with pinkish tinge. Occasionally large flocks during migration. Food, seeds. Call soft *purrrr*. Wood Pigeon similar, much larger.

Black-winged Stilt

adult

Lesser Black-backed Gull

1st winter

adult   juv.

Ringed Plover

male   female

Kentish Plover

juv.

Little Tern

adult

summer

Redshank

winter

summer

Black Tern

adult

Rock Dove

1st winter

Mediterranean Gull

Turtle Dove

Cuckoo *Cuculus canorus*
Sp. Cuco **L 33**
Summer visitor. All types of country preferring open woodland. Grey, heavily barred breast, long tail. Nest parasite; never incubates own eggs. Food, insects, hairy caterpillars. Call: male, the familiar *cuc-coo*, female series of bubbling notes. Sparrowhawk similar, more rapid flight, hooked raptor beak

Swift *Apus apus*
Sp. Vencejo Común **L 17**
Common summer visitor. Seen everywhere especially over towns. Very dark plumage, long scythe-like wings. Extremely acrobatic and fast; spends most of life on the wing. Very gregarious. Hunts aerial insects, gliding effortlessly, high in the sky. Call a shrill scream. Pallid Swift similar, slightly paler brown with pale throat.

Kingfisher *Alcedo atthis*
Sp. Martín Pescador **L 18**
Common resident along rivers, lakes and seashores. Brilliant blue-green above, bright orange chest, heavy head and long bill. Dives from branch after fish, sometimes hovers, fast flight. Nests in holes in river banks. Call, high-pitched whistle.

Bee-eater *Merops apiaster*
Sp. Abejaruco **L 28**
Common summer visitor. Prefers areas with plenty of sandy banks, where they usually make their nest holes. Brilliantly coloured plumage, pointed wings and long tail. Acrobatic flight; perches on wire or branch awaiting prey, mainly wasps, bees, other flying insects. Call, liquid *phrupp*.

Hoopoe *Upupa epops*
Sp. Abubilla **L 28**
Common partial migrant. Open woodlands, golf courses and agricultural land. Unmistakable cinnamon, black-and-white plumage, long bill, large crest, broad wings. Flapping flight. Frequently probing moist mown lawns and leaf-mould under trees. Food, worms, ground insects, amphibians. Call, tri-syllabic *poo-poo-poo*. No similar species.

Great Spotted Woodpecker *Dendrocopos major*
Sp. Pico Picapinos **L 23**
Common resident. Deciduous and coniferous woodland. Black-and-white spotted plumage, male has red nape patch, both sexes red under tail. Undulating flight. Frequently drums on trees. Food: summer, insects; winter, seeds. Call, loud *kick*. Lesser Spotted Woodpecker similar, considerably smaller.

Crested Lark *Galerida cristata*
Sp. Cogujada Común **L 17**
Common resident. Open country and farmlands. Buff, streaked with brown, very conspicuous pointed crest. Often seen running up sandy paths, very fluttering flight. Food, insects and seeds. Call *chee-chee-chu*. Thekla Lark similar, greyer under wings, different song, more open rocky ground.

Woodlark *Lullula arborea*
Sp. Totovía **L 15**
Common resident, in scattered open woodland and scrub. Plumage basically buff, streaked with brown. Black-and-white spot at 'elbow' of wing. Undulating song flight. Often gregarious in autumn. Food, seeds and insects. Song, melodious *hwoo-loo-ee*. Skylark similar, lacks wing spot.

Skylark *Alauda arvensis*
Sp. Alondra Común **L 18**
Common resident in open agricultural land, scrubland and hills. Pale brown, heavily streaked, white edge to tail, small crest. Forms flocks in autumn. Food, insects and seeds. Song usually heard overhead, a vast outpouring of liquid bubbling notes. Woodland Lark similar, smaller, lacks white tail feathers and crest.

Meadow Pipit *Anthus pratensis*
Sp. Bisbita Común **L 14.5**
Winter visitor. Meadows, marshes, scrubland and open hillsides. Grey-brown with pale breast streaked with brown, pale legs, white outer-tail feathers. Often in large flocks in agricultural land. Food, insects. Call *tzi-tzi-tzi* usually in display flight. Tawny Pipit similar, much larger, paler and more wagtail-like.

female

male

male

Cuckoo

Great Spotted Woodpecker

Swift

Crested Lark

Kingfisher

Bee-eater

Woodlark

Skylark

crest raised

Hoopoe

Meadow Pipit

Crag Martin *Hirundo rupestris*
Sp. Avión Roquero **L** 15
Fairly common resident. In summer breeds in mountainous craggy areas, in winter inhabits lowland and coastal areas. Ashy-brown plumage, pale below, square-cut tail. Often seen in large flocks during winter. Food, insects. Call, soft twittering. Sand Martin similar, dark breast band.

Swallow *Hirundo rustica*
Sp. Golondrina Común **L** 19
Common summer visitor. Farmland, open spaces, gardens. Dark steel-blue, deeply forked tail, underparts pale cream, red chin. Fast flying, narrow wings. Frequently skims water. Nests in barns, garages on beams, ledges. Food, flying insects. Voice, soft twittering. Red-rumped Swallow, shorter tail, lacks breast-band, rusty rump.

House Martin *Delichon urbica*
Sp. Avión Común **L** 14
Common summer visitor. Glossy black, white rump and underparts, forked tail. Mainly near human habitation, nesting under house eaves. Fast flyer, often very high, catching insects on the wing. Voice a chattering twitter. Sand Martin similar, brown, lacks white rump.

Yellow Wagtail *Motacilla flava*
Sp. Lavandera Boyera **L** 16.5
Western European, blue-headed form depicted. Common summer visitor. Marshes, agricultural land. Male, blue-grey head, brilliant yellow underparts, green-yellow above. Female paler. Very active. Call, shrill *chip-chip*. Food, insects, small seeds. Grey Wagtail similar, grey back and head, frequents fast-flowing streams and rivers.

Nightingale *Luscinia megarhynchos*
Sp. Ruiseñor Común **L** 16.5
Common summer visitor. Woodlands with plenty of undergrowth, bramble-covered streams. Dull brown, reddish tail. Sings, day and night, well concealed in undergrowth. Food, insects. Voice rich variety of notes, very variable, extremely melodious. Robin similar, considerably smaller with red breast.

Black Redstart *Phoenicurus ochruros*
Sp. Colirrojo Tizón **L** 15
Common resident. Rocky hillsides, cliffs and broken ground. Male, black, red tail, white wing bar, greyer head. Female, browner. Briefly perches on stones. Very active, often confiding. Food, insects. Call a shrill high *sip*. Redstart similar, paler, reddish underneath. Male, white forehead.

Stonechat *Saxicola torquata*
Sp. Tarabilla Común **L** 12
Common resident. Farmland, scrub with low bushes, hillsides. Male very colourful, black head, white collar, reddish breast. Female, duller. Perches conspicuously on top of bushes, stones and wires. Food, insects. Call, harsh *chak* (like two stones knocked together). Whinchat similar, white eyestripe, more mottled plumage, white outer feathers at tail base.

Black-eared Wheatear *Oenanthe hispanica*
Sp. Collalba Rubia **L** 14.5
Common summer visitor. Cultivated areas and grasslands. Male striking black and cream plumage, conspicuous white rump when flying. Female, paler, pinkish tinge. Usually flies low from stone to stone. Food, insects. Voice, squeaky warble. Wheatear similar, grey head and back, buff breast, dark wings, also with white rump.

Wren *Troglodytes troglodytes*
Sp. Chorchín **L** 10
Common resident. Scrub, woods, hills and gardens. Diminutive dumpy brown bird, with cocked tail. Secretive, often hunting in low scrub. Food, mainly insects. Voice, surprisingly loud for such a small bird, a scolding *churr*.

Great Tit *Parus major*
Sp. Carbonero Común **L** 14
Common resident. Well-wooded areas and orchards. Black-and-white head, yellow breast with black central stripe, greyish back and wings. Active within trees and bushes. Food, insects, seeds. Song a distinctive *teecher-teecher-teecher*, also a loud *churr*. Blue Tit similar, smaller, with blue on head, wings and tail.

Nightingale

Crag Martin

Swallow

House Martin

female

male

Black Redstart

female

male

Stonechat

female

male

Black-eared Wheatear

male

female

Yellow Wagtail

Wren

Great Tit

Fan-tailed Warbler *Cisticola juncidis*
Sp. Buitrón **L 10**
Common resident in most of Spain. Marshes, farmland and scrub. Very small brown bird, heavily striped back, fan-shaped tail. Distinctive, jerky, undulating display song-flight. Food, insects. Call *zip-zip* in flight, one *zip* per bounce. Reed Warbler similar, summer visitor, larger with uniform plumage.

Great Reed Warbler *Acrocephalus arundinaceus*
Sp. Carricero Tordal **L 19**
Local summer resident. Marshes with extensive reedbeds. Largest warbler in the area. Dull reddish brown, cream underparts, prominent eye stripe. Frequently seen perching on high reeds. Food, insects. Song, loud far-reaching, very frog-like, *kara-kara, kree-kree, kirk* and various croaks. Reed Warbler similar, much smaller.

Sardinian Warbler *Sylvia melanocephala*
Sp. Curruca Cabecinegra **L 13**
Common resident. Gardens, scrubland and woods. Male, red eye-ring, black head, white breast, grey back. Female, red eye-ring, greyer. Very active within bushes. Food, insects. Call, agitated *chak-chak*, also a musical warble. Dartford Warbler similar, slightly smaller, maroon chest, cocked tail.

Short-toed Treecreeper *Certhia brachydactyla*
Sp. Agateador Común **L 13**
Common resident. Woodland, both coniferous and broad-leaved. Small brown bird with longish bill. Seen running up trunks of trees, flying to base of next to continue up again. Food, insects. Call, a high-pitched *teeut*. Treecreeper very similar, paler without buff flanks. Found only in north.

Golden Oriole *Oriolus oriolus*
Sp. Oropéndola **L 24**
Summer visitor to orchards, broad-leaved woods. Male unmistakable, bright-yellow body, black wings, red bill. Female, greenish yellow, streaked breast. Very difficult to see within the tree foliage. Undulating flight. Food, fruit and insects. Call, a distinctive, far-reaching *wee-oo*.

Jay *Garrulus glandarius*
Sp. Arrendajo Común **L 35**
Common resident. Woods and agricultural land. Pinkish brown body, black tail with conspicuous white rump. Wings black and white, with well-known blue barred feathers. Sometimes forms groups in spring. Food, varied, seeds, fruit, worms, young birds and eggs. Call, a raucous screech. No similar species.

Azure-winged Magpie *Cyanopica cyanus*
Sp. Rabilargo **L 35**
Local resident in southern Spain. Cork woods, orchards, and mixed forest. Striking black head, buff-pink body and powder blue wings. Gregarious and noisy. Food, fruit and seeds. Call, harsh *zo-whee*. Magpie similar, larger, black and white.

Magpie *Pica pica*
Sp. Urraca **L 45**
Common resident. Farmland, gardens, woods. Black head and tail (half of length is tail), black-and-white wings, white chest. Perches on wires and posts, hops sideways on ground. Fairly gregarious. Food, carrion, young birds, eggs and seeds. Call, a harsh *chait*. Azure-winged Magpie similar, smaller, with blue wings.

Jackdaw *Corvus monedula*
Sp. Grajilla **L 33**
Common resident. Agricultural land, old buildings and sea cliffs. All black with grey head. Gregarious, fairly confiding, can be noisy in flight. Food, worms, seeds, small animals, eggs and birds. Call, harsh *jack*. Carrion Crow and Rook similar but much larger. Chough, red bill and feet, buoyant flight, larger.

Raven *Corvus corax*
Sp. Cuervo **L 65**
Widespread resident of open country, rocky hills and mountains. Large, black with strong bill. Often seen soaring in pairs with widespread wings. Food, carrion, eggs, birds and mammals, also seeds. Call, harsh but low *karr-karr*. Carrion Crow similar, smaller. Jackdaw even smaller. Chough, red bill and feet.

song flight

Fan-tailed
Warbler

Jay

Great Reed
Warbler

Azure-winged Magpie

female

male

Sardinian Warbler

Magpie

Short-toed
Treecreeper

Jackdaw

male

female

Golden Oriole

Raven

Great Grey Shrike *Lanius excubitor*
Sp. Alcaudón Real L 24
South Iberian, pinkish-tinged breast form depicted. Common resident. Open country, agricultural land. Grey and black, mask-like black eye stripe, sharp beak. Sits on wires and bush tops, pouncing on insects, in spring impaling them on thorns. Food, insects, small mammals, birds. Call, shrill *shreek*. Woodchat Shrike similar, smaller, chestnut crown and nape.

Woodchat Shrike *Lanius senator*
Sp. Alcaudón Común L 19
Summer visitor. Open and wooded country. Pale breast, black-and-white wings, rich chestnut crown and nape, sharp bill. Sits on wires and posts. Food, insects, small birds. Call, mimicry, more melodious than Great Grey Shrike, which is similar, larger, without chestnut crown on head.

Spotless Starling *Sturnus unicolor*
Sp. Estornino Negro L 21
Common resident. Open countryside, agricultural land, gardens, villages. Dull black with yellowish bill. Congregates in large flocks, roosting on wires, trees and reed beds. Food, insects, seeds and fruit. Call, loud mimicry, chattering. Starling similar, iridescent spots, winter visitor.

Tree Sparrow *Passer montanus*
Sp. Gorrión Molinero L 14
Local resident. Open woodland, scrub, orchards. Chestnut crown, white collar, black patch on cheek, paler underneath. Usually gregarious. Food, seeds and insects. Voice, *chip-chip*. House Sparrow similar, found around human habitation, grey crown. Male larger, black bib.

Serin *Serinus serinus*
Sp. Verdecillo L 11
Common resident. Woodlands, orchards, most cultivated land. Yellow breast, grey and black streaks on back, prominent yellow rump. The Canary Islands form is the ancestor of the cage canary. Gregarious. Food, seeds. Call, high-pitched twittering. Siskin similar, winter visitor, has a dark crown.

Greenfinch *Carduelis chloris*
Sp. Verderón L 14.5
Common resident. Open woodland, orchards, villages. Yellow-green with prominent yellow wing bar. Gregarious, often forming flocks with other finches. Food, seeds. Call, drawn out *cheee-ee*, and various twitterings. Female Linnet similar, but is brown, and female House Sparrow, brown and lacks yellow wing bar.

Goldfinch *Carduelis carduelis*
Sp. Jilguero L 14
Common resident. Open woodland, farmland, orchards, gardens. Adult striking, with red face; black on head, wings and tail; brown back; bright yellow wing bar. Gregarious, often with other finches. Food, seeds, especially thistle and teasel. Call, variation on a jingling twitter. Greenfinch similar, lacks red on face, larger, uniform green.

Linnet *Carduelis cannabina*
Sp. Pardillo Común L 13
Common resident in open woodland, heaths and scrub, agricultural land. Male rich streaked brown, red breast and forehead. Female lacks the red. Gregarious, often with other finches, sometimes in large flocks. Food, seeds. Call, twittering in flight. Female House Sparrow similar, paler underneath, lacking red on breast and face.

Rock Bunting *Emberiza cia*
Sp. Escribano Montesino L 16
Local resident. Summer, hillsides and mountains with rocks and trees; winter, lower down. Variations in brown, grey head with three prominent black stripes, chestnut rump. Food, seeds. Call, a bubbling twitter. Corn Bunting similar, lacks the grey head and black markings; larger.

Corn Bunting *Miliaria calandra*
Sp. Triguero L 18
Common resident. Agricultural land, scrub, hillsides. Largest bunting, streaked brown. Sits on wires, when flying the legs often hang down. Food, seeds. Song, distinctive, from a wire or post, resembles the jangling of a bunch of keys. Rock Bunting similar, has black stripes on head.

female

Greenfinch

male

Great Grey Shrike

male

female

Woodchat Shrike

Goldfinch

female

male

Linnet

Spotless Starling

female

Rock Bunting

male

Tree Sparrow

male

Serin

female

Corn Bunting

Hedgehog *Erinaceus europaeus* Sp. Erizo Común
Body 22–28, tail 2.0–3.5, weight 0.5–1.25
Common, scrub, wood fringes, orchards, gardens.
Mainly active from dusk throughout the night.
Iberian form is lighter coloured than the northern
one. Rolls into a prickly ball when in danger.
Hibernates. Food, insects, worms, snails, eggs.
Voice, grunts and snores. Vagrant or Algerian
Hedgehog similar, much paler, inhabits Mediter-
ranean coastline.

Noctule Bat *Nyctalus noctula* Sp. Nóctulo
Común **Body 7–8, tail 4–6, weight 15–40g**
Common. Open woods, agricultural land, orchards. Flies earlier in the evening than other bats,
and fairly high. Hibernates in hollow trees, stone
buildings, not in eaves. Usually in large groups.
Often migrates vast distances. Food, insects.
Voice, high-pitched squeak. Pipistrelle similar,
considerably smaller.

Rabbit *Oryctolagus cuniculus* Sp. Conejo
Body 34–45, tail 4–8, weight 1.50–2.25
Common. Woods, hills, open parkland, mainly
sandy land. Breeds in large colonies in burrows.
Tends to be nocturnal, but often feeds at dawn
and dusk. Food, plants, will eat tree bark. Voice,
gives loud screams when frightened, mainly silent.
Thumps with hind legs as warning. Dives for
undergrowth or burrow when disturbed. Brown
Hare similar, larger, dark tips to ears.

Brown Hare *Lepus capensis* Sp. Liebre
Body 48–68, tail 7–11, weight 2.5–6.5
Common. Agricultural land and open grasslands.
Usually solitary except in breeding season. Does
not burrow, but rests in a depression (form) on
the ground. The Iberian race is smaller than the
northern European race. Mainly nocturnal, but
often seen feeding in fields. Food, plants. Is
mainly silent. Rabbit similar, smaller, lacks dark
tip to ears.

Red Fox *Vulpes vulpes* Sp. Zorro
Body 60–70, tail 35–48, weight 6–10
Locally common. Woods, scrubland, tall vegeta-
tion. Mainly nocturnal, sometimes hunts during

daytime. Iberian species is smaller and greyer than
the northern European species, always with a
white tail tip. Food, varied: carrion, fruit, birds,
rodents, eggs. Voice, barks, vixen wails in mating
season. Wolf similar, much larger, no white tail
tip.

Weasel *Mustela nivalis* Sp. Comadreja
Body 16–24, tail 6–6.5, weight 60–130g
Local. Prefers sandy, dry agricultural lands, scrub,
open woodland, villages. Male considerably larger
than female. Smallest of the group known as
martens. Mainly nocturnal but also hunts by day.
Food very varied, always carnivorous, birds, mice,
rats, rabbits. Stoat similar, larger and found only
in northern Spain.

Beech Marten *Martes foina* Sp.Garduña
Body 42–48, tail 23–26, weight 1.70–2.25
Local. Rocky outcrops, cliffs, rough hillsides,
sometimes barns. Nocturnal. Mating occurs in
summer. Three to four kittens are born the
following spring, about 250 days gestation. Food,
mainly rats, birds, also fruit. Pine Marten similar
having a yellowish-cream bib, and is found in
extreme north of Spain.

Otter *Lutra lutra* Sp. Nutria
Body 62–83, tail 36–55, weight 5.5–15
Local. Streams, rivers, lakes, marshes. Mainly
nocturnal. Swims powerfully with webbed feet
and can remain underwater for some time. Often
makes lengthy expeditions overland to find new
feeding grounds. Playful, slides down banks.
Food, mainly fish, occasionally crustaceans, eels,
frogs. Voice, drawn-out whistle. Egyptian Mongoose similar, smaller, tuft at end of tail.

Brown Rat *Rattus norvegicus* Sp. Rata Común
Body 21.5–27.5, tail 17–23, weight 0.25–0.50
Common. Fields, farmyards. During winter,
buildings and villages; spring and summer, fields
and river banks where it makes its nest. Mainly
nocturnal but often seen by day. Food varied,
refuse, small animals, birds, grain, eggs. Voice
loud squeaks and squeals. Black Rat similar,
darker, smaller, longer tail.

Hedgehog

Red Fox

Noctule Bat

Weasel

Rabbit

Beech Marten

Brown Hare

Otter

Brown Rat

Wild Cat *Felis silvestris*
Sp. Gato Montés
Body 48–80, tail 26–37, weight 5–10
Local, rare. Woods, scrub, rocky hills, mountains. Nocturnal, hunting at dawn and dusk. Rests in holes in trees and rocks or lies along branches in daytime. Very fierce (kittens cannot be domesticated), but will mate with household cats. Food, birds, mammals, reptiles, fish. Voice, mews, purrs. Domestic cat similar, smaller, with longer thinner tail.

Badger *Meles meles*
Sp. Tejón
Body 61–72, tail 11–19, weight 10–22
Local, never abundant. Open woodland with plenty of undergrowth. Prefers soft sandy or chalky soil to build its extensive set. Very clean; nest lined with bracken, leaves and grass which is thrown out when soiled. Nocturnal, playing and hunting in moonlight. Food, earthworms, insects, small mammals, eggs, berries, plant roots. Voice, noisy, mixture of growls, snores, sometimes a scream. No similar species.

Egyptian Mongoose *Herpestes ichneumon*
Sp. Meloncillo
Body 51–55, tail 33–45, weight 7–8
Common southern half of Iberia. Scrub, open woodland, marshes, river banks. Mainly nocturnal, but does hunt by day. Often seen in family parties of mother and up to four young; the litter remains with the mother after the next litter is born. Food, snakes, amphibians, eggs, birds, rodents. Voice rarely heard. Otter similar, but larger, lacks bushy end to tail.

Genet *Genetta genetta*
Sp. Gineta
Body 47–58, tail 41–48, weight 1.00–2.25
Common but seldom seen. Woods, scrub, rocky stream beds. Exclusively nocturnal and mainly solitary; spends a lot of time moving noiselessly through the undergrowth or branches of trees. Food, small mammals, eggs, birds, insects, reptiles. Domestic cat similar, much longer legged and not spotted.

Wild Boar *Sus scrofa*
Sp. Jabalí
Body 110–115, tail 15–20, weight 35–175
Common. Woods with plenty of undergrowth, marshes. Likes to wallow in muddy ponds, especially in summer. Can cause considerable damage to farmland by uprooting and eating roots and vegetables. Mainly nocturnal, tends to rest in bramble-covered valleys during the day. Food, mainly vegetation, roots, seeds. Voice, grunts and snorts. No similar species.

Spanish Ibex *Capra hircus*
Sp. Cabra Montés
Body 130–145, tail 12–15, weight 50–120
Rare, confined to summits of high sierras where it shows amazing ability to maintain footing on precipitous mountainsides; most numerous in the Sierra de Gredos. Almost extinct until King Alfonso XIII controlled hunting in 1905. Food, grass and mountain vegetation, coming down to pasture-land in winter. Voice, a short loud hiss. Chamois similar, smaller with slender horns.

Chamois *Rupicapra rupicapra*
Sp. Rebeco
Body 110–130, tail 3–4, weight 25–50
Rare, mainly in high Pyrenees and Cantábrican mountains; prefers coniferous woodland just within the treeline. Feeds during morning and evening, usually rests during middle of the day. Goes down to pasture-land during winter. Food, vegetation, seeds. Voice, rather goat-like bleat, but mainly silent. Spanish Ibex similar, larger, longer curved horns.

Roe Deer *Capreolus capreolus*
Sp. Corzo
Body 95–135, tail 2–3, weight 15–27
Widespread in open woodland. The commonest Spanish deer. Feeds at dawn and dusk, also active at night. Conspicuous white patch around tail, especially during winter. Food, grass, leaves, shoots, berries. Voice, deep bark if startled, usually silent. Red Deer similar, much larger, with large branched antlers on the male. Fallow Deer, larger, with the stag having palmate antlers.

Wild Cat

Spanish
Ibex

male,
summer

Badger

Egyptian Mongoose

summer

Genet

Chamois

male

Wild
Boar

male,
summer

Roe
Deer

Fire Salamander *Salamandra salamandra*
Sp. Salamandra Común **L 20–28**
Local. Usually in forests, woods, hilly country but always where it is damp and near water. Highly colourful, black body with yellow, orange or red spots and blotches. Entirely nocturnal. Often gives birth to live young (viviparous). Food, invertebrates. No similar species.

Striped (Common) Tree Frog *Hyla arborea*
Sp. Ranita de San Antonio **L 5**
Common. Marshland with tall reed beds, bushes, trees. Climbs well. Usually bright green. Blue, yellow or brown forms are known. Mainly nocturnal. Rests on leaves in sunlight. Food, insects. Call, loud *krak-krak* during breeding season. Stripeless Tree Frog similar, lacks flank stripe.

Natterjack Toad *Bufo calamita*
Sp. Sapo Corredor **L 7–10**
Common locally. Mainly sandy areas, sand dunes near sea or quite high in mountains. Nocturnal, tends to run instead of hop. Spends day in holes or under stones. Food, mainly insects, caterpillars, worms, snails. Call, loud *errr-errr* during mating season. Common Toad similar, but considerably larger.

Common Toad *Bufo Bufo*
Sp. Sapo Común **L 15**
Common. Almost any locality, fields, scrub, hillsides, woodland; during breeding season, ponds and marshes. Largest European toad, female can become massive (15cm long). Mainly nocturnal. Food, insects, worms, snails, slugs, caterpillars, all of which must be live. Call, croak during mating season. Natterjack Toad similar, but smaller.

Marsh Frog *Rana ridibunda*
Sp. Rana Común **L 15**
Common. Ponds, lakes, rivers, marshes. Rests on banks, jumping into water at the slightest disturbance. Frequently seen with just nose and eyes above water. Food, insects, snails, crustaceans. Call very noisy, day and night during mating season. Other frogs similar, smaller.

European Pond Terrapin *Emys orbicularis*
Sp. Galápago **L 20**
Common. Slow-moving rivers, ponds, lakes. Sun themselves on river banks, very timid, sliding into water if disturbed. Swim with only head and neck showing. Food, aquatic insects, invertebrates, snails. Stripe-necked Terrapin similar, but with striped neck. Spur-thighed Tortoise, terrestrial, larger, vegetarian.

Ocellated Lizard *Lacerta lepida*
Sp. Lagarto Ocelado **Body 20, tail 30–40**
Common. Agricultural land, scrub, woodlands, hillsides. Brilliant green with large blue spots along side. Largest European lizard, gives a nasty bite if cornered. Powerful and sharp claws. Food, large insects, worms, eggs, birds, small mammals and in autumn fallen fruit. Green Lizard similar, smaller.

Moorish Gecko *Tarentola mauritanica*
Sp. Salamanquesa Común **L 15**
Common. Dry walls, rocky land, houses, often seen around lights at night. Mainly nocturnal, highly territorial, especially the males. Climbs walls by its adhesive foot pads; often enters houses. Many myths surround the gecko, but it is harmless. Food, insects, hunted by sight. Turkish Gecko similar, smaller.

Montpellier Snake *Malpolon monspessulanus*
Sp. Culebra Bastarda **L 200**
Common. Scrub, marshes, agricultural land, sand dunes, woods. Venomous, unlikely to bite unless picked up, fangs placed very far back. Hisses if threatened. Food, lizards, mammals up to small rabbit size, birds, eggs. Other large snakes similar, but lack prominent ridge above eye.

Ladder Snake *Elaphe scalaris*
Sp. Culebra de Escalera **L 160**
Common. Stony rocky ground with bushes, walls, scrubland. Large non-venomous snake, kills prey by constriction. Lies in the sun near bushes. Food, mammals up to small rabbit size, birds, grasshoppers. Montpellier Snake similar, larger, prominent eye ridges.

Fire Salamander

European Pond Terrapin

Stripeless
Tree Frog

Ocellated Lizard

male
in song

Natterjack Toad

Moorish Gecko

Common Toad

Montpellier Snake

adult

Ladder Snake

young

Marsh Frog

Swallowtail *Papilio machaon*
Sp. Macaón **W 6.4–10.0**
Common. Meadows and gardens. Main flight periods April/May and July/August. Caterpillar large, bright green, with a black transverse band in each segment, broken by a series of red spots. Food, Umbelliferae especially Fennel and Wild Carrot. Scarce Swallowtail similar, has more striped markings.

Scarce Swallowtail *Iphiclides podalirius*
Sp. Podalirio **W 6.4–9.0**
Locally common. Open woodlands and orchards. Flight period March to September. Caterpillar up to 4cm long, fat and green with oblique yellow lines down middle of back. Food, fruit trees, mainly in the *Prunus* group. Swallowtail similar, brighter yellow, less striped, shorter tails.

Spanish Festoon *Zerynthia rumina*
Sp. Arlequin **W 4.4–4.6**
Common. Hillsides, especially near the sea. Flight period early in the year, February to May. Caterpillar pale buff with black spots, two rows of reddish black-tipped stiff hairs. Food, various species of *Aristolochia* (birthwort). Southern Festoon similar, but lacks red markings on forewing.

Black-veined White *Aporia crataegi*
Sp. Blanco del Espino Albar **W 5.6–6.8**
Common. Fields and orchards. Can become a pest. Flight period May/June. Caterpillar hairy, grey, with black band running down back, with two lines of orange markings. Food, Cherry, Hawthorn and other fruit trees. Large White similar, has black wing spots.

Large White *Pieris brassicae*
Sp. Mariposa de la Col **W 5.7–6.6**
Very common. Prominent dark tips to white wings. Gardens and agricultural land; sometimes causes serious damage. Flight period April to August. Caterpillar green with black markings down the sides and a broad yellow stripe down the back. Food, cabbage and other *Brassica* species. Small White similar, 1–2cm smaller.

Green-veined White *Pieris napi*
Sp. Blanca Verdinervada **W 3.6–5.0**
Local. Usually found north of Madrid, more plentiful near Santander. Flight period March to August. Caterpillar, green with small black spots, slightly hairy. Food, cabbage and other *Brassica* species. Small White similar, does not have the green-grey veins on underneath of hind-wings.

Clouded Yellow *Colias crocea*
Sp. Colia Común **W 4.6–5.4**
Common. Scrubland and open farmland. Flight period April/May and then later with a succession of broods. Caterpillar green with fine black spots and yellow line down each side. Food, clovers and vetches. Large White and Small White similar, but lack the yellow markings.

Cleopatra *Genepteryx cleopatra*
Sp. Cleopatra **W 5.0–6.8**
Common. Open woodland and agricultural land. Large orange area on forewing. Flight period May/June and later. Caterpillar basically green, finely marked with black, shading to blue-green along back. Food, Buckthorn and Alder. Brimstone similar, but lacks orange markings on forewing.

Wood White *Leptidea sinapis*
Sp. Blanca Esbelta **W 3.6–4.8**
Common. Woodlands and scrub. More delicate than other whites. Flight period May/June and later with two or more broods. Caterpillar small, green with a darker line down middle of back and yellow line along the side. Food, bird's-foot trefoil, vetches and related plants. Large White and Small White similar, but both are larger.

Spanish Purple Hairstreak *Laeosopis roboris*
Sp. Moradilla del Fresna **W 2.4–3.0**
Local. North and central Spain, in mountainous areas up to 1500m (5000 feet) altitude. Flight period May to August. Caterpillar short, maximum 15mm length, brown with grey-brown line down middle of back. Food, Ash. Purple Hairstreak similar, has greyer underwing lacking orange-spotted border.

Swallowtail

Scarce Swallowtail

Spanish Festoon

Black-veined White

Large White

Green-veined White

Clouded Yellow

female   male

Cleopatra

Wood White

Spanish Purple Hairstreak

Small Copper *Lycaena phlaeas*
Sp. Manto Bicolór   **W 2.4–2.8**
Common. Especially in flowery meadows. Flight
period from March to October. Caterpillar small
and fat, but tapering at head and tail. Green with
a pale purple line running along the back. Food,
sorrel and species of dock. Sooty Copper similar,
but is rare, the male having sooty-brown fore-
wings.

Escher's Blue *Agrodiaetus escheri*
Sp. Fabióla   **W 3.4–4.0**
Locally common. Rocky hilly areas up to 2000m
(6560 feet) altitude. Flight period June/July.
Caterpillar small and fat, usually green with a dark
brown line running down the middle of the back,
but very variable. Food, milk-vetch. Adonis Blue
similar, smaller and without the violet hue.

Spanish Chalk-hill Blue *Lysandra albicans*
Sp. Ninfa Coridón   **W 3.6–4.2**
Local. Restricted to limestone hillsides from sea
level to 2000m (6560 feet) altitude. Flight period
July/August. Caterpillar small, green with two
yellow lines along back and a double yellow line
along the sides; very variable. Food, vetch species.
Chalk-hill Blue similar, smaller and much more
blue.

Two-tailed Pasha *Charaxes jasius*
Sp. El Bajá   **W 7.6–8.3**
Local. Restricted to coastal areas, especially where
the food plant is plentiful. One of Europe's largest
butterflies. Flight period May/June and August/
September. Caterpillar large, green, with two
yellow spots ringed with black in middle of back.
Two prongs at tail and four large backward-
pointing horns at back of head. Food, Strawberry
Tree. No similar species.

Red Admiral *Vanessa atalanta*
Sp. Vulcana   **W 5.6–6.3**
Common. Gardens and orchards. Flight period
May to October. Migratory. Caterpillar medium
sized. Two colour forms; the most common, dark
grey with black hairs and yellow patches at side of
body. Food, nettle. No similar species.

Painted Lady *Cynthia cardui*
Sp. Cordera   **W 5.4–5.8**
Common. Hillsides and pasture-land. Strongly
migratory. Flight period April to October. Caterpillar medium length, black with fine white spots
and black hairs. Fine yellow line down lower side
of body. Food, nettles and thistles. American
Painted Lady similar, much smaller, occasional
migrant.

Queen of Spain Fritillary *Issoria lathonia*
Sp. Sofia   **W 3.8–4.6**
Common. Meadows and scrubland. Migratory.
Wings more pointed than other fritillaries. Flight
period February/March sometimes later. Caterpillar medium sized, black with fine white spots
and a double white line along middle of back;
brown hairs all over. Food, violets. Most species of
fritillaries are similar.

Meadow Fritillary *Mellicta parthenoides*
Sp. Minerva   **W 3.0–3.6**
Common, flying close to the ground on hills and
mountains up to 2500m (8200 feet) altitude.
Flight period May to August. Caterpillar medium
sized, black with small white spots and dark hairs.
Food, scabious and plantain. Most species of
fritillaries are similar.

Great Banded Grayling *Brintesia circe*
Sp. Rey Mozo   **W 6.6–8.0**
Common. Woodlands up to 800m (2600 feet)
altitude. Flight period June/July. Caterpillar medium sized, tapering towards the tail where there
are two small prongs. Pale brownish-grey to
greenish-grey, but variable. Food, grasses. The
Hermit is similar, but smaller and paler.

Meadow Brown *Maniola jurtina*
Sp. Loba   **W 4.0–5.8**
Common. All grassy places up to 2000m (6560
feet) altitude. Flight period June to August. Caterpillar medium sized, tapering towards the tail
where there are two small points. Yellowish-green
with a covering of white hairs. Food, grasses
especially meadow grass. There are many other
browns, and ringlets are similar.

Small Copper

male

female

Escher's Blue

Spanish Chalk-hill Blue

Painted Lady

Queen of Spain Fritillary

Meadow Fritillary

Two-tailed Pasha

Great
Banded Grayling

Red Admiral

Meadow Brown

Stone or Umbrella Pine
Pinus pinea
Common, especially near the coast on sand or alluvial soils. A large handsome evergreen tree, up to 30m high with an umbrella-shaped crown. The fruiting cone is almost spherical. The seeds are hard shelled. The pine kernel which is edible is a delicacy.

Beech
Fagus sylvatica
Common. Forms forests in the north and mountainous areas. A large deciduous tree up to 30m high. The leaves become beautifully golden-brown before falling in the autumn. The seeds (mast) are relished by rodents, especially squirrels. The hard durable wood is used for furniture making. Also excellent for fuel, giving great heat with little smoke.

Sweet or Spanish Chestnut
Castanea sativa
Common. A large deciduous tree, up to 40m high. Has long leathery leaves with finely serrated edges. The catkins are followed by edible nuts, harvested in autumn; many exported to northern Europe. The hard durable wood is used for furniture or fencing.

Holm or Ilex Oak
Quercus ilex
Common. Large evergreen found in most parts, especially the centre and south. Livestock estates use them for shelter. These trees are often severely pruned, the offsets used for charcoal. Herds of pigs feed on the acorns. A valuable hard timber used for building and furniture.

Cork Oak
Quercus suber
Common. Evergreen oak from the warmer areas, up to 25m tall. The thick outer bark (cork) is skillfully removed every eight to ten years. The catkins are followed by large acorns relished by pigs. The very hard wood is used for floors and furniture. Cork forms an important part of the economy.

Fig
Ficus carica
Small deciduous tree, common in the warmer areas, reaching a height of 4m. The large green leaves appear early in spring followed by a crop of fruit, sometimes with a second crop two months later. No visible typical flowers. The wood is soft and of no commercial value.

Oriental Plane
Platanus orientalis
Common in the cooler northern towns. A native of eastern Europe normally grown as an avenue tree. Deciduous and sheds its bark in patches. The fruit clusters are usually in pairs. It will grow to 60m but is usually extensively pruned. The hard durable wood is often used for furniture.

Japanese Loquat
Eriobotrya japonica
Native to Japan but often cultivated in warm gardens as an evergreen ornamental fruiting tree. 5–10m tall with large leathery dark-green leaves with rusty undersides. The sweet-smelling white cluster is produced in early winter followed by large yellow plum-shaped sweet fruit.

Carob Tree
Ceratonia siliqua
Native of eastern Mediterranean, grown in most warmer parts. Slow-growing evergreen up to 10m. Dark shiny leaves, the flowers are often seen together with the long black pods. Fruit used for animal feeds or as a chocolate substitute. Hard wood used for fuel and furniture.

Olive
Olea europaea
Cultivated in vast plantations in warmer parts, Andalucía in particular. Attractive evergreen, up to 10m tall with grey-green leaves. Small white flowers produced in spring, green fruit turning black when ripe, harvested in autumn. Olive oil forms important part of the economy. Wood hard, beautifully grained, used for carving.

Stone or Umbrella Pine

Holm or Ilex Oak

Cork Oak

Beech

Fig

Japanese Loquat

Sweet or Spanish Chestnut

Carob Tree

Oriental Plane

Olive

Almond
Prunus dulcis

Cultivated deciduous tree in southern warmer areas, up to 10m. Attractive pink to almost white flowers appear in early spring before the leaves, followed by hard wrinkled edible nuts encased in a leathery skin, harvested in autumn. The hard durable wood is used for fuel and veneers.

Judas Tree
Cercis siliquastrum

Attractive ornamental deciduous tree common in warmer areas. Up to 10m. The magenta, pink or white pea-shaped flowers appear in early spring before the leaves. The large pod-shaped fruit hang until well into autumn. The hard fine-grained wood is used for furniture making.

Mimosa
Acacia retinodes

Common small ornamental tree, native to Australia, frequently planted in gardens. Reaches a maximum height of 10m producing clusters of globular pale-yellow flowers on the ends of the flexible branches throughout the year. The bark is rich in tannin and the wood hard.

Prickly Pear
Opuntia ficus-indica

Native to the Americas. This cactus is frequently planted in gardens for ornament in the warmer south. Often cultivated for the fruit. The jointed stems reach 3m. Orange or yellow flowers are produced on the edge of the pads, followed by yellow or orange fruit.

Pomegranate
Punica granatum

Small attractive deciduous shrub or tree, 2–5m tall. Cultivated for their fruit or planted in gardens for their attractive scarlet flowers which are produced in profusion in early summer. These are followed by the well-known, hard-skinned fruit.

St Dabeoc's Heath
Daboecia cantabrica

Local heather-type plant of the north and west of Iberia, usually on low acid heathlands free from severe frosts, and with plenty of moisture. Small neat perennial shrub normally not more than 60cm high. Evergreen, it produces attractive purple flowers over a long period, mainly June to October.

Strawberry Tree
Arbutus unedo

Common small evergreen tree up to 8m tall. Seems to prefer a slightly acid soil. The flowers in autumn are creamy drooping bells (rather like Lily-of-the-Valley). The round rather rough reddish-yellow fruit takes a year to ripen. Sometimes collected to make a very strong spirit. Food plant of the spectacular Two-tailed Pasha butterfly.

Tree Heather
Erica arborea

Common evergreen heather usually growing up to 2.5m, but in favourable conditions can be even taller. Prefers a calcareous soil in southern areas. Produces masses of white flowers during winter. Roots are very hard and are used to produce the finest briar tobacco pipes.

Oleander
Nerium oleander

Strong-growing evergreen shrub, 3–4m high. Usually found growing in dried-up river beds, especially in the hot arid south. Used extensively in Andalucían motorway landscaping. Usual colour is pink but red, white, apricot and double-flower forms have been developed for horticultural use.

Shrub Tobacco
Nicotiana glauca

A slender shrubby perennial from South America which has naturalised in many areas in the south, on waste ground, old rubbish dumps and dry scrublands. Small grey-green leaves. The tubular yellow flowers are produced almost throughout the year. Very small seeds.

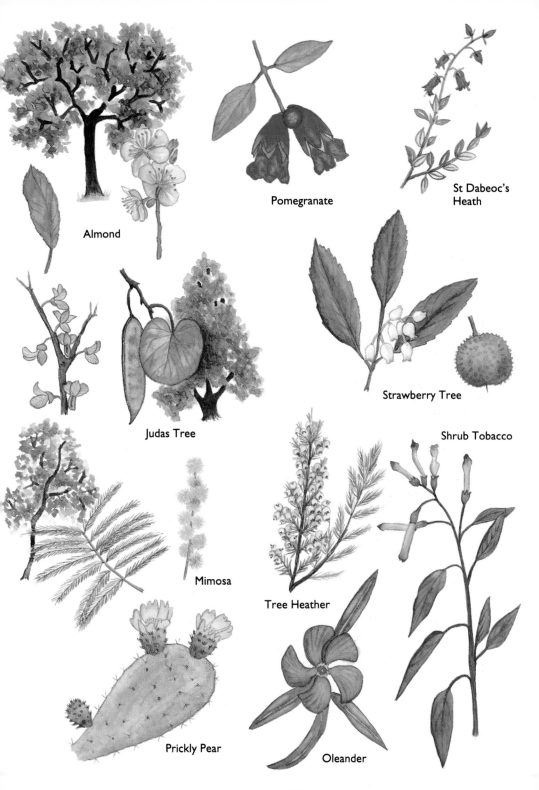

Pomegranate

St Dabeoc's Heath

Almond

Judas Tree

Strawberry Tree

Shrub Tobacco

Mimosa

Tree Heather

Prickly Pear

Oleander

Cytinus ruber

Striking parasitic plant found in all regions except the north. Grows on cistus and *Halimium* roots, from which it gains all its nourishment, preferring *Cistus crispus*. It is devoid of chlorophyll and pushes its short stem up through the soil under the shrubs. The flowering head is cream with each flower encased in a scarlet bract.

Pheasant's Eye

Adonis annua

Common annual plant of the fields and roadsides. Up to 40cm high with fine feathery grey-green foliage. The flowers during April to June are up to 2.5cm in diameter, bright red, often with a black spot at the base of the petal.

Corn Poppy

Papaver rhoeas

Common scarlet poppy seen in fields and roadsides throughout the region. Annual, up to 90cm tall, which exudes a white latex if cut. Flower is large, up to 10cm diameter, often with a dark patch at the petal base. Seed capsule large with flat top, seed very small.

Sea Stock

Matthiola sinuata

Common plant in coastal areas, either on rocky shoreline or sandy dunes. Perennial or biennial up to 60cm tall. Leaves are thick and grey-green with wavy edges. Lilac sweet-scented flowers are produced from March to June followed by 12cm-long seed pods.

Sweet Alison

Lobularia maritima

Common throughout near the coast, usually on sandy road edges, rocky hillsides and in scrubland. A low spreading perennial with small pale-green leaves. The small white scented flowers are produced almost throughout the year and are followed by small elliptical seed pods.

Upright Mignonette

Reseda alba

Local along the southern coastline. Annual, biennial or perennial depending on growing conditions. Up to 50cm in height with a tall flowering stem. Flowers are produced in a conical spike; each individual white flower is almost 1cm in diameter. Seed pods up to 1cm long.

Pyrenean Saxifrage

Saxifraga longifolia

Local plant of the high Alpine mountains in the Pyrenees. Beautiful silver-leaved rosette up to 12cm in diameter growing in the tight crevices of rocks. Monocarpic (dies after it flowers) perennial which eventually produces a long graceful flower-spike of cream flowers.

White Spanish Broom

Cytisus multiflorus

Common in most areas. Beautiful graceful shrub up to 3m high. The long slender but stiff branches are covered with white pea-shaped flowers in early spring and summer. The leaves are small and covered with white hairs. Used in motorway landscaping.

Greenweed

Genista cinerea

Common in any limestone areas amongst rocks. Grey-green shrub up to 2m high, with long thin much-branched stems. Flowers, yellow, pea-shaped in clusters of one to five followed by a pod up to 1.5cm long. Flowering period March to June.

Spanish Broom

Spartium junceum

Common on scrubland, mainly on limestone soil over most of Spain. Rush-like plant with stiff branches and stems up to 3m high. Flowers pea-shaped, up to 2cm long, yellow and fragrant, followed by 8cm-long black pods. Flowers May to August.

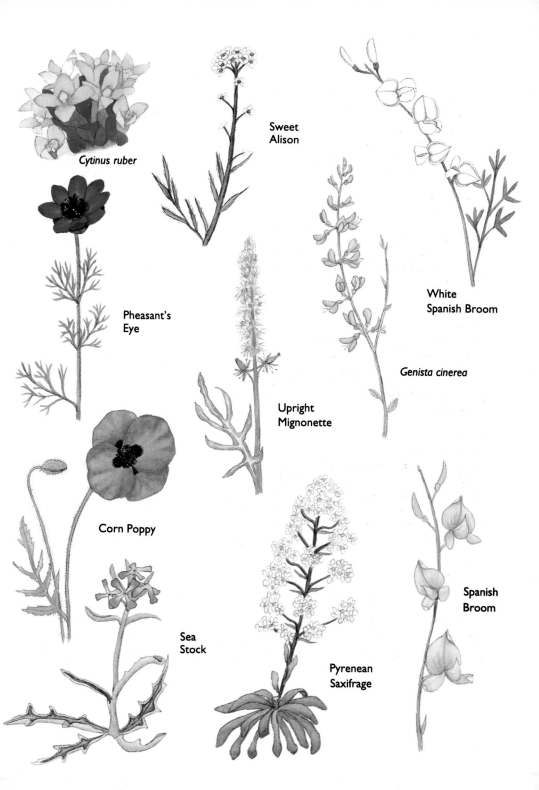

Cytinus ruber

Sweet
Alison

White
Spanish Broom

Pheasant's
Eye

Genista cinerea

Upright
Mignonette

Corn Poppy

Spanish
Broom

Sea
Stock

Pyrenean
Saxifrage

Hottentot Fig
Carpobrotus edulis
South African succulent plant of the *Mesembryanthemum* family. Used as ground cover and sand-binder in southern coastal areas. Fleshy triangular leaves; the stems run along the ground rooting at the nodes. The cream flowers are 4cm in diameter; followed by fat seed pods which can be eaten.

Pitch Trefoil
Psoralea bituminosa
Common in dry sandy areas mainly in the south. A dark-green straggling perennial with stems up to 1m long. When crushed gives off a tar-like smell. Leaves are trifoliate. The blue flowers are produced on long stems in terminal clusters from April to June.

Tangier Pea
Lathyrus tingitanus
Common in coastal areas of the south and east. An annual scrambling vetch with large purple flowers up to 2cm in diameter produced from May to June; shiny seed pods. This plant is often cultivated and is now naturalized in many places.

Sea Medick
Medicago marina
Common on sandy beaches and dunes where it can cover large areas. An attractive creeping plant with clear lemon-yellow flowers produced from February to May, which are followed by 'corkscrew' seed pods. The whole plant is covered with fine white down-like hair which gives it a silvery appearance.

Star Clover
Trifolium stellatum
Common in dry sandy areas, roadsides and fields. Distinctive annual up to 25cm high, with globular, pink, multi-flowered heads, followed by a seed head which spreads out into a star form. The leaves are trifoliate and have short silky hairs. Flowers from March to June.

Bermuda Buttercup
Oxalis pes-caprae
Common. Attractive herbaceous perennial with a mass of brilliant-yellow flowers from January to April. The trifoliate leaves (similar to Shamrock) can be eaten by livestock. Because it produces bulbils at the stem base as well as seeds, it is difficult to eradicate, causing a weed problem.

Large Mediterranean Spurge
Euphorbia characias
Fairly common perennial found in most maquis scrub areas. Large herbaceous plant up to 80cm. Exudes milky sap when bruised. Typical *Euphorbia*-like flowers with brownish-red bracts from March to May. Fruit, covered with soft hairs, 'explode' and scatter seeds when ripe.

Mastic Tree
Pistacia lentiscus
A common shrub of maquis scrub. Evergreen, it eventually reaches 3m in height. The catkin flowers from April to July are followed by a bunch of small pea-sized fruit. Mastic, a form of resin, is produced from the cut bark; used in the pharmaceutical industry.

Grey-leaved Cistus
Cistus albidus
Common and beautiful small perennial shrub. Found in maquis scrub mainly on limestone. The leaves are hairy, grey-green and white beneath. The colourful rose-magenta flowers, 6cm across, are produced early in the year, over a two-month period, each lasting for only one day.

Gum Cistus
Cistus ladanifer
Very common shrub, often the main constituent of a maquis habitat. The plant is up to 2m high with thin sticky branches and leaves. The large white flowers, up to 10cm in diameter, usually have a purple spot at the base of each petal. Flowers from May to June.

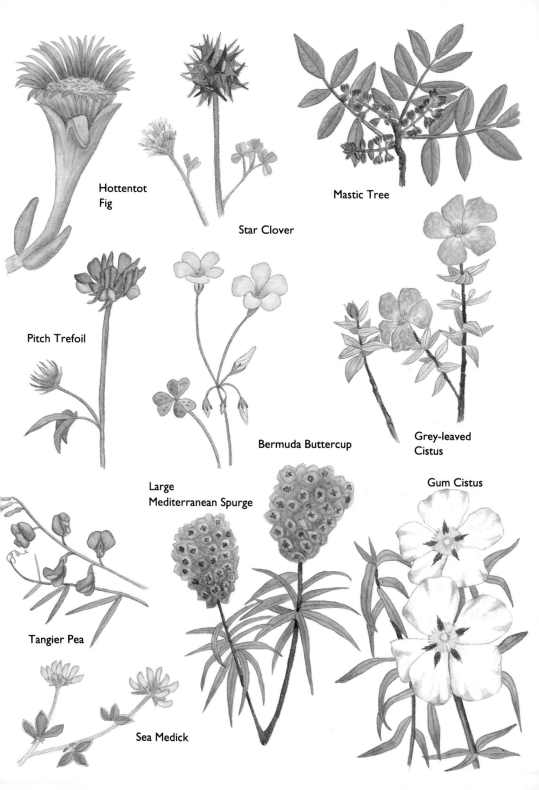

Hottentot
Fig

Star Clover

Mastic Tree

Pitch Trefoil

Bermuda Buttercup

Grey-leaved
Cistus

Gum Cistus

Large
Mediterranean Spurge

Tangier Pea

Sea Medick

Squirting Cucumber
Ecballium elaterium
Common in the south on roadsides and waste places. A poisonous cucumber-like perennial with long fleshy stems up to 80cm long. Small yellow flowers produced from March to September are followed by hairy 'sausage-shaped' fruits which explode when touched, distributing seeds within a liquid spray over a wide area.

Shrubby Pimpernel
Anagallis monelli
A beautiful common plant of rocky and waste places, roadsides and sandy areas. Low spreading perennial with dark-green leaves and stems up to 50cm long producing a profusion of large vivid-blue flowers with a violet-hued centre, up to 1.5cm in diameter. Flowers between March and August.

Common Centaury
Centaurium erythraea ssp. grandiflorum
Fairly common herbaceous plant in the south. Scrub and cultivated land. An erect plant with a neat rosette of pale green leaves. A large much-branched head, up to 60cm high, of vivid pink flowers, each 1cm in diameter. Albino forms are frequent. From June to September.

Intermediate Periwinkle
Vinca difformis
A locally common plant of wet river banks, stream beds and damp field edges. Long and trailing up to 50cm, with dark shiny thick evergreen leaves. The solitary flowers are 5cm in diameter, pale blue with a paler centre, produced February to May.

Bristly-fruited Silkweed
Gomphocarpus fruticosus
Local. Unusual, striking medium-sized shrubby perennial of South African origin. Damp areas and river beds. The umbel of small white flowers from June to September is followed by large prickly balloon-shaped fruits containing seeds attached to long silky filaments, which aid distribution by wind.

Mallow-leaved Bindweed
Convolvulus althaeoides
Common, usually near the sea in scrub or on cultivated ground. A hairy trailing olive-green perennial up to 100cm long. Flowers, which are produced in profusion from April to June, are a beautiful pink colour, 4cm in diameter, with a darker centre.

Borage
Borago officinalis
Common plant of the roadside, wasteland and on the edge of cultivated fields. An annual up to 60cm high with thick branched stems and long egg-shaped leaves. The flowers, on a branched stem, are 2cm in diameter, bright blue with purple anthers. Often cultivated as a culinary herb.

Large Blue Alkanet
Anchusa azurea
Common plant of wasteland and the sides of cultivated ground. Handsome perennial covered with short stiff hairs with quite long lanceolate leaves. The attractive flowers on a branched stem are up to 1.5cm across and are bright blue. Flowers April to June.

Scrambling Gromwell
Lithospermum diffusum
Common shrub in scrubland and on the edge of pine woodland in the north, centre and west of Spain. Spreading stem, up to 80cm long with slightly hairy leaves. The flowers are 2cm long, funnel shaped and a brilliant blue from April to July.

Purple Viper's Bugloss
Echium plantagineum
Common plant found on waste ground, road edges and in pastureland, especially on calcareous soils. Biennial with spreading branches up to 60cm long. Large slightly hairy leaves. Flowers are large, up to 3cm across, long and reddish-blue. Flowers March to June.

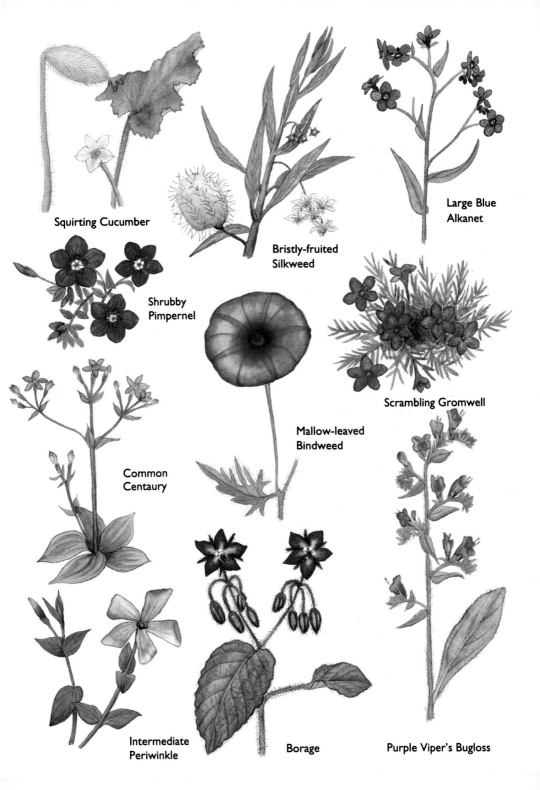

Squirting Cucumber

Bristly-fruited
Silkweed

Large Blue
Alkanet

Shrubby
Pimpernel

Scrambling Gromwell

Common
Centaury

Mallow-leaved
Bindweed

Intermediate
Periwinkle

Borage

Purple Viper's Bugloss

Rosemary
Rosmarinus officinalis
Common shrub in maquis scrub and hillsides especially near the sea. Evergreen up to 150cm high, with very aromatic leaves used for culinary purposes. Flowers in clusters at the end of the branches, very variable in colour but mainly pale violet. Flowers throughout the year.

French Lavender
Lavandula stoechas
Common shrub in the centre and south on siliceous soils. Distinctive perennial up to 60cm high, with soft narrow leaves; very aromatic. The flower heads are long and square in cross section with a tuft of long violet bracts at the top. Flowers from February to June.

Purple Phlomis
Phlomis purpurea
Local plant in rocky areas in the south. Perennial with felt-like leaves looking like Sage; grey-green in colour. The flowers are a series of whorls up to the flowering stem which is 60cm high. The pale purple flowers are borne in May and June.

Snapdragon
Antirrihinum majus
Fairly common in dry and sandy land. Perennial but fairly short-lived (the parent of the garden Snapdragon). Often grows up through maquis scrub bushes. The long stems, up to 80cm high, have many lance-shaped smooth leaves. The magenta-coloured flowers are formed in a terminal spike, each flower 4cm long; from March to July.

Red Valerian
Centranthus ruber
Widespread on old walls and roadsides. A smooth blue-green perennial with strong stems up to 80cm tall and with terminal clusters of deep-pink flowers, liked by butterflies. The individual flowers are only 5mm in diameter and highly scented. Flowers from March to September.

Curry Plant
Helichrysum stoechas
Common in rocky and sandy places. Very aromatic plant, smelling of curry when flowers are crushed. Perennial with many white felt-like stems which are topped by groups of small round yellow flower heads. These are papery, often used as 'everlasting flowers'. Flowers from May to September.

Corn Marigold
Chrysanthemum segetum
Very common annual found in grain fields, wasteland and roadsides. An attractive plant up to 50cm high with bright-yellow flower heads up to 4cm in diameter. Upper leaves lance shaped but the lower ones deeply cut. Flowers from April to August.

Crown Daisy
Chrysanthemum coronarium
Very common annual growing in profusion in grain fields, fallow land and roadsides. A large colourful plant up to 80cm high, well branched with finely cut leaves. The flowers are deep golden-yellow, 6cm in diameter. There is also a common form with bi-coloured ray florets. Flowers April to July.

Milk-thistle
Silybum marianum
Common plant of waste ground and track sides. Biennial with an attractive over-wintering rosette of white and green mottled leaves (the midribs can be used for salads). The flowering stem is stout up to 2m in height, with large purple flower heads up to 8cm in diameter are produced from April to August.

Spanish Oyster Plant
Scolymus hispanicus
Very common thistle-like plant of waste ground and roadsides. A very spiny biennial with a strong flowering stem up to 80cm high. The individual flowers are stemless, situated in the axels of the leaves. These are bright yellow, 1.5cm in diameter and found from May to August.

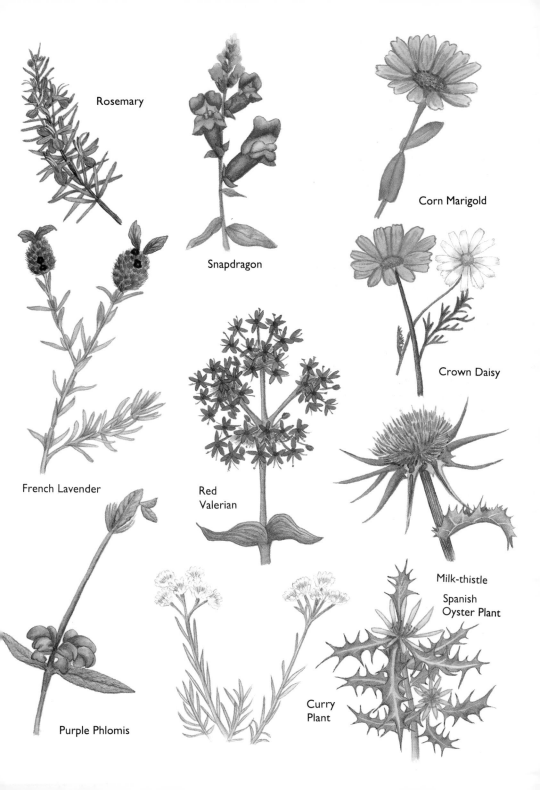

Rosemary

Snapdragon

Corn Marigold

Crown Daisy

French Lavender

Red
Valerian

Milk-thistle

Spanish
Oyster Plant

Purple Phlomis

Curry
Plant

Branched Broomrape
Orobanche ramosa
Common parasitic plant found in cultivated ground, often living on the roots of tomato, potato and other plants. It is usually branched from the base, with flowering stems up to 30cm high completely devoid of chlorophyll. Pale-blue flowers 1cm long are arranged up the stem during May to September.

Asphodel
Asphodelus aestivus
Common. Wasteland and rocky scrub. Perennial with a large tuber which starts into growth early in the season. Long sword-shaped leaves up to 100cm in length. The branched flower stalk grows to 150cm tall. Individual flowers are 1.5cm in diameter, white with brown veins. Flowers from April to June.

Hollow-stemmed Asphodel
Asphodelus fistulosus
Common on dry cultivated land and road edges. The fibrous rooted perennial is small and delicate with rush-like hollow leaves 50cm tall. The flower stem is sparsely branched with flowers 2cm in diameter, white with a pink vein. Flowers from March to June.

Rose Garlic
Allium roseum
Common on rocky hillsides and cultivated land. The bulb produces many small bulbils around the base. The few leaves are long and linear; when bruised produces a strong garlic smell. The flower stem, up to 60cm tall, carries a large globular head of pale pink-violet flowers from April to July.

Spanish Snake's Head
Fritillaria hispanica
Local on scrubland, grassy hillsides and mountains in the south. A bulbous plant which produces slender leaves up to 30cm long. The flower is large and bell-shaped, very variable in colour but usually maroon-brown with a yellow-green midstripe, not chequered; from April to June.

Tulip
Tulipa australis
Locally common in the south amongst rocks and scrub. The stem is slender, 60cm high with a single flower 2–3cm long with pointed segments. Outer petals are reddish-yellow whilst the inner ones are clear yellow and only open fully in bright sunlight during March to May.

Tassel Hyacinth
Muscari comosum
Common in orchards and cultivated grasslands. A large grape-hyacinth which has striking flowers on the top of a 40cm flowering stem. The topmost flowers are bright blue, sterile and turned upwards; the fertile flowers lower down the stem are brownish-blue. Flowers from April to June.

Century Plant
Agave americana
Common. Gardens and countryside. Introduced from America. Monocarpic (dies after flowering); flower stalk appears after 12–15 years, attaining 10m in a month. Flowers are green-yellow and small for the size of the plant. Fertile seed is not produced in Europe (requiring a special moth for fertilization). Propagation by many offsets.

Dwarf Trumpet Narcissus
Narcissus asturiensis
Local in the mountains of Cantábrica. This is the smallest of the trumpet daffodils, only reaching a height of 10cm, a true miniature. Only two leaves, 0.5cm broad and 8cm long. Large trumpet-shaped flowers are produced on minute stems from March to May.

Hoop Petticoat Narcissus
Narcissus bulbocodium
Common. Meadows, grassy hillsides and road edges. Flower very variable in shape and colour, ranging from deep golden-yellow to pale lemon. Leaves are thin, often lying prostrate on the ground. The bulbs divide rapidly, soon forming large clumps. Seeds readily. Flowers from January to March.

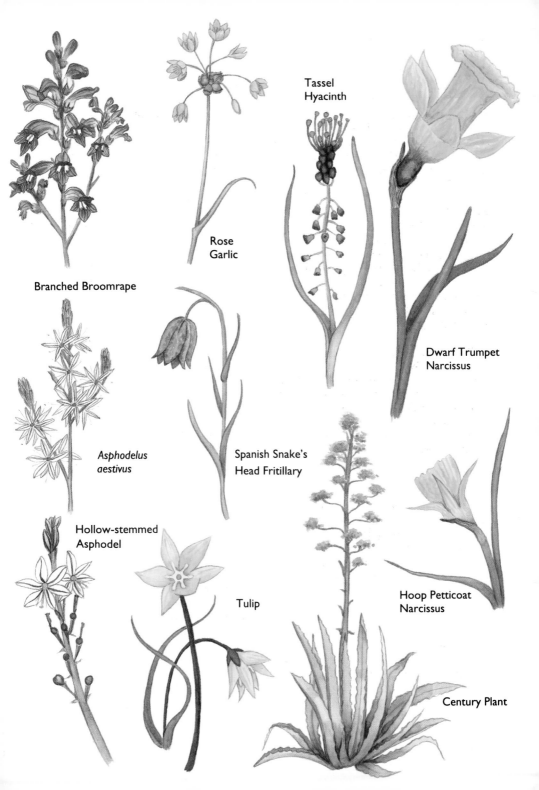

Branched Broomrape

Rose Garlic

Tassel Hyacinth

Dwarf Trumpet Narcissus

Asphodelus aestivus

Spanish Snake's Head Fritillary

Hollow-stemmed Asphodel

Tulip

Hoop Petticoat Narcissus

Century Plant

Barbary Nut

Iris sisyrinchium

Common on dry sandy pathways and hillsides. One of the smaller irises with stems up to 40cm high and a cluster of blue flowers with white centres. Each flower opens for a day but only in the afternoon. Leaves are thin and wavy. Flowers from February to April.

White-flowered Iris

Iris florentina

Fairly common on rocky ground. Grown for ornamental purposes in gardens and was possibly introduced by the Arabs. A strong plant up to 60cm high with many large white flowers, sometimes with blue veins. The leaves are broad and sword shaped. Flowers from March to May.

Field Gladiolus

Gladiolus segetum

Common in cornfields and cultivated lands. From a small corm the long sword-shaped leaves reach up to 50cm, between which a terminal flower spike rises to 80cm. The flowers, up to ten in number, are 5cm long and a beautiful cerise. Flowers from April to June.

Dwarf Fan Palm

Chamaerops humilis

Common in coastal areas on uncultivated and dry land. The only native European palm. The tough fibrous stem is short up to 1m high, producing a number of fan-shaped leaves. Flowers are yellow, in a dense cluster at the base of the leaves, followed by shiny brown date-like fruit. Flowers in July and August.

Giant Reed

Arundo donax

Common at river edges and often used as a windbreak in rice-growing and horticultural units. Large bamboo-type plant up to 6m high arising from tuberous roots. Long strap-shaped leaves. Flowers in dense terminal plumes. Used for basket making, mats and fishing rods.

Friar's Cowl

Arisarum vulgare

Common on uncultivated land and scrubland. Unusual herbaceous perennial. The flower, 4cm in length, is striped in white and dull purple. The shape is tubular but turned over at the top to form a hood. The leaves are arrow shaped and bright green. Flowers during winter and early spring.

Sawfly Orchid

Ophrys tenthredinifera

Local on dry hillsides and on grassy road edges. A beautifully flowered orchid. Very variable in height from 10–30cm. The large flowers have bright pink sepals; the oblong lip is 2cm long, yellowish-green with a brown central patch and very hairy. Flowers from March to June.

Tongue Orchid

Serapias lingua

Local on scrubland and on the edge of woods, mainly on sand. A slender orchid with unusual reddish flowers. The lip is long and narrow like a tongue. Very variable in both colour and shape. Flowers from March to June.

Wavy-leaved Monkey Orchid

Orchis italica

Local. Grassy calcareous hillsides in the south. Large handsome orchid up to 60cm tall, arising from a rosette of wavy-edged leaves. The bright-pink flowers form a large compact head. The lip is large and can be likened to a naked man. Flowers from April to May.

Limodore

Limodorum abortivum

Local in pine woods on calcareous soils. Un-usually, it has no leaves, but stout 30–80cm green-violet stem and large violet-coloured flowers, 5cm across. The roots are deep and thick and are probably saprophytic on decaying pine needles. Flowers from April to July.

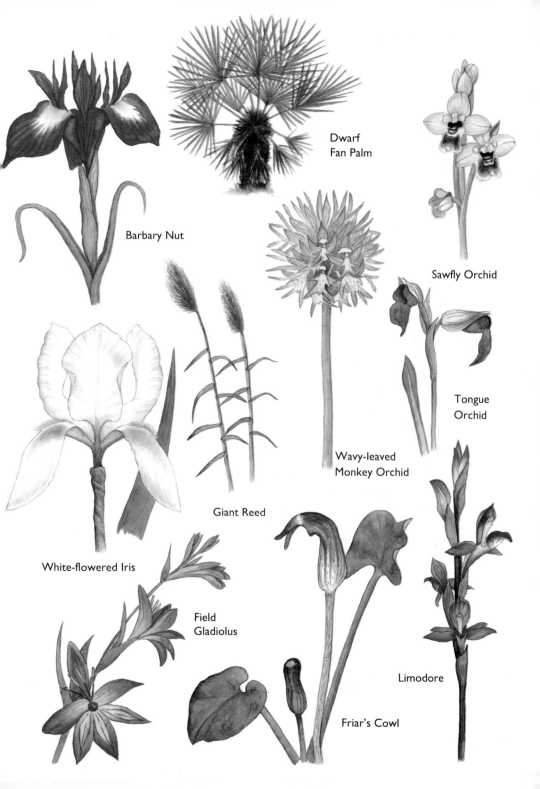

Dwarf
Fan Palm

Barbary Nut

Sawfly Orchid

Tongue
Orchid

Wavy-leaved
Monkey Orchid

Giant Reed

White-flowered Iris

Field
Gladiolus

Limodore

Friar's Cowl

SITE SUMMARY

The following table lists all the main sites described in Section II in alphabetical order. For each one a star rating of between zero and three is given, indicating how good the site is for birds (Bi), mammals, reptiles and amphibians (M), butterflies (Bu) and wild flowers (Fl).

SITE	SITE No.	STAR RATING				HABITATS
		Bi	M	Bu	Fl	
Acosta		see Gata, Salinas del Cabo de				
Adelantado, Parador el		see Cazorla y Segura, La Sierras de				
Ademuz, Rincon de	73	☆		☆	☆	maquis scrub, coniferous forest
Aiguamolls de l'Empordà, North	83	☆☆☆	☆☆☆			freshwater marsh
—, South	84	☆☆☆	☆☆			freshwater marsh
Aigües Tortes and Estany de Sant Maurici, Parque nacional	38	☆☆	☆	☆☆☆	☆☆☆	Alpine
Albarracín, Sierra de	72	☆☆		☆☆☆	☆☆☆	Alpine, coniferous forest
Alcántara, Embalse de	58	☆☆☆				lake
Alcázar de San Juan, Lagunas de	75	☆☆☆			☆	lake
Alcudia, Albufera de	144	☆☆☆				freshwater and saltwater marshes
Alto Campóo	8	☆			☆☆	Alpine
Alto Pallars-Aran, Reserva nacional de	39	☆☆	☆☆	☆	☆☆	Alpine
Alto Tajo, Parque Natural del	70	☆☆	☆	☆☆	☆☆	coniferous forest
Ancares Leoneses, Reserva nacional de los	2	☆	☆		☆☆	deciduous broad-leaved forest, maquis scrub
Andratz, Puerto de, and environs	140	☆☆☆				sea cliffs
Aran, Vall d'	37	☆☆☆	☆☆	☆☆☆	☆☆☆	Alpine, coniferous forest
Badajoz, Río Guadiana	61	☆☆☆	☆	☆	☆	river
Barbate, Marismas de	103	☆☆	☆		☆	saltwater marshes
Bárdenas Reales	25	☆☆☆		☆		steppe
Belchite	28	☆				steppe
Benasque, Reserva nacional de	36	☆	☆	☆☆	☆☆☆	Alpine
Beseit, Reserva nacional de Puertos de	89	☆		☆	☆	maquis scrub, mixed lowland forest
Beyos, Desfiladero de los		see Picos de Europa				

SITE	SITE No.	STAR RATING Bi	M	Bu	Fl	HABITATS
Bonanza, Salinas de, with nearby coniferous forest	99	☆☆				salt-marshes, coniferous forest
Boquer Valley	143	☆☆☆				maquis scrub
Bornos, Embalse de	100	☆				lake
Bosque, El	see Grazalema, Sierra de					
Boumort, Sierra del	40	☆☆		☆	☆☆	Alpine
Cabrera, Isla de	150	☆☆	☆			sea cliffs
Cabrera, Sierra de la, and Valle de Sanabria	10			☆	☆	maquis scrub, Alpine, lake
Cadi, Sierra de	41	☆☆	☆	☆☆☆	☆☆☆	Alpine
Cádiz, Salinas de	102	☆☆☆				salt-marsh
Cameros, Reserva nacional de	23	☆		☆	☆☆	Alpine, maquis scrub, coniferous forest, deciduous broad-leaved forest
Castilla, Mar de	71	☆☆☆				freshwater lake
Castronuño	44	☆☆				river, freshwater marsh
Cazorla y Segura, Las Sierras de; Hornos and the Eastern Banks	133	☆☆	☆☆	☆☆	☆☆☆	coniferous forest, freshwater lake
—, Parador el Adelantado Route	135	☆☆	☆	☆☆	☆☆☆	coniferous forest, mixed lowland forest
—, Information Centre at Torre del Vinagre	134	☆☆	☆☆☆	☆☆	☆☆☆	coniferous forest
Chorito, Sierra del	64	☆☆☆				mixed lowland forest
Cies, Islas	9	☆☆☆	☆☆		☆	sea cliffs
Circos, Reserva nacional de los	35	☆	☆	☆☆	☆☆☆	Alpine
Contreras, Embalse de	74	☆☆☆		☆	☆☆	freshwater lake
Corchuela Road	60	☆☆☆	☆			lowland mixed forest
Cordoba, Lagunas de	113	☆☆☆				fresh- and salt-water lakes
Covadonga	see Picos de Europa					
Cuenca, Serranía de, La Ciudad Encantada	80	☆		☆	☆☆☆	coniferous forest
—, Parque Cinegético del Hosquillo	78	☆	☆☆☆	☆	☆☆	maquis scrub, coniferous forest
—, Hoz del Júcar	79	☆☆		☆	☆☆	deciduous broad-leaved forest, river
—, Uña and Embalse de la Toba	81	☆☆☆	☆	☆☆	☆☆	freshwater lakes

SITE	SITE No.	STAR RATING				HABITATS
		Bi	M	Bu	Fl	
Cuenca Alta del Manzanares, Parque Regional de la Pedriza de Parque Regional de la	51	☆☆	☆	☆☆	☆	Alpine, coniferous forest, maquis scrub
Daimiel, Tablas de	66	☆☆☆				freshwater marsh
Degaña, Reserva nacional de	4	☆☆	☆	☆☆	☆☆	deciduous broad-leaved forest
Demanda, Sierra de la	22	☆☆☆		☆	☆☆	Alpine, coniferous forest
Despeñaperros, Desfiladero de	112	☆			☆☆	maquis scrub
Doñana, Coto, Marismas of the North Pre-park	111	☆☆☆		☆	☆	freshwater marsh
—, Rocina Hides and Palacio del Acebrón	108	☆☆☆	☆	☆	☆	coniferous forest, river, mixed lowland forest
—, 'The Bridge', El Rocio	109	☆☆☆				freshwater marsh
—, Coto del Rey	110	☆☆☆	☆☆	☆☆	☆☆	mixed lowland forest
—, Safari Tour and the Acebuche Hides	107	☆☆☆	☆☆☆	☆☆	☆☆	dunes, salt- and freshwater marshland, mixed lowland forest, beach
Duratón, Cañon de	46	☆☆		☆☆		maquis scrub, steppe
Ebro, Parc Natural del Delta del, Northern Side	94	☆☆☆	☆☆	☆	☆	freshwater marsh, beach, sand dunes
—, Southern Side	95	☆☆☆	☆☆	☆	☆	freshwater marsh, beach, sand dunes
Elche	91					palm forest
Encantada, La Ciudad	see Cuenca, Serranía de					
Esla de Ricobayo, Embalse del	see Villafáfila, Salinas de					
Espuña, Reserva nacional de Sierra de,	93	☆☆	☆☆	☆	☆	lowland mixed forest, coniferous forest
— Filabres, Sierra de los	126	☆		☆	☆	steppe
Formentera, Isla de	149	☆☆			☆	sea cliffs
Freu, Cabo del	see Porto Cristo					
Fuente de Piedra, Laguna de	115	☆☆☆	☆☆☆			saltwater lake
Gallocanta, Laguna de	69	☆☆☆				freshwater lake
Garrotxa, Parque Natural de la Zona Volcanica de la	42		☆☆☆			deciduous broad-leaved forest
Gata, Sierra de	56	☆☆	☆			maquis scrub, mixed lowland forest

SITE	SITE No.	Bi	M	Bu	Fl	HABITATS
Gata, Sierra del Cabo de	129	☆☆			☆☆	maquis scrub, steppe, sea cliffs
Gata, Salinas del Cabo de, and Acosta	130	☆☆☆	☆			saltwater lake and marsh
Gernika, Ria de	16	☆☆☆				river estuary
Gibraltar	120	☆☆☆	☆		☆	sea cliffs, maquis scrub
Gorramakil, Monte	17	☆☆		☆	☆	deciduous broad-leaved forest
Grazalema	121	☆☆☆	☆	☆☆	☆☆☆	Alpine
Grazalema, Sierra de, El Bosque	123	☆☆	☆	☆☆	☆☆☆	coniferous forest
—, Grazalema to Ubrique	122	☆☆		☆☆	☆☆☆	Alpine, maquis scrub
—, Grazalema to Zahara	124	☆☆☆	☆	☆☆	☆☆☆	Alpine, maquis scrub, coniferous forest
Gredos, Sierra de, Guisando	55	☆☆☆	☆	☆	☆☆	maquis scrub, coniferous forest
—, Northern Slopes	53	☆	☆	☆	☆☆	Alpine, maquis scrub
—, Puerto del Pico	54	☆☆	☆		☆☆	maquis scrub, coniferous forest
Guadarrama, Sierra de	52	☆☆			☆☆	Alpine, coniferous forest
Guadiana, Río		see Badajoz				
Guadix		see Sierra Nevada				
Guara, Sierra de	32	☆	☆	☆	☆	maquis scrub, coniferous forest, Alpine
Guisando		see Gredos, Sierra de				
Hermida, Desfiladera de la		see Picos de Europa				
Hornos,		see Cazorla y Segura, Las Sierras de				
Hosquillo, Parque Cinegético del		see Cuenca, Serranía de				
Huebra, Río	48	☆	☆			river
Ibiza	148	☆	☆			maquis scrub, sea cliffs
Janda, La	104	☆☆		☆☆	☆☆	pasture-land
Júcar, Hoz del		see Cuenca, Serrania de				
Levante, Salinas de, to Cabo Salinas	146	☆☆☆				saltwater marsh
Leyre, Sierra de	19	☆☆☆	☆	☆	☆☆☆	lake, lowland mixed forest
Mallorca, North-east Coast	142	☆☆☆			☆☆☆	sea cliffs
—, North-west Coast	141	☆☆☆	☆	☆	☆☆☆	sea cliffs

SITE	SITE No.	STAR RATING Bi	M	Bu	Fl	HABITATS
see also Andratx, Puerto de; Boquer Valley; Alcudia, Albufera de; Porto Cristo; Levante, Salinas de						
Medes, Islas	85	☆☆☆				sea cliffs
Medina, Laguna de	101	☆☆☆☆	☆	☆		freshwater lake
Menorca	147	☆	☆☆☆		☆☆	maquis scrub, sea cliffs
Mini Hollywood		see Tabernas				
Moclin	114	☆				coniferous forest
Moncayo, Parque Natural de la Dehesa del	27	☆		☆	☆☆☆	Alpine, maquis scrub, coniferous forest
Monfragüe, Parque Natural, Santuario de Monfragüe	68	☆☆☆	☆☆	☆☆	☆	maquis scrub, mixed lowland forest
—, The Tajo Tiétar	67	☆☆☆	☆☆☆	☆☆	☆☆	river, maquis scrub
Montejo de la Vega	47	☆				river, steppe
Montsant, Sierra de	88	☆☆		☆	☆☆	lowland mixed forest
Montseny, Parque Natural del	86			☆☆	☆☆	coniferous forest
Montserrat, Sierra de	87			☆☆	☆☆☆	Alpine, maquis scrub
Muela de Cortes, Reserva nacional de la,	77	☆☆	☆	☆	☆	river, lowland mixed forest
Muniellos, Coto nacional de	3	☆	☆		☆	deciduous broad-leaved forest
Níjar, Campo de	128	☆			☆☆	steppe
Odiel, Las Marismas del	98	☆☆☆				river, salt- and fresh-water marshes
Ordesa, Parque nacional de	33	☆☆	☆	☆☆	☆☆☆	Alpine, coniferous forest
Orduña, Puerto de	20	☆		☆☆☆	☆	Alpine
Ortigueira Estuary	1	☆☆☆				sea cliffs, river
Pancorbo	21	☆☆				maquis scrub
Pedriza, Parque Regional de la,		see Cuenca Alta del Manzanares				
Peña de Arias Montano	96	☆		☆	☆☆	lowland mixed forest
Peña de Francia, Sierra de la	57	☆	☆			Alpine, lowland mixed forest
Picos de Europa, Desfiladera de los Beyos	11	☆☆	☆	☆	☆☆☆	Alpine, coniferous forest, river, deciduous broad-leaved forest
—, Covadonga	12	☆☆☆	☆☆	☆☆	☆☆☆	Alpine, lake, coniferous forest
—, Desfiladera de la Hermida	13	☆☆	☆☆	☆☆	☆☆☆	river, deciduous broad-leaved forest

SITE	SITE No.	STAR RATING Bi	M	Bu	Fl	HABITATS
—, Potes	14	☆☆☆	☆☆	☆☆☆	☆☆☆	Alpine
Pico, Puerto del		see Gredos, Sierra de				
Piedras, Embalse de	97	☆				lake, coniferous forest
Porto Cristo to Cabo del Freu	145	☆				sea cliffs
Potes		see Picos de Europa				
Puente de la Cerrada, Embalse de	125	☆☆				river, freshwater lake
Punta Entinas-Sabinar	131	☆☆☆				saltwater marshes, beach
Quintos de Mora, Coto nacional de los	65	☆☆				maquis scrub, mixed lowland forest
Rey, Coto del		see Doñana, Coto				
Riaño, Reserva nacional de	6	☆	☆	☆☆☆	☆	Alpine, freshwater lake
Rocio, El		see Doñana, Coto				
Roncesvalles	18	☆☆☆		☆☆	☆☆	coniferous forest
Ronda Gorge	118	☆				maquis scrub
Ronda, Reserva nacional de Serranía	119		☆	☆	☆☆	coniferous forest, maquis scrub, Alpine
Roquetas de Mar, Las Marinas de	132	☆☆☆				saltwater lake, marshes
Roses, Golfo de, the Northern Rocky Cliffs	82	☆☆			☆☆	sea cliffs
Ruidera, Parque nacional de las Lagunas de	76	☆☆				lakes, steppe
Saja, Reserva nacional de	7	☆	☆		☆☆	deciduous broad-leaved forest, maquis scrub, Alpine
Salinas, Cabo		see Levante, Salinas de				
Sanabria, Valle de		see Cabrera, Sierra de la				
San Juan de la Peña	29	☆☆		☆	☆	coniferous forest, maquis scrub
Santa Pola, Salinas de	92	☆☆☆				saltwater lake, marsh
Santillana, Embalse de	50	☆☆☆				freshwater lake
Santo Domingo de Silos	26	☆☆☆		☆	☆☆☆	deciduous broad-leaved forest, maquis scrub, river
Santoña, Las Marismas de	15	☆☆☆				saltwater marsh
Santuaria de Nossa Señora de la Luz Valley	106	☆☆☆	☆	☆	☆	maquis scrub, lowland mixed forest

SITE	SITE No.	Bi	M	Bu	Fl	HABITATS
Serena, La	63	☆☆☆				steppe, lake
Sierra Nevada, Guadix	139	☆☆		☆	☆☆	steppe
—, Northern Higher Slopes	137	☆☆		☆☆☆	☆☆☆	Alpine
—, Northern Lower Slopes	136	☆☆		☆☆☆	☆☆☆	lowland mixed forest, maquis scrub
—, Southern Slopes	138	☆☆		☆☆	☆☆☆	Alpine, maquis scrub
Somiedo, Reserva nacional de	5	☆	☆	☆☆	☆☆☆	Alpine, deciduous broad-leaved forest, lakes
Somport, Puerto de	30	☆☆	☆	☆	☆☆	Alpine, coniferous forest
Sonsaz, Reserva nacional de	49	☆☆				deciduous broad-leaved forest, maquis scrub
Tabernas/Mini Hollywood	127	☆☆		☆		steppe
Tarifa Beach	105	☆☆☆			☆	beach, sand dunes
Tajo, Río (near Almaraz)	59	☆☆		☆		river
Teba Gorge	116	☆				maquis scrub
Toba, Embalse de la		*see Cuenca, Serranía de*				
Torcal de Antequera, El	117	☆		☆	☆☆	maquis scrub
Torre del Vinagre		*see Cazorla y Segura, Las Sierras*				
Trujillo and environs	62	☆☆☆				lowland mixed forest, steppe
Ubrique		*see Grazalema*				
Uña		*see Cuenca, Serranía de*				
Urbión, Laguna Negra de	24	☆☆☆		☆☆	☆☆☆	Alpine, coniferous forest
Valencia, La Albufera de	90	☆☆☆				freshwater lake
Vellos, Río	34	☆			☆☆☆	Alpine, river, maquis scrub
Villafáfila Plain	45	☆☆☆	☆			steppe
Villafáfila, Salinas de, and Embalse del Esla de Ricobayo	43	☆☆☆				saltwater lake, freshwater, lake, steppe
Viñamala, Reserva nacional de	31	☆☆	☆	☆	☆☆☆	Alpine
Zahara		*see Grazalema*				

USEFUL ADDRESSES

Sociedad Española de Ornithologia
Faculdad de Biologia Planta 9
Ciudad Universitaria
28040 Madrid

National Institute for the Conservation of
Nature (ICONA)
Gran Vía de San Francisco 35
28079 Madrid

Dirección General del Medio Ambiente
Paseo de la Castellana 67
28046/28071 Madrid

The Gibraltar Ornithological and Natural
  History Society
The Gibraltar Museum
18–20 Bomb House Lane
Gibraltar

Alpine Garden Society
Lye End Link
St John's
Woking
Surrey GU21 1SW

BIBLIOGRAPHY

d'Aguilar, J. & Dommanget, J-L., *A Field Guide to the Dragonflies of Britain, Europe and North Africa* (Collins, 1986).

Aritio, L.B. *Guia de los Parques Nacionales Españoles* (Incafo, 1981).

Arnold, E.N. & Burton, J.A. *A Field Guide to the Reptiles and Amphibians of Britain and Europe* (Collins, 1978).

Blanchard, J.W. *Narcissus: A Guide to Wild Daffodils* (Alpine Garden Society, 1990).

Buttler, K.P. *Field Guide to Orchids of Britain and Europe* (The Crowood Press, 1991).

Carter, D.J. & Hargreaves, B. *A Field Guide to Caterpillars of Butterflies and Moths in Britain and Europe* (Collins, 1986).

Chinery, M. *A Field Guide to the Insects of Britain and Northern Europe* (Collins, 1973).

Corbett, G. & Ovenden, D. *The Mammals of Britain and Europe* (Collins, 1980).

Grey-Wilson, C. & Blamey, M. *The Alpine Flowers of Britain and Europe* (Collins, 1979).

Grunfeld, F.V. *Wild Spain* (Ebury Press, 1988).

Heinzel, H., Fitter, R.S.R. & Parslow, J. *The Birds of Britain and Europe* (Collins, 1979).

Higgins, L.G. & Riley, N.D. *A Field Guide to the Butterflies of Britain and Europe* (Collins, 1970).

Humphries, C.J., Press, J.R. & Sutton, D.A. *The Hamlyn Guide to Trees of Britain and Europe* (Hamlyn, 1989).

Jones, D. *A Guide to Spiders of Britain and Northern Europe* (Hamlyn, 1989).

Manley, W.B.L. & Allcard, H.G. *A Field Guide to the Butterflies and Burnets of Spain* (Classey, 1970).

Michelin, *Spain: Green Tourist Guide* (Michelin, 1987).

Michelin, *Red Guide España Portugal* (Michelin, 1990).

Polunin, O. & Huxley, A. *Flowers of the Mediterranean* (Chatto and Windus, 1990).

Polunin, O. & Smythies, B.E. *Flowers of South-west Europe* (OUP, 1988).

Reichholf-Reihm, H. *Field Guide to Butterflies and Moths of Britain and Europe* (The Crowood Press, 1991).

INDEX

Bold page numbers refer to main entries and *italic* numbers refer to illustrations.

PHOTOGRAPHIC ACKNOWLEDGEMENTS

All photographs by the author except for those on the following pages:
JM Benington 178, 180, 181, 182 (left), 183, 185; **Bruce Coleman Ltd.**: LR Dawson 129; JLG Grande 138; **Natural Image**: R Gibbons 4–5, 63, 81 (left), 96 (lower), 153; **Nature Photographers**: CS Bisserot 167, 176; K Blamire 115; M Bolton 112, 127; K Carlson 70, 73, 87, 94, 125, 132, 142; C Carver 144; RS Daniell 84; EA Janes 92; LG Jessop 25; WS Paton 67 (lower); JF Reynolds 96 (upper); P Sterry 12 (upper and lower), 49, 51, 106, 186; EK Thompson 150; R. Tidman 56, 123 (right), 148.